SO THAT
YOU MAY BE
ONE

Holy Man of Crete

SO THAT YOU MAY BE ONE

from the Visions of

JOA BOLENDAS

Translated by John Hill

LINDISFARNE BOOKS

Published in the United States by Lindisfarne Books
3390 Route 9, Hudson, New York 12534

Library of Congress Cataloging-in-Publication Data

Bolendas, Joa.
    [Ein fels.   English]
    So that you may be one / from the visions of Joa Bolendas; translated
from the original German version by John Hill.
        p.   cm.
    Includes bibliographical references.
    ISBN 0-940262-85-1 (pbk.)
    1. Bolendas, Joa–Diaries. 2. Mystics–Switzerland–Biography.
3. Private revelations. 4. Visions. 5. Spiritual life. I. Title.
BV5095.B75A3   1997
248.2'9–dc21   96-40526
                                                                CIP

Cover art by Joa Bolendas
Cover design by Paul Perlow
Typography and interior design by Rob Baker/Watersign Resources

10 9 8 7 6 5 4 3 2 1

Printed in the United States of America.

CONTENTS

THE VISIONS OF JOA BOLENDAS

AN INTRODUCTION   II

Robert Sardello

TRANSLATOR'S FOREWORD

John Hill   30

I HEARD THE CALL OF THE SERAPH

WORKING WITH THE VISIONLIEDER OF JOA BOLENDAS

Therese Schroeder-Sheker   46

ABOUT THESE VISIONS   71

Joa Bolendas

PART ONE
THE EARLY VISIONS

PREFACE TO PART ONE   74

FROM MY JOURNALS   75

PART TWO
FOR THE UNITY OF THE CHURCHES, FOR THE PEOPLES OF THE WORLD

THE GRAIL LEGEND   136

THE ROSARY   140

ICONS   145

OUR LADY OF FEODOR   146

THE MOTHER OF GOD OF KURSK   148

JESUS CHRIST—BLESSING   150

THE CRUCIFIX   152

MARY'S DEATH   154

THE ASCENSION OF ELIJAH   156

VIRGIN AND CHILD   158

THE PRESENTATION   160

THE MOTHER OF GOD OF PHILOTHÉOU   162

SAINT BASIL, SAINT GREGORY, AND SAINT JOHN CHRYSOSTOM   164

SAINT CYRILL OF BELOOZERO   166

THE GREEK AND RUSSIAN FATHERS   168

SAINT ZOSSIMA AND SAINT MARY THE EGYPTIAN   170

THE CRUCIFIED SERAPH   172

THE VIRGIN AND CHILD WITH THREE SAINTS   174

TEN MESSAGES OF WISDOM   177

1. ASKING FOR THE HOLY SPIRIT   178

2. WHILE IN PRAYER   179

3. WATER FOR LIFE   180

4. AT ONE WITH GOD AND CREATION   181

5. GOD BETWEEN YOU AND YOUR NEIGHBOR   182

6. ON TIME   183

7. BINDING AND RELEASING   184

8. THE BREAD OF LIFE   186

9. THE DEATH AND RESURRECTION OF JESUS   187

10. PRIMAL LIGHT   188

TREASURES OF THE FAITH

192

PENTECOST   192
BAPTISM   194
REPENTANCE AND RECONCILIATION   195
PRAYER   197
THE LAWS   199
ECUMENISM   200
EUREKA!   202

RISEN FROM THE DEAD

208

PREFACE   208
THE FIRST ANSWER   211
THE SECOND ANSWER   212
THE THIRD ANSWER   213
THE FOURTH ANSWER   215

PEOPLES OF THE EARTH

217

A SIOUX SPOKE   217
THE AGES   218
THE STONE AGE   220
THE AGE OF THE PLANTERS   220
THE AGE OF THE ASTRONOMERS   220
THE BEGINNINGS IN THE OLD AND NEW TESTAMENTS   221
THE PEOPLE OF AFRICA   222
THE PEOPLE OF CHINA   223
THE INDIAN PEOPLE OF NORTH AMERICA   225
INDIA   226
ISRAEL   227
THE AGE OF THE CELTS   228
EUROPE   228
THE UNITED STATES AND CANADA   231
LET US REPENT   232

GOD 236

PART THREE

ON THE OLD AND NEW TESTAMENTS

PREFACE TO PART THREE 240

THE UNIVERSE 241

THE OLD TESTAMENT 245

GENESIS 245

Abram's Hymn 251

ISAAC 252

ISAAC'S SONS ESAU AND JACOB 254

JOSEPH, SON OF JACOB AND RACHEL 258

THE SECOND BOOK OF MOSES 260

Sing, Sing 261

THE TEN COMMANDMENTS 263

THE LAWS 265

THE ADORATION OF THE GOLDEN CALF 271

THE THIRD BOOK OF MOSES 274

THE FOURTH BOOK OF MOSES 281

THE FIFTH BOOK OF MOSES 291

JOSHUA 292

THE BOOK OF JUDGES 296

THE BOOK OF RUTH 299

THE FIRST BOOK OF SAMUEL 299

SAUL 300

DAVID 301

THE BOOK OF ESTHER 302

THE BOOK OF JOB 303

THE PSALMS 303

THE BOOK OF PROVERBS 303

ECCLESIASTES 303

THE SONG OF SONGS 303

ELIJAH   304

ELISHA   304

THE LAMENTATIONS   304

JOEL   304

OBADIAH   305

JONAH   305

MICAH   305

NAHUM   305

ZEPHANIAH   305

MALACHI   305

ISAIAH   306

OTHER PROPHETS   307

**THE NEW TESTAMENT:
THE FOUR EVANGELISTS**   309

MARK THE EVANGELIST   309

MATTHEW THE EVANGELIST   312

LUKE THE EVANGELIST   313

    In the Middle of the Night   317

    Glory to you, O Christ   331

JOHN THE EVANGELIST   340

**THE NEW TESTAMENT:
THE ACTS OF THE APOSTLES**   360

**THE NEW TESTAMENT:
THE REVELATION OF JOHN**   383

TWELVE VISIONLIEDER   395

HOVER YE ANGELS   396

HONOR TO YOU O CHRIST   398

THREE MYSTICAL SONGS   400

    Em e re re re   401

    Ro ho–ro ho   402

    Romio   403

EL—EL—EL—EL   404

10 • **CONTENTS**

JESUS CHRIST, WE PRAY TO YOU   406

JESUS, I LOVE YOU   408

FATHER—FATHER—OUR FATHER   411

PRAISE, PRAISE BE TO YOU, MARY   414

TWO SONGS TO PRAISE AND THANK MARIA   416

    Maria, Maria, You Maiden of the Lord   *417*

    Honor to You, Maria   *420*

NOTES   423

ABOUT JOA BOLENDAS   429

A Martyr

THE VISIONS OF JOA BOLENDAS

AN INTRODUCTION

Robert Sardello

This work is a remarkable collection of very unusual records of conversations and a journal of visions, telling of the connections between an individual, here called Joa Bolendas, and spirit beings who have been appearing to her since 1957. These beings range from angels to Mary, Joseph of Arimathea, Jesus, unnamed saints, Matthew, Mark, Luke, and John, and several individuals that Joa Bolendas has known who have died. I know practically nothing about this woman; I have never met her, nor have I corresponded with her. I first heard about her from my friend and colleague, Therese Schroeder-Sheker, who does know her, has visited her several times in Switzerland, and first told me about this remarkable woman in 1990. What most impressed me—and the reason I am involved at all—is that Joa had told Therese that it was *most* important that these records be published in America. Therese conveyed this appeal to me with such intensity and urgency that I immediately said I would be more than happy to do whatever I could to help. This brief introduction constitutes a continuation of my promise.

First, let us try to clarify the genre of these writings. They do not belong to what these days is known as channeled information.

There are indications in the writings themselves that Joa is in a completely awake state during the visions and conversations. Her body is not taken over by spirit beings. She retains her own voice, and the voices of those with whom she communicates are apparently experienced as quite independent of her own psychic being. These spirit beings cannot be heard by anyone around Joa when they manifest, and others also cannot see what she sees. Nor do these conversations belong to the related realm of mediumism. A medium, or a seer, reports only what takes place within her or his own inner psychic being, even though this is more than mere subjective reporting and usually involves a capacity to sense in more subtle ranges of perception than are available to most people. Mediums report what they see. What is seen, however, does not in turn operate as an interactive partner, adding, modifying, or correcting the medium's experience.

These conversations and visions are also different from initiation experiences, in which the initiate goes through a long physical, psychic, spiritual, and moral training that makes it possible to enter other realms and modes of experience completely unfamiliar to ordinary experience. Contact with spiritual realms and beings achieved through initiatory experience must then be translated into ordinary human terms and ideas. The boundaries among these types of experience are not fixed; neither, however, should they be confused and considered basically the same. The experiences reported here most clearly belong to the realm of visionary experiences, which differs in important respects from any of the above-mentioned forms of spirit communication.

The visionary mode of experiencing other realms is quite unusual in the modern age. The figures that appear and speak do so in a way that is similar, or analogous, to ordinary perceptual experience. In several places, Joa Bolendas begins, for example, with brief descriptions of what one of these beings looks like, is wearing, or how tall it is. On the other hand, the visions are not at all limited by the laws of physical reality as we know them; she sometimes describes a mist or a veil that covers the entire inner space of a church, or sees the extension of a being ranging from one continent to another. The main question is whether these appearances are visions or hallucinations, and this is the same as asking whether what is seen originates from within or from without. The difference between hallucinations and visions is that in the former the subject involved is a distorted sensation of physical reality, whereas in the latter the subject exists in a world other than physical reality. The difference cannot be comprehended by saying that in visions something "real" is experienced, whereas in hallucinations something not "real" is perceived. If I were there with Joa in a church in Switzerland, and she was experiencing a vision, and I could not see nor hear what was going on, it would not be justifiable to say that she was hallucinating and that what she saw was not real. Perhaps she sees things that I am not capable of seeing. Further, the visions recorded in these writings lack characteristics that typically accompany hallucinations—namely, a severe change in the experience of one's own body, a confusion of subject–object boundaries in which the subject fuses with the environment, a destabilizing of everything being sensed, the stoppage of time, a boundlessness of space, and the disintegration of the order of experiential connections. In the auditory realm, in hallucinations one hears voices, but not the voices of people speaking. Even when the hallucinating person can identify the voices in a general way as male or female, loud or soft, clear or scarcely distinguishable, it is the voice that presses in, as if from all sides. Hallucinatory voices also typically deride, persecute, and command. There is no indication of any sort in the body of the text that the freedom of the person receiving these visions has been interfered with in any way. A great deal of care and discipline is displayed in the writing and in the ongoing records kept by this individual for nearly forty years.

Finally, we may consider if this writing is in the genre of imaginal dialogues—that is to say, the conversations have been created solely out of imagination. Perhaps the conversations are a variation of what Jung spoke of as active imagination, a procedure of either taking an image from a dream or fantasy life or of conjuring up an image and then initiating a conversation with an imaginal figure as if it were real. The primary reason that this is probably not the case here is that in such imaginal conversations the images do not cross the boundaries of their own world and intermingle with outer reality; their reality remains clearly psychic. Visions are not so clearly a part of an inner world. Some of the visions here, for example, take the form of Joa Bolendas seeing a halo of light around a priest saying mass or around a minister preaching a sermon; and such appearances, as described in the text, seem to occur spontaneously.

Still, searching through all of the possibilities, it must be stated that there is no way to prove conclusively or even to say very much about the reality of the beings who form the content of these visions. The intention of going through these possibilities, in fact, is not to attempt such proof. Rather, the aim is to make some positive suggestions concerning how to approach such a text. First, I suggest that the organ that perceived these visions is not the physical eye, but rather the heart. Such a suggestion is made, not to evoke a sympathetic response, but to indicate that this body of work is best read by engaging the heart, in order to see what is actually present. Moreover, the text itself can serve to educate one into the reality of the heart as an organ of perception; it resists a purely mental engagement, and remains forever closed to that point of view.

The suggestion that one approach this text through the heart and that by doing so one also develops the capacities of the heart, is not a call to sentimentality. The heart evoked here is the *thinking heart*, not emotional response. The first page of the text tells us something about what is needed for a proper relation to this kind of writing. Joa Bolendas is being spoken to, according to the text, by one who has risen from the dead; Joa is being instructed about the reception of visions, as are we who read the visions:

> Revelations have another wavelength.
> The words, images, sounds (the hymns) come
> over an extended period of time——with great intervals——
> which demand a lot of energy from those who receive them.
> Devotion and concentration are needed.
>
> Whenever someone receives revelations, the brain
> works more quickly and the heart beats more slowly.

The particular form of visions recorded in this work are referred to as *revelations*. This designation indicates, *I believe*, that nothing was done on the part of the recipient to make these visions occur. They began spontaneously, and are not the result of any particular inner training or practice beyond a devout practice of prayer and a sincere belief in God and the revelations of the Old and New Testaments. That these visions are termed revelations does not imply that they have the same status as the revealed word of God, or biblical texts; it does mean that the initiation of the experiences was on the side of the spiritual worlds and that these experiences are evidently intended to increase and renew the connections between human beings and the spiritual worlds. The significant aspect of the above statement, however, concerns the conditions under which the visions occur—that is, devotion and extended concentration.

The attitude of devotion belongs to the capacities of the heart. Devotion means constant and fully engaged attention, such as, for example, the physical organ of the heart itself constantly gives to the circulation of the blood through the body. The heart, unlike any other muscle of the body, never ceases its work, even for a brief moment. We are thus led to conclude that these visions did not occur outside of the important context of a life lived in a constant attitude of love. It is far-fetched, I am sure, to imagine that these visions occurred to one who lives a life forgetful of the divine order of all of creation, needing to be reminded periodically by jolts from the heavens. These visions are more like momentary episodes in an ongoing life of dedication to communion with the spiritual worlds. Thus, the indication that concentration is a condition for the reception of the visions is not limited to the actual moments of the visions, but also signifies a life orientation. From the text alone, we do not learn much concerning this extremely important context, but it seems crucial to be able to imagine the kind of life that must go along with these experiences, to be able to visualize that they are not episodic intrusions, but episodic concentrations within a life dedicated to bridging the seen and the unseen.

The passage quoted also hints at the specific alteration of attention needed for the reception of visions. More important, for the reader of these documents, this same passage indicates something of what is required for a right understanding of the work. The reader must recognize that reception becomes possible when "the brain works more quickly and the heart beats more slowly." If the text is read primarily by means of the brain—that is, through mental capacities alone—very little will be gained. A speeding up of the brain implies that another level of mental work is going on, a level that is bypassed entirely when the text is read in the ordinary way. In practice, if the text is read in that manner, extraordinary nuances are read as ordinary words, and their deeper significance goes unnoticed. To properly understand this sort of text, we are effectively told that the heart must beat more slowly. Reading must occur at a different pace, or different rhythm, than is usually asked for in reading. In fact, the key to benefiting spiritually from spending time with the text is found in the way the words are savored and felt, in the way readers allow themselves to be touched by what is said. If we approach revelation as new information, frustration follows. If we, on the other hand, approach the text with the possibility that untouched levels of our being can be moved and new capacities awakened, then something entirely different results. I want to explore this difference in detail.

The Difference between Information and Transformation

In this age of information there is a very great danger that abstraction will effectively seal off the possibility of learning anything truly new. Such a statement sounds strange indeed, for it would seem that the whole idea of the information revolution is to make it possible to know, in a broader sphere, what was previously known only by a very few. The inherent deception, however, is that knowing new information has little to do with learning. Learning is the transformation of our body and soul and the vivifying of our spirit through the development of otherwise dormant capacities. Knowing more and more information only adds, in a cumulative fashion, to the stock of available facts at our disposal. Information allows us to become more clever, perhaps more inventive, even more practical in certain realms, but it does not help us to become more human, or to realize what it means to be human. The intent of information is power, and power has become coupled with speed.

One might argue that I have just conveyed information. Information certainly is involved, but here information does not do business on its own. Information serves as a medium through which other, more subtle qualities can find a habitation and expression in the world. And, in the visions of Joa Bolendas, the informational content is further reduced while subtle qualities of soul and spirit are increased. I am not suggesting here that information is of no value; it is a necessary medium, but the problem arises when, as Marshall McLuhan said, the medium becomes the message. For example, the corporate head of Microsoft, the principal maker of computer software in the world, has tried to buy the rights to photograph all of the great art of the world in order to create a software program to display these paintings and other works of art on home computer screens. Such an achievement would make "information" available to vast numbers of people, but would this make art more available in the world? Would not these high-quality digital graphics increase the distribution of art that would remain otherwise largely unavailable? A most difficult question indeed. Answering in the affirmative neglects the fact that a work of art is not just a thing, even a beautiful thing; it neglects the reality of a work of art as having body, soul, and spirit. A work of art is a living being—not a human being, but more than a picture. A picture is the informational part of a work of art. I am not suggesting that the project of making digital reproductions of art is of no value; it has value as long as the makers of the product are clear that they are making only a certain version of art available—not the experience of viewing the paintings themselves. But, if this is not clearly stated, the result may be that art will become an abstraction; we may all *know* a great deal more about art, but it is likely that its transformative capacity will be curtailed. We are already in the habit of living with secondhand versions of things, which unfortunately leads to a basic incapacity to deal with the original. We want information *about* the spirit, but do not know what to do with its actual presence. What I feel urged to do, in a first gesture toward Joa Bolendas's visions, is to struggle against the likelihood of their being approached as information, attempting to open up a space where they may be considered with a fresh attitude instead of our habitual mind-set.

Information has become so widespread that there is a strong tendency to approach things that are not so easily codified as if they should be mere data. If a reader takes up these writings of Joa Bolendas infected with an attitude of seeking information, there is nothing much to be learned. In a certain sense, these writings are not about the reality of spirit; they are rather living manifestations of spirit, and thus must be read through presence of soul and spirit. The informational content is minimal; the transformational value is enormous. But, if they are to become available for their transformative value, it is necessary to dwell with them and not approach them as simply ideas or facts.

The reader is advised to refrain from coming to this book with the same attitude with which one approaches other books. A reader ordinarily believes that a book is already finished, completed, and self-contained. Such technical reading assumes that through reading one can possess the content of a writing. In general today, writing has taken the place of speaking, and reading has taken the place of listening. This book, however, has to be heard, even though the hearing comes through the process of reading; and, further, one hears not just his or her own inner voice, but also the voice of the ineffable. The noisiness of the knowing mind, with all of its curiosity and questions, has to be stilled; the will to hear must supersede the will to know. In an attitude that wills to hear rather than to master, the reader manifests a willingness to be modified by what is heard. The understanding that the reader brings to the text, which enables one to read at all, is placed at risk; suddenly we are placed in a space of unknowing receptivity. This kind of reading takes place between the familiar and the strange, the known and the unknown. One opens to the possibility of being transformed rather than informed.

What does it mean to dwell in the presence of these words, these visions? Whereas the aim of gathering information is to increase a sense of our own power, the aim of reading something communicated as a vision is to yield to its power. Here we become more by becoming less; we are required to grow beyond our own egotism in order to learn. We have to give up the expectation of gaining something for ourselves from the text, entering its being as much as possible, and what may then happen is an increase, a development, of our own inner being, which is far greater than mere ego. Having done so, we may well be unable to say very much about what we have learned, but we experience in a most immediate way that we are different as a result of having relinquished, for a while, our own special interests. We are more open, more present to the moment, less self-involved, closer to a true impression of the spiritual worlds; new, inner capacities can be felt, in which we sense ourselves as more than we ever imagined we could be. Of course, these newfound capacities can also be used in an egotistical manner. We can begin to feel special, gifted, and spiritually astute. Thus, to allow ourselves to be formed by an original document of the sort presented in this series of visions also carries an attendant responsibility. The responsibility involves—in perhaps small and imperceptible ways, as far as the rest of the world is concerned—continuing in life with the ever-present challenge of gradually releasing the acquisitive act of wanting to add to our store of information. To relinquish this form of greed is not the end of learning, but rather its true beginning.

Observations Concerning the Manner of the Visions

The journal of Joa Bolendas contains entries from 1957 through 1990, and continues this journal writing into the present. The conversations with spiritual beings concerning the creation of the universe and the Old and New Testaments are not dated. Visions are presented without interpretation.

I would like to draw attention to the particular quality of the relationship between Joa and the spiritual beings who come to her. On her part, there is a deep attitude of reverence and respect, but she does not abdicate her own personality. In the conversations there is a remarkable air of what can only be called an equality of relationship. For example, as a member of the Reformed church,

Joa at first has a difficult time handling the many appearances of Mary. These appearances often take place in a Catholic church, and Joa comes to a point when she tells Mary that she will no longer visit this church as it causes her to struggle with her own beliefs. Mary then accuses Joa of betrayal. Joa answers: "Mary, I will not betray you! I will write down everything, about your love, your light and your greatness. I will not betray my church. I will betray no one. I only want to serve. Understand me—forgive me. Do not withdraw from us. Give me and all the others time. I beg you—forgive me!" Notice the strength in the conversation. Mary does not coddle this woman. On the other hand, Joa does not simply prostrate herself in submission either. She says she will not betray Mary, nor will she betray her church, and in fact will betray no one. This response indicates a truly free person, or, even better, a moment of becoming truly free. She discovers her freedom in speaking what she really wants—to serve—and this is possible without betraying either Mary or the Protestant church.

Could the essence of such interactions between Joa and these many spiritual beings have to do with discovering that the spiritual worlds do not want anything from us beyond a free and completely open relationship with them, one in which we are exactly who we are, which requires putting aside all that we think we are? Joa at first thinks of herself as a member of the Protestant church, a church that says, "Christ must increase, Mary must decrease." She discovers that she can love and honor Mary and still belong to this church, but now, for her, this has become a free association; this is not a matter of her thinking whatever she wants, in spite of what the church might hold. Something far deeper is involved, a deeper sense of what constitutes *church*. But, such an understanding of church cannot be arrived at by logical thought; rather, this comprehension is encompassed in the vision itself. Mary does not say that Joa betrays her by choosing the Protestant Church instead of devotion to her. The one word spoken by Mary, "Betrayal!" does not even indicate that it is Mary who feels betrayed. She could as well be indicating to Joa that to choose one, the church, over the other, Mary, is a self-betrayal of Joa herself; or it could indicate a betrayal of both Mary and the church. Mary speaks in a wonderfully objective manner; it is, I think, this objective way of speaking that makes possible Joa's discovery of freedom; it is not given to her, for no one, not even a spiritual being of the highest rank, can give one freedom. Rather, Mary here speaks in a way that opens a space for the possibility of discovering true freedom. Further, as we read this section of the text, it becomes clear that this moment of discovery emerged from a larger context, a context of struggle, of trying to find words for experiences that do not yield easily to words, of discarding more and more of what one could say, and of finally speaking when one does not want to speak at all—a long process of distillation of the heart: "I tore out page after page from my notebooks and rewrote them again. It is simply so difficult to put into words one's experiences with God. If only I could paint, maybe then I could pass on the visions in a better way—but that would be a never-ending task. I have taken so much out of the books about Mary and Holy Communion, but I can't leave out everything, when God wants me to write it."

The single instance described above shows the direct, frank, open form of the conversations between Joa Bolendas and spiritual beings, which is multiplied in many places throughout the text; it creates a tenor for the whole of the text. Joa, for the most part, says little, but her questions are direct, and sometimes a little argumentative. The spiritual beings always speak very directly, without elaboration or any rhetoric that could excite the personal imagination of the listener. The statements are almost oracular, so clearly stated and lacking in ambiguity that there is no need for any analysis. Nothing is presented in a convoluted manner; this is true even when quite esoteric notions are discussed. For example, in one conversation with an unnamed saint, the saint explains what is meant by Holy Communion. This figure instructs Joa to open her eyes, to see what is really before us when we are with another human being. At that moment, Joa sees the life energy of the person she was with the previous day: "And I 'saw' the same Hannes as yesterday, except that his body—his arms, legs, and head—was full of small rays of light, like small lines of light. The trunk of his body was darker than the other parts. I 'saw' an aura around his body consisting of thin, short, intensive rays of silver. And when Hannes spoke, all this light was in movement—like active energy." The saint is then able to go on and say that Holy Communion is the life of Christ. Here, there is no elaborate explanation of etheric bodies, astral bodies, and such. The most esoteric of topics is discussed with such immediacy that one does not even stop to think that what is being presented is out of the ordinary. The effect of this mode, this tenor, is that the spiritual worlds are experienced as being right here, united and one with our own world.

Whereas the effect of the tone of these visions is to unite us with the spiritual worlds, I do not intend to imply that this result is brought about by a deliberate use of a particular form of address. One never feels manipulated reading these visions. It must then be concluded that, if we only had eyes to see and ears to hear, we would, indeed, experience the spiritual worlds as all around us. By means of these visions recorded by Joa Bolendas, we may at least have an inkling of what this would be like. The journal and con-versations have transformative power because of this immediacy of the reality of a spiritual universe, which is right here. Through a meditative reading of this work, it seems that sacred stories, angels, saints, and divine beings—realms that have, for some at least, been a matter of belief, even intense belief—suddenly come near—almost near enough to touch. This transformation comes about almost imperceptibly; what was previously more or less remote, becomes close. On the one hand, a more vivid insight into the nature of belief becomes apparent. Belief is like seeing something very far in the distance, knowing that it is indeed there, but not being able to get to it, as if an impenetrable veil spreads out in front of us and blocks our way to the objects believed in. As the reading of this text proceeds, it is as if this veil is gently lifted, and what we may have known as true all along in our heart is clarified, despite the confusions brought about through our mind. On the other hand, as belief is transformed, we must look carefully into the precise nature of this transformation. I do not think of it as a transformation into immediate perception, but rather as a transformation into a new way of knowing, a knowing that may best be called *faith*.

For those who approach these writings in an attitude of radical receptivity, belief can be transformed into faith. Belief and faith are often thought of as virtually the same, but whereas belief gives an indication of something beyond the veil, faith is a way of knowing; with belief we do not yet know, but with faith there is certainty. This certainty is, however, of a different type than that given when we apprehend something in the physical world through the senses, or when we grasp something in an inner way with our reason.

Faith is a much more intimate way of knowing; it is as if the senses and reason are circumvented in favor of a more direct connection with the heart and spirit. To *circumvent* means either to go around or to encompass; it is the latter that I think applies here. We are not asked to close our senses or to stop thinking while reading this material. Rather, faith is opened, which also produces an alteration of sensing and thinking; they become more capable, as if augmented by a new inner capacity.

Faith is something like a first level of higher ways of knowing. Joa Bolendas, it seems, was born with a high potential for this capacity, and it seems to have awakened through a dream that occurred when she was sixteen. In the introduction, we are told this dream: "In the middle of the night, men came walking on a stone path. They carried wooden poles, upon which were stone plates. On the plates was written: 'Wake up, keep watch, and pray.'" She did not understand the dream but simply put it into action. To "wake up" is to enter into faith as a mode of knowing, and the principle way of strengthening this capacity is through prayer. The intermediary act between faith and prayer is keeping watch. Faith can go back to sleep, and usually does so in the particularly devastating sense that we do not even know we have fallen asleep. Joa is quite aware of this possibility, for there are times in the conversations when she is praying but realizes there is for her no living force in her words. This plight causes her severe agitation.

What do we learn concerning the character of prayer from these visions? Many times in the text we observe that a vision begins while Joa prays. But we can also feel, from the whole tone of the visions, that Joa is always praying; prayer is a state of the soul, not merely an external act. When she sometimes finds herself praying as an external act, she is merely talking to herself. Prayer, it seems, is the soul's mode of conversation with the spirit. It is not performed primarily with the lips nor with the mind, but is more like an action of the soul's breathing. As such, prayer has its own particular quality of rhythm. At one point, in a conversation with Mary about the Hail Mary prayer, Joa says to Mary that she finds this prayer decidedly uninteresting. Mary's reply is that the rhythm of the prayer is exactly right; and she says to Joa that her questioning of the prayer in this manner hurt God. Thus, to pray, it seems, involves establishing a rhythm in the life of the soul so that it becomes capable of spirit consciousness. Prayer is a way of exercising the capacities of the soul. And prayer is a completely free human act.

What could Mary be referring to when she says that the rhythm of the Hail Mary prayer is exactly right? First, it seems to mean that we are taken out of our established life rhythms, which have accumulated as habits over the years. We freely allow ourselves to be set within a different kind of movement and a different kind of space, which follows laws that are different from the laws of the physical world. For example, the rhythm of prayer decidedly partakes of a much slower movement than the events, experiences, and occurrences of ordinary waking life. If, for example, these visions are not approached in a prayerful attitude, then we will find our reading advancing too quickly. The rhythm of prayer thus refers first to its own particular time, which is very different than linear or clock time. Then, a second aspect of rhythm requires that every word is in its right place. When Mary says that the rhythm of the Hail Mary is exactly right, she is also referring to the particular placement of the words, which is to say that time is also a place; get the right timing and you find yourself in a different place. If we always pray by making up our own prayers, seeking for something from the spiritual worlds, it is likely that our timing will be off, and we will find ourselves exactly where we started. Formulated prayer thus has the important aspect of learning to become accustomed to a different mode of time. One can then go on from there and improvise according to one's own idiom, but the soul has to be strengthened first, or else we constantly fall back into ordinary consciousness.

The matter of prayer is relevant because this whole text of Joa Bolendas can be considered prayer. We could say, in fact, that *vision* is just another term for prayer. Prayer launches the visions, which are more intense modes of praying. This central characteristic of this text and the years of effort represented in this work, more than anything else, separate these visions from channeling and mediumism. If we imagine a progression of human connections with the spiritual worlds, it might well be channeling, mediumism, active imagination, prayer, vision, and initiation.

Working toward Unity

We may now explore the purpose of these visions. The title itself gives us our starting place—*So That You May Be One*. This title is brilliantly ambiguous; it can refer to the individual, to all the peoples of the earth, or to the church; it can also be something told to Joa Bolendas, having to do primarily with her, or suggesting that any greater unity begins with her. What we feel through the visions is the gradual unification of all of these spheres, and that unification in one sphere alone is illusory. Let us start, however, with the one sphere that is perhaps the most problematic—the unity of the churches.

In 1993, I attended the Parliament of World Religions in Chicago. The apparent aim of this huge weeklong gathering was to open lines of conversation that might eventually bring about a sense of unity. I was more than surprised, as I am sure many others were, to see the attitudes displayed among the many sects as each attended the showing of its wares to the others. In some sessions, bitter fighting erupted; I vividly recall one confrontation between Native Americans and an Islamic sect. At the same time, once I got over being overwhelmed by the multifarious costumes and displays of incredibly strong tendencies to hold onto the past, and began to meet individuals, I found that conversations were possible and fruitful. We are, however, apparently light-years away from achieving anything resembling a unity among religions. And yet, for nearly forty years, the visions of Joa Bolendas have concentrated on this one theme.

One might wonder what one individual could possibly contribute to the unity of the churches. A meditative reader of these visions would conclude, I believe, that any possible unity will not come from the churches as organizations. By *church*, Joa does not seem to mean an organization. Over half of this text concentrates on the Old and New Testaments, and we are presented with nothing about the sacred texts other than those of the Christian religion; this does not necessarily imply that unity ultimately means that all religions will be absorbed by Christianity as we now know it. Joa works toward the question of unity from this background because it is her background. Much of what occurs in the visions of the Old and New Testaments consists of an angel or a saint saying to Joa that one thing or another is unimportant, that it belongs to the times when the Bible was written. The purpose of the communications does not center on doctrinal concerns. Rather, one of the central purposes of the biblical visions seems to be to help develop a symbolic imagination, particularly a capacity to sense the symbolic as true. Thus, purely historical matters are not excluded, but the focus is on how such matters are presented symbolically. A saint, for example, says, "The story of Adam and Eve—is not a legend. It is symbolic! A story that was told over and over again—from tribe to tribe: they, the tribes, eventually turning it into their own Hebraic history. Therefore it is both true and symbolic." Repeatedly, in these conversations, history and symbol are seen to be intertwined. But, apparently some things are only history, and have changed in the course of evolution; other things—those that are symbolic—are still meant to be observed today and contribute to the unification of the churches. Concerning Passover, a saint tells Joa, "Celebrate it—the Passover—in the language of today, with the Jews! (It is to be part of the one unifying church.)"

So That You May be One thus seems to be a title that conveys the possibility of developing the capacity to distinguish the essential from the nonessential; first, it is an individual capacity, one not easy to acquire. If we look at these visions in a certain way, seeing a unity between the visions and the questions Joa brings to those who appear to her, we see that two capacities combine to form a new capacity. On the one hand, there is the questioning—the quest—which must issue from a desire of the heart. On the other hand, there is the capacity of vision, of coming into connection with the spiritual beings, the reality that one quests to know and to understand. There is guidance that stems from a life of concentrated prayer, the inbreathing and outbreathing of the soul in communion with the spiritual worlds. In order to become One, we first need to establish a unity of mind, soul, and spirit. Prayer and questioning indicate the method. The new capacity that can develop out of such a practice is symbolic vision—not argument, logic, discussion, or philosophy. If individuals are disposed to be one within themselves and then to come together, a similar unity of quest and vision can take place in community. What has happened to this one person, Joa Bolendas, could happen for everyone; that, I suggest, is the purpose of these visions.

Robert Sardello is a psychologist and the author of Facing the World with Soul *and* Love and the Soul. *A Fellow and former Co-Director of the Dallas Institute for Humanities and Culture, and a faculty member of the Chalice of Repose Project, he is co-founder of the School of Spiritual Psychology, which seeks to revision psychology and spirituality in the light of phenomenology and Rudolf Steiner's anthroposophy.*

TRANSLATOR'S FOREWORD

John Hill

In writing this foreword I wish to express my gratitude to a woman of extraordinary character. I have known Joa Bolendas for twenty-eight years. I have had many opportunities to witness her great joy and despair as she chartered her ship across the unsettled and unpredictable waters of our times. What treasures has her voyage discovered? As requested, I have outlined some of them in this introduction. During the many years I have worked with Joa, I have become convinced that God's word can still speak directly to the human being—perhaps the most valuable treasure she has unfolded. Sometimes Joa's gifts can be ablaze with such vitality that her words and intentions have been misunderstood. I remember the day when Joa was full of joy as she saw many saints of the Orthodox Church working for peace in Yugoslavia. As we were coming out of the church, she met an acquaintance and told her the great news. The lady we met looked at me askance, having not understood the context of Joa's experience. On several occasions, her work was rejected because it was too Gnostic, too Catholic, too Protestant. These were the storms, which nearly threatened to wreck the ship. She cried out to the heavens and let herself be guided by the winds and tides of God. She learned to become an excellent helmswoman. It is thanks to her courage and her loyalty to these invisible forces that her ship has been guided to a safe port, and some of its treasures are now to be unloaded. This is the background to the publication of this book.

With these visions, Joa Bolendas offers us insight into a world that we can only dimly perceive. For the most part, it remains invisible and inaudible. Often I have sat near Joa in various churches, while she prayed and received messages from the heavens. Gradually a spiritual landscape has opened up for me—a landscape peopled with many wonderful beings of light and energy. Due to my Christian upbringing, this landscape was not unfamiliar. I began to understand the influence these beings have had on my own life and the lives of those who are close to me, not to mention the political and social events of our time. The figures of light witnessed in these visions are here to help us. At times I have felt their presence, believed in them, doubted them, ignored them, or refused them. Despite the fluctuations of my own spiritual life, I am deeply grateful to have had the opportunity to participate consciously in this greater life, while here on earth. These visions have brought God's world closer to me. They have been my source of strength, support, and consolation. Joa has received God's words for us all.

I would like to add that my affirmation of this material has not been without struggle. There was my struggle with the language of the visions. Statements were unclear, and subject to all kinds of interpretation. Often I had to ask Joa for further elaboration, and sometimes another wording of the original statement proved to be a clearer description of what was witnessed in visions. I struggled with the meaning of these visions, too. I had to meditate on the short cryptic messages in order to appreciate their symbolic meaning, and not assume that they would materialize in concrete form. Obviously, the active participation of the receiver is necessary so that each can evaluate these statements in his or her own way. Nevertheless, I must say that I and others who have known Joa Bolendas have again and again had the experience of visions coming true. In the spring of 1968, Joa saw that the Soviet armies would crush the freedom of the Czechoslovakian people, which was confirmed several months later. Already in 1973, she saw that dangerous solar rays would penetrate the ozone layer of the earth's stratosphere and threaten life on earth—a prophecy that was soon to become public knowledge. Many times she has seen individuals who carry within themselves some potential illness. When they consulted a medical practitioner, the illnesses were discovered, and lives were saved. These are but a few examples of innumerable incidents where Joa has participated in a great struggle for the well-being of humanity. Her life and work express a deep concern about the collective dangers that threaten our planet, as well as a motherly care about the sufferings of individuals.

A New Theology

Joa Bolendas's words are a human testimony about God's revelation. Several of her texts refer to the spiritual understanding of the early church that we seem to have lost and need to find again. Many will recognize familiar Christian truths formulated in new ways. What Jews and Christians have long believed comes to life again through a direct encounter with the source of their faith. When I read the texts, it is not just the words that strike me but the space between them. In this space I encounter the spirit of the holy. Joa Bolendas does not attempt to contain these experiences in an interpretation, concept, or dogma. Her task is to serve—to pass on her experiences to others in a clear and unadulterated form. It is not her task to make people believe. The decision to believe is up to the individual. This testimony offers us an opportunity to meet the living God, who is closer than we imagine. We may see, hear, and be moved by God's world.

This volume of Joa Bolendas's work opens with extracts from her journals. In these early texts, we catch glimpses of a long struggle to accept what was given to her. Trials followed the initial joy of witnessing God's light and presence in her own Swiss Reformed Church. Beholding in vision Christ's suffering for humankind, the spiritual strength of his resurrection, Mary's loving presence, and the pleadings of the saints, Joa Bolendas's heart was moved so that she could say yes to aspects of Christianity not rooted in her own church. It was not self-evident that she would participate in the Mass, say the rosary, or pray to the saints. Her struggle with the churches and her assent to the spirit of ecumenism pervading these visions so transformed her that she could embrace not only the traditions of the Protestant and Catholic Churches but also those of the Eastern Orthodox Church, as witnessed in her words on the icons.

In the visions on the Grail, rosary, and icons, we can discern essential attributes of the three churches. These attributes are not to be understood as belonging exclusively to one church or the other, but enable us to catch glimpses of Joa's spiritual journey. In her text on the Grail, primal light received through the eucharistic meal becomes a theological extension of Joa Bolendas's own Protestant background. The significance of Mary and the rosary highlights Joa's initiation into the rich symbolism and rhythms of prayer contained in Catholic liturgy, adding a freshness and immediacy to older forms of worship. I can remember how joyful Joa Bolendas was when she first discovered the icons of Ireland. She was overwhelmed by their beauty and depth. Through visions, she learned that these treasures of the Orthodox Church are not to be appraised for their aesthetic value only; icons have a lasting and transformative effect on the human soul.

The volume then expands on two themes that seem essential for the coming unity of the churches: asking for the Holy Spirit and receiving primal light at Communion. We are asked to pray to the wise saints (*startsi*) of the Orthodox Church so that we may be strengthened by those who were guided by the direct inspiration of God's Spirit. The visions tell us that, since Pentecost, every human being is entitled to ask Christ for the gifts of the Holy Spirit. The Holy Spirit acts directly on the human spirit, moving it, changing it. One of the key teachings of Johannine Christianity is that, when the human spirit is united with God's Spirit, a great spiritual unfolding will take place and, we are told, the peoples of the earth will learn to share the many gifts of life with their fellow human beings.

One of the earliest visions of Joa Bolendas was of a shining light surrounding the eucharistic bread. Later she witnessed Christ's physical suffering and sacrifice on the cross and, after taking this within herself, she could experience the spiritual strength of his resurrection. It is the risen Christ who is present in the eucharistic celebration. The Johannine understanding of Communion implies that, through the life of the risen Christ, the primal light of creation is passed on to human beings, strengthening them to participate in God's creation as people of light. This is God's gift to every individual, and by participating in this mystery with our whole self we become conscious of what this gift means. Every person can experience a direct relationship with Christ through the eucharistic meal. Joa Bolendas once told me that the greatest task of the coming church will be to discern the many different ways that human beings can receive God's primal light.

Through this work, we may contemplate the mysteries of revelation. The initial visions in part three of this volume reveal God's greatness in the story contained in the Old Testament: God's omnipresence in the creation of the world, in the development of the spirit of man and woman, in the Ten Commandments, in the celebration of the Feast of the Passover, in the life of the prophets. Then follow visions on the life and work of Jesus in the New Testament, witnessed in different ways by the Four Evangelists: Mark as the companion; Matthew as the artist; Luke as the narrator of Christ's mission to the poor, those who seek justice, truth, and love; and John as the one who prepares the way for the coming, unifying church—a serving church that will encourage each individual to develop in freedom as a person of light. John invites us all to come to the table of the wise and participate in the ongoing process of creation. The Johannine teachings presented here are holistic. Living in revelation provides space for the human body, soul, and spirit to meet God's Spirit.

In these visions we are exhorted to learn the language of symbols—a language of the soul that helps us express many things in few words. In the visions on John's Revelation, Luke tells us that symbols reveal the greatness of God but also may fade in significance, according to their relevance to a specific culture. Symbols are not an end in themselves; they serve to express mysteries that cannot be grasped by the normal processes of reasoning. It is clearly implied that these mysteries not only reflect inner states of consciousness but reveal truths about God's world, even though the ways those truths are expressed may differ among individuals and cultures. I remember the day when Noirin ni Riain, the well-known Irish vocalist, Joa Bolendas, and I went to church and prayed. Quite spontaneously Noirin began to sing the hymns of Joa. I was struck by the beauty and deep Celtic resonance of Noirin's interpretation. Joa was impressed by the quality of Noirin's singing but upset because her songs were not sung in the way she had received them. As we continued to listen, Joa passed me a note containing the following words of a saint:

> It is the Irish soul that sings your hymns in this way. In Africa you will experience them in still more different ways—with drums and movements of the body. Give thanks!

Some of Joa's visions refer to coming events. Here it is impossible to make a definite judgment about them, for we as human beings cannot know the future; only God does. These predictions anticipate what lies ahead and therefore are to be understood as possibilities that may or may not come true. Rather than interpreting these prophecies as giving precise information about the future, it is wiser to understand them as exhortations to prayer. We are told that prayer changes the world. We are to struggle so that God's world comes to earth, whereby heaven and earth are linked, thus giving individuals and the different cultures the opportunity of recognizing and cultivating this link according to their own understanding.

This work has much to say about our attitude toward religious experience. We are exhorted not to cleave to the traditional laws of men but to recognize the signs of the times and the signs of the living God, who meets us in so many unexpected ways. We learn that prayer is not prattle but a struggle with darkness. Joa Bolendas receives instructions to pray that wars, violence, famine, and natural disasters do not ravish humankind. She is specifically instructed to pray for a particular land or group of people who are in danger. This task remains a heavy burden for her to carry. Throughout her visionary life, Joa Bolendas has continued to struggle daily until her prayers are heard and she sees God's light descending on the people, bringing relief to the suffering and distressed.

> *Called to this living source, we creatures still*
> *Darkly may feed hereon and take our fill,*
> *Although it is night.*

This poem by John of the Cross[1] seems to reflect much of Joa's approach to spiritual life. In the struggle with darkness, she too has been accompanied by God's light, visible in those who have risen from the dead. Already in 1966, in the last vision noted down in her journals, she beheld the figures of heaven clothed in black. In anguish she asked why they were all in black, and the answer was: "Light is within us. We suffer for humankind." And Joa responded: "I bend before you, and I will remain with you."

The new theology contained in these visions assures us that sacramental life is not to be confined within narrow definitions. The spirit of baptism is understood in a simple, direct way. In repentance and reconciliation, we are to ask our brother or sister to pray to Christ for forgiveness. The ordination of a priest should be simplified so that it will bring forth many wonderful fruits. The faith must not become sterile. We are not to make laws about what comes first or what comes last. We are to remember that there are many who are far away from the churches, yet close to Christ. By returning to the basic Christian truths, the many words that separate will fall away. We can no longer limit these truths to their dogmatic formulations. They are an expression of an encounter with the living God—an expression of the dynamic, ongoing process of creation itself. They are far greater and more mysterious than their formulation or ritualistic enactment. Mary Magdalene tells us, through Joa Bolendas, not to be small-minded but rather open and generous. John the Evangelist relates to us how from the ancient Greeks he learned to stay in the midst of life and discuss religious experiences in an unprejudiced way. Let us see with our eyes and listen with our ears to God's presence in the whispers of the human soul. The Christian faith is a living faith: a faith lived with the body, soul, and spirit—with the whole human being.

Faith and Experience

When I started my training as a Jungian analyst, I was afraid that the analyst I chose would expose my faith as a fraud or a massive defense system. I feared that I would be unable to articulate or defend my own religious belief. To my surprise, these fears were alleviated by the unconscious itself, which came to my rescue by means of a dream. In this dream I saw a large stone altar surrounded by four pillars supporting a roof, a simple version of the baldachin of St. Peter's, Rome, which was in need of repair. A voice said, "The altar is religion, the four pillars are psychology." When I awoke, the holy atmosphere surrounding the altar impressed upon me the necessity of maintaining my religious perspective, and I understood the altar to be a symbol of my own immediate relationship with God. I recognized the mandala structure of the baldachin as a symbol of the wholeness of the personality. This would be the subject matter of analysis. It could be renewed and strengthened so as to act as a support, protection, and means of communication of the altar mysteries, which at times were too powerful to be contained and expressed through faulty structures of my personality. This dream has remained with me throughout my life, pointing to a distinction between religion and psychology and the need to recognize their complementarity.

Up to recent times, faith has been largely a matter of tradition that has allowed little space for personal experience. Today faith has become taboo. People find it difficult to speak about this subject. On the one hand, people are critical and unimpressed by the authority of parents, state, or any religious institution. In discussions, knowledge of facts and an ability to reason are decisive. Faith is regarded as naive, childish, sometimes illusory. On the other hand, the longing for security, trust, and love render people without roots susceptible to all kinds of irrational experiences. There is a hunger for spiritual meaning and a turning toward the Unconditional, as understood by Paul Tillich.[2] This hunger can be manipulated by secular or religious sectarianism. Yet it cannot be overlooked that often in the most bizarre experiences many encounter the reality of the soul—the reality of themselves. Religious institutions cannot overlook these social and psychological upheavals. Religious traditions can no longer ignore the discoveries of depth psychology and its tolerance of inner transcendent experiences.

I have been asked to write a Jungian commentary on these visions, in this short foreword. For various reasons, I will not attempt an interpretation of them. Considering the openness of Jungian psychology to this kind of phenomenon, I would prefer to sketch a possible attitude that Jung might have had to this material.

C. G. Jung's reflections on his earliest religious impressions antici-
pated many of today's problems in this area. At an early age, Jung, like
so many people of our time, could no longer follow the example of his
father, who told him not to question the theology prescribed by the traditions handed down by his forefathers. He understood his earliest religious experiences as a reaction to this lifeless theology. God revealed
himself to Jung as an archaic, vital subterranean force, visiting him in
the mysteries of nature or the images of dreams. God was a psychological reality, an immediate, living experience which, in the last
instance, remained unknown and indefinable. Like those of Joa
Bolendas, Jung's religious experiences taught him that God refuses to
abide by the traditions of men:

> I was certain that this was the wrong way to reach God, for
> I knew, knew from experience, that this grace was accorded
> only to one who fulfilled the will of God without reserva-
> tion. This was preached from the pulpit, too, but always on
> the assumption that revelation had made the will of God
> plain. To me, on the other hand, it seemed the most obscure
> and unknown thing of all. To me it seemed that one's duty
> was to explore daily the will of God.[3]

These early impressions remained with him throughout his life,
and he always reacted strongly against an intellectual belief that
was divorced from a personal experience of God. Faith should not
forestall such experiences.

Jung was critical of any claim to a universal truth, not because of
its content but because of the inherent human tendency to pre-
sume to possess the truth and so exclude the validity of religious
experiences of other people and other cultures. He was well aware
of the destructive aspect of power in religious thinking and how it
limits the freedom of the human spirit. Many of the followers of
religious traditions, who have not sufficiently recognized split-off
parts of the psyche within themselves, are all too disposed to project

evil onto others who are not in agreement with their own religious thinking. As a psychiatrist, Jung was also aware of the overwhelming power of the unconscious and its capacity to destroy the individual personality.

It is with caution that I invoke the spirit of Jung, and in doing so I do not imply that Jung's and Joa Bolendas's anticipations of the future of Christianity are identical. Jung took to task a Christianity that emphasized the light principle because of the inherent human tendency to deny the darker, unrecognized or unwanted parts of the self. Joa's concept of light is not equivalent to the light of a one-sided attitude of the conscious mind, nor does it signify a rational approach to religion, often the target of Jung's critique of religious practices. Primal light, according to the Johannine teachings in Joa's texts, approximates to the transcendental and metaphysical light of the mystics; it is an expression of the very essence of God and all of creation, including the darkness of night.

Despite these reservations, I have little doubt that Jung, as a man who foresaw the religious predicaments of our times, would have been convinced of the importance of these visions as private revelations. For Joa Bolendas did not blindly follow the traditions of her faith but had the courage to act upon her own religious experiences. She did not interpret the experiences so as to fit collective expectations. At no point has her personality been absorbed in the numinosity of her visions. She has retained her individuality and with it a recognition of her failings and limitations. She has maintained her role as mother, pastor's wife, and active member of a busy community.

Jung would have recognized not only the personal but also the collective significance of this work. I believe he would have taken seriously a vision of Christianity that is not just a matter of human opinion but a direct experience of the original mystery of God's relationship to humankind. He would have welcomed a message that asks the churches to move with the spirit of the times and encourages each individual to seek the truth in his or her own way. He would have certainly supported the attitude of ecumenical tolerance expressed through Mary's words in the section, "Risen from the Dead":

> Hold on to this: The new church, the unified church, is all that makes men and women into people of light! Holy Scripture and the truth of the Old and New Testament will remain. The church that has grown and developed will remain. Repentance and reconciliation, baptism and the eucharistic meal, will remain. To be left open are the ways in which different types of people will develop. Do not be small-minded; be open and generous! You will discern all things through love!

A Message of Hope

Reflecting on the difference between an illusion and a healing religious experience, Jung[4] came to the conclusion that no one can know what these ultimate things are:

> We must therefore take them as we experience them. And if such experience helps to make life healthier, more beautiful, more complete, and more satisfactory to your self and to those you love, you may safely say: "This was the grace of God."

That was the same conclusion that Gebhard Frei, the well-known Catholic theologian who had the privilege of knowing Carl Jung and Joa Bolendas, reached in his assessment of her private journals in 1962. Following the criteria of John of the Cross, Frei found no evidence for disintegration of the personality. On the contrary, he was moved by this woman's love and active work for her family, parish, and fellow human beings. He was impressed by the courage, energy, and strength that she gained from her religious experiences to deal with the troubles, fears, and concerns of daily life; by her ability to accept sacrifice and suffering; by her prayerful attitude toward those who were near as well as important issues in the community, the church, and the world. Regarding the content of these visions, he asked:

> *How can this Protestant woman arrive at insights and convictions which at times contradict those assimilated in her youth, or, better said: which extend so thoroughly her image of Christianity that they could not have come from her personal unconscious?*[5]

He found Joa Bolendas's writings on Christ, Mary, the Mass, and life after death in accord with the teachings of the Orthodox and Roman Churches. Frei was convinced that this Protestant woman had been predisposed toward an inner living Christian mysticism. He concluded that her journals reflect the experience of a spiritual reality which, in its dynamism as a living organism, expresses the mystery of Christ's love for humankind.

What has been said about the journals in 1962 might well apply to the present work. Joa Bolendas's religious formation in the journals now finds its flowering in *So That You May Be One*. The message of this book is a plea to Christians and Jews to return to the origins of their faith, to their first love, and from that basis to begin again and find the one rock—the coming unifying church. The reader does not have to accept everything in this work, but is asked to read it critically. In Joa's commentaries on the Old Testament, an angel commends us to discern between what belongs to the spirit of the times and what is of God's Spirit. When Joa inquired about the tribe of Jit, an angel answered that it was not important to argue over this matter. We are not expected simply to believe, but are invited to open ourselves to the reality of faith and to the

experience of God's immense love for humankind, for all creatures, for the entire living cosmos. We are not expected to follow
blindly the traditions of the past, but are invited to seek the truth
and participate in the ongoing process of creation. The Johannine
teaching of this book tells us that the wholeness of the human
being is a process—the history of human spirit relating to God's
Spirit. We are not to become resigned and isolated or think that
we alone possess the truth. In a true and authentic way and in the
freedom of spirit, we are to pray, ask for forgiveness, live in community with our fellow humans and those risen from the dead,
and be receptive to God's primal light so that the mystery of God's
word may abide in us and be passed on to all the peoples of the
earth. This is a message of hope and renewal for the individual,
the churches, and the cultures of the world.

Such may be the intimations of this book. The impact of Joa Bolendas's visions on the future remains to be seen. In this critical age of
doubt and disbelief, we may ask if heaven itself has come to its own
rescue? Has the ultimate source of being spoken to humankind
through the words of a woman, trained as a secretary, whose soul and
spirit seem to have been called to a higher purpose? Do the Evangelists continue to speak to us at a time when contemporary historical criticism is questioning their existence? Do the words of Joa
Bolendas testify to the ongoing transformative truth contained in the
Old and New Testaments? These among others will be the questions
for the future. Perhaps in the end there is no proof or disproof, only
the hope that through Joa Bolendas's visions, the living source of all
life may work on the human soul, bringing it and the world one step
closer to a recognition of truth and fulfillment.

This Translation

The original German text, *Ein Fels*, was privately printed in 1988
and finally published in 1992. Although I have used that text as the

basis for the present translation, the English version differs in two ways: "The Rosary" and "Risen from the Dead," as well as some additional material in "From My Journals," have been included; and some visions have been extended by Joa Bolendas from answers received to questions about this translation.

Joa Bolendas's style of writing is direct, spontaneous, and at times telegraphic. Its beauty lies in its simplicity. It is not the language of the Greek or Latin theologians. It is not a language of definitions, nor does it use the notion of substance. Joa Bolendas receives answers that explain not just what things are but also what they do. According to Hans Küng,[6] this kind of language is closer to the spoken language of biblical times. Wherever possible, I have tried to retain this original style. Changes have been made only where the full meaning could not be contained in a direct rendering of the German text—and these changes only with the permission and help of the author. It should be noted that words in bracketed italic print were not directly spoken in the visions but were implied. It is also important to remember that much space lies between these words. I have often sat in a church with Joa Bolendas for more than an hour, during which time she wrote down a mere five to ten lines of vision. Most of this time was spent in beholding a spiritual presence in prayer and silence.

This translation would not have been possible without the help of Christopher Mason, Lela Fischli, Franziska Piderman, Liza Burr, and AnneMarie Hill.

NOTES

1. E. Allison Peers, *Saint John of the Cross* (Hertfordshire: Anthony Clark, 1974), p. 432.

2. Paul Tillich, *What Is Religion?* (New York: Harper, 1973), p. 76.

3. Carl Gustav Jung, *Memories, Dreams, Reflections* (New York: Vintage, 1963), p. 46.

4. Carl Gustav Jung, *Psychology and Religion*, coll. works, vol. 11 (New York: Bollingen Series XX, 1969), p. 105.

5. Gebhard Frei, *Beurteilung*, unpublished, p. 3.

6. Hans Küng, *On Being a Christian* (London: Fount Paperbacks, 1985), p. 325.

Educated in Dublin and at the Catholic University of America in Washington, D.C., John Hill is a Jungian analyst in private practice in Zürich, Switzerland. He is the author of numerous articles on Jungian themes and is a lecturer at the C. G. Jung Institute in Zürich.

I HEARD THE CALL OF THE SERAPH

WORKING WITH THE VISIONLIEDER OF JOA BOLENDAS

Therese Schroeder-Sheker

In writing about the mystical songs and prayers of Joa Bolendas, I don't want to present readers with a musicological commentary on the nature of hymnody, but rather with a meditation on the fusion of two distinct fields: song and prayer. I am concerned here only with the capacities required to work with and live in *sung prayer*. Joa Bolendas's songs (which *are* prayers) are central to her mysticism. The songs-as-prayers and the visions are united, comingled and cannot be separated—hence, the term *visionlieder*.

The singing of prayer is central to all human religious experience, regardless of creed, ethnicity, or locality. All spiritualities have chant traditions, in one form or another. One might assume that the two realities of song and prayer would simply merge in an ideal synergy, which would then be propelled along (perhaps joyously carried away) by the energy of the marriage. But that would be like assuming a genuine marriage could take place by a simple combining of financial assets, without communion or devotion or conscious awareness of the commitment being made or the responsibilities freely held by the two people. It would also overlook the ongoing renewal of relationship that must occur in endless stages of growth.

Sung Prayer and the Mystical Marriage

In this context, the mystical marriage can symbolize at least two realities, if not three. The first is the union of the soul and the spirit, a true *interior communion* which takes place very gradually within the human individual; such communion is the fruit of prayer. The second concerns the *grounding* of either silent or sung prayer into the fabric of our daily lives; this is the marriage of contemplation and action, in which any tendency to dualism is transformed. Such mysticism is more than metaphoric, for interhuman marriage can be incarnational of both. Ultimately then, nuptial mysticism is profoundly creative and radiates hope: one can be inwardly *and* outwardly married.

This analogy is furthermore disconcertingly valid in describing the repeated challenge of a commitment to daily prayer, whether sung or not. There is a honeymoon phase, and then there is a real shakedown period. During the shakedown phase of a marriage, the glamor of falling in love can fade; distractions are eventually stripped away to reveal essentials. As the two people land (for better or worse), strengths and weaknesses emerge with all their potentials, the shadow material is uncovered, and there, in the boundary zone where the tension lies, is the material and the opportunity for growth. At that point, the task is to see if transformative but tumbleweed passion can grow into enduring rooted, grounded, fruitful love. The couple must consciously discover what it is they really are doing together, and why, and how.

Marriage is also a sensitive and delicate way of describing the impediments to and joys of prayer, silent or sung. In the beginning or honeymoon phase, at the point of entry, we may be given this gift (of either music or prayer or sung prayer) by pure grace. Initially, we may be infused with sung prayer by virtue of community activities in a *schola cantorum* or even astonished in blessed hours of solitude. This kind of musical epiphany has its parallel to the experience of romantic love, of falling in love. While it is true that one must carve out spaces in the day reserved wholly for prayer or for music, this infusion, this sacramental indwelling or pure gift that parallels "falling in love" does not happen because it is scheduled in a daily planner. Mystery is involved; it happens, initially, in the honeymoon phase, as a gift, by virtue of the fact that you showed up, and often when you least expect it. For the lover, "falling" involves being in the right place at the right moment. A hundred things could happen to prevent the meeting, and yet, a miracle occurs: two people meet and the meeting changes their lives. We have all heard someone describe the simplicity of walking into a room, meeting someone unexpectedly, and, inch by inch, the heart starts to open. The gift of love is nothing short of a miracle, and the same is true for the experience of the singer who works with prayer: sung prayer is one of many ways in which love is made audible and brought into the fullness of life.

The greatest *schola* masters are really truly "in love" with the sung prayer of the liturgy. They bring the capacities for fervor and devotion and care and attention into every note, but the "falling" imagery may not be the same. For the singer, one must first show up, and then one must risk. In sung prayer, one must risk burning and one must risk soaring, nothing less. Whether one falls in love or whether one sings in love, surrender is an elemental teacher, and eventually one learns to stand in love, to be and to radiate love. In the case of the musician, this is done through the medium of music. In the case of a truly musical person, this can even be achieved through a silence which radiates interior harmony and, by extension, brings peace to those surrounding them.

In music, in sung prayer, the elevation and expansion that brightens, softens, and makes transparent the human body and soul also vivifies the spirit. This gift which seems to come so effortlessly in the beginning is more difficult with the passage of time; it cannot be programmed or demanded, but happens sometimes in spite of us, despite our weariness, boredom, conflicts, and human brokenness, not to mention pitch problems, sympathies and antipathies. We are daily surprised by the vivifying, renewing, refreshing aspect of sung prayer. Furthermore, it's difficult to separate sung prayer from love, for one embodies the other. But as relationships progress, sustained over years, daily sung prayer doesn't just "happen" any more than marriage just "happens." Sung prayer is a field that must be carefully tended and cultivated, because it is relationship-centered. The relationship between the individual singer and the body of prayer to be sung must be allowed to alternate between periods of activity and rest, and it must be constantly renewed. Periods of reflective silence must flow between the periods of praise or lamentation. Practically translated into daily life, that means that the geography of the musical soul must include silence and sounding.

Taking the metaphor of the mystical marriage to its completion, we do well to give consideration to the higher purposes of music. What is the role of the inner life for the serious musician? And what role does the reorganization and reharmonization of body, soul, and spirit have in the outpouring of this living, streaming music? Sound reorganizes matter and it reorganizes us as human beings. Living in a musical tradition (be it psalmody, hymnody, art or love song) over time changes the musician completely, in subtle and not-so-subtle ways. Not only do pitch, hearing, and listening become more acute, but the ability to actually experience music increases in dimension, including height, depth, width.

In alchemy, a perfect metaphoric language to describe the journey leading up to the mystical marriage, we are continually encountering the processes that separate what is essential from the nonessential, that separate what is gross from what is refined. This can occur through heating processes, in which the rigid, solid state of matter softens, melts, eventually becomes liquid, and even vaporizes. From the spirits or vapors come essential oils, fragrances, and medicines; from these essentials tinctures are made. What is dense and non-essential settles to the bottom of the crucible, and what is pure and transparent rises. Music has the same possibilities within the human soul and also affects our physiological parameters to a profound degree. The entire combination of body, soul, and spirit (each inter-penetrating one another) forms the human crucible. In the alchem-ical picture of the mystical marriage, opposites gradually achieve union because a complete harmonization process has become suc-cessful. The individual, wholly unified, becomes virginal again, in soul and spirit. We can accurately use the same language of nuptial mysticism to describe what happens when the singer has become reorganized by sung prayer. Another way of saying it: we become what we love. The singer becomes one with the prayer. The activi-ties and beings become one.

The *visionlieder* of Joa Bolendas are only possible because she did tremendous inner work over many years. She had to gradually har-monize the interior conflicts and tempests that occurred as she was asked to grow and pray and work in new ways, ways previously unknown to her. The visions published here relate these struggles humbly, honestly, and musically.

Visionlieder and Bridge-Work

If sung prayer requires alternating periods of song and silence, we must also remember that the prayers are by their very nature identi-fied with specific religious identities, liturgies, and rituals (Buddhist, Jewish, Christian, Islamic, and others). Furthermore, prayers are intimately related to the liturgical year. It is valid then to ask if there are other subtleties and nuances of intention involved in singing the *visionlieder*. It isn't specific to one particular liturgical impulse, and it is profoundly Christian. One might say that Joa's entire mystical life has been devoted to repairing fragmentation. She is a kind of spiritual physician. Her legacy, musical and mystical, is about bridging — building bridges that allow individuals and groups and cultures (yes, even churches) to connect despite differences, to love and honor and cherish the differences; building bridges that allow the communities of the living and the communities of the dead to work and assist one another; and building bridges that connect the human and the divine, the earth–sky axis.

Meeting differences and building bridges *so that we may be one* is not about uniformity, or slighting important distinctions that support healthy identities, and it is not a nostalgic longing for blissful unconscious merging. Its greatest potential is about the miracle of love in a constantly deepening humanity and experiencing the presence of God within that humanity. Jean Vanier, the founder of the international L'Arche home movement (nurturing the dignity of the disabled) says that God is not simply present in acts of healing or in capacities to heal, but rather *in the need to be healed!* Our wounds and our differences in fact create the opening for the theophany to occur. He does not underestimate the value of differences and bridge-work: "We can only truly love people who are different; we can only discover that difference is a treasure and not a threat," he said, in the Harvard Wit Lecture of 1992.[1]

Over the better part of a decade, in American and European concert settings and in the world of palliative medicine, I have experienced the ways in which the *visionlieder* of Joa Bolendas build bridges between individuals of great spiritual and cultural diversity, and between the living musician-clinicians who serve the needs of the dying and those individuals who are living with their dying.

Perhaps the readers wonder if the comments here are formed of a combination of scholarship and prayer, out of which one might be tempted to theorize. In light of that, it seems useful to say a few words about the personal relationship and bridges between Joa and myself. There are not so many details, but they are vivid, spiritually demanding, and life-affirmative. My initial encounter with the mystical work of Joa Bolendas involved seeing a reproduction of one of her paintings in Brussels. This depicted the Christmas angel who visits her. Stunned, I excused myself from a crowded room and spent the night changing. Having seen her seraph, even on paper, what else could I do? Meeting this woman came later.

Joa stresses that her private life is not so important; the message is. I take her indication and would say, simply, that when we met, we got right down to business. That is to say, she gave me very personal guidance about interior prayer and sung prayer. She cautions about polar tendencies: Be serious, but go neither toward severe austerity to find God nor toward the casual or sloppy, which breed spiritual superficiality. When she prays, she is fierce in her ability to attend to the moment with total surrender and focus. She is fierce, like fire, yet humble, like a candle, only brighter. She can argue; she can ask the most of you when she knows there is more of you to give. She comforts many; she is a tremendously warm and animated woman, who has the love of a lively family network. I sought her out and asked to be received in the late 1980s. She prayed for a week and then told me where and when to arrive. She has never been my spiritual director, and yet she has informed my life and work very deeply, very generously, helping me through illness and interior crisis, and celebrating with me in joy. This strong woman is clear, direct, yet supportive, and when I describe her to people, I stress that she is indeed very serious (even demanding) about her commitment and spirituality, that she has suffered and struggled physically and spiritually through the decades with a most particular and charismatic vocation, but that she embodies a tremendous capacity for joy.

The Spirituality of Listening in Joa Bolendas

The reception of this music comes to Joa quietly, slowly, as if one could hear the extended but certain approach of a choir traversing a body of water, coming from far distances. Joa, the receiver, is best understood as a solitary figure waiting on an unsullied shore, attentive, peering as if to pierce the mist, listening with her entirety. She is particularly sensitive to pitch, timbre, and the feeling of the key of each scale, down to the minutiae of vibration. As the boat holding the mystical *schola* draws near, the intensity increases. Over time, she can discern the melodies and countermelodies as if they were currents in the water, the currents allowing the movement of the boat to take place. These currents can allow the mystical ship to approach without being propelled by manmade devices, without tension or even steering. The same is true for the *visionlieder*; if the human body ensouled is the little ship and the hymns are the currents, the *visionlieder* allow movement (and progress) to take place within the human soul and spirit. After many years of living with these hymns, I suspect they reorient and open the human heart as well.

One must not understand these hymns as "compositions" in the modern sense of the word, as the intellectual property and fruit of a musically informed and highly educated individual who will sign her name to the work and own the copyright. Joa is not a composer; she is a hearer and a listener. She turns to listen, to hear, and in doing so, the music is received and revealed, from angels; it is neither conceived nor composed. The voices of the singers ring—the angels repeat the hymns over and over until she can hold the content and understand the inner relationships. The chorus is kind to Joa, a servant who loves song but who is completely unlearned in music notation, theory, harmonic analysis, or schools of composition. These hymns are revealed to her because she listens faithfully, and not because she wants to compose a hymn of praise to Mary or

Christ. Sometimes, she asks the heavens for a song that will convey what words alone cannot, and she does this for specific situations; the heavens then shower her with song.

In a world of ambient music, atmosphere music, elevator music, the music of so-called "distraction therapy," and general sensory overload, listening (as activity and as capacity) is undervalued and underestimated. When it is valued psychologically, it is understood as an essential piece in relationship building and in conflict resolution. People today in a competitive corporate secular world are not encouraged to take up listening *as a spiritual practice*, but it has always been implicit as that in temple and monastic cultures. It requires tremendous life forces *to listen*, to become inwardly still, to suspend self-talk and arrogant critical and judgmental tendencies and to be present to another person or reality. In this "higher octave" listening, one selflessly comprehends the acoustic event, but the locus of the activity seems to be the heart, not only the mechanical instrument of the ear. The rudiments of spiritual (or other) knowledge may be received through the ear, but when these ideas penetrate the heart and are apprehended by the *oculus cordis*, then *hearing becomes vision*. For these reasons, I have only been able to describe the hymns of Joa Bolendas by coining a new word to characterize an entire genre: *visionlieder*.

Listening as Spiritual Activity

Mystics—those who have had the simultaneous experience of knowing, loving, and sensing the presence of God in their lives—link listening with the active reception of God. Entire treatises have been written about the care of the senses in the cultivation of the spiritual life. Saint Maximus (580–662) of the Eastern Orthodox tradition emphasizes the primacy of the senses in the development of holiness: "The powers of soul expand and develop through the senses."[2]

The words of Isaiah the prophet are clear: "Hear, and your soul shall live" (55:3). The contemporary physician Alfred Tomatis says, "Listening is the royal route to the divine."[3] In Hebrew, to be heard is already to be answered, and to listen is to obey. The central affirmation in Judaism is: "I am heard." David Wolpe tells the story of Rabbi Harold Schulweis: "If you ask me—is prayer heard? I'll ask you—are you listening?"[4]

The early church father Origen (c.185–c.254) understood hearing as "inner readiness" and listening as an "attitude of soul" toward God for the inner dialogue which takes place without sound from the soul to God, and from God to the soul.[5] "Sin" (literally: alienation, being off the mark) causes "deafness in the soul." For Origen, "quiet readiness" brings about a mysterious close union with God, but this spiritual hearing can only be maintained when "linked with action." Any such inspired "action," of course—some intentional or contemplative work that serves the soul of the world—prevents this interior listening from retreating into elitist privatism. This spirituality of listening linked with "action" is immediately put to the test, for example, in the use of music and sung prayer in the care of the dying.

For the Benedictine abbess Hildegard of Bingen (1098–1179), hearing is receiving; not being able to hear or receive is wilderness, wasteland, desert. "We would be vacant if we were unable to hear and perceive," she says.[6] She sees the inability or unwillingness to hear as a closure. Furthermore, she understands not listening as a hearing disturbance and the cause of illness. She says that we take what is sacred in with our ears; with sight we come to know, but with hearing, we come to understand. In her vision of the end of time, she *hears* the body of Christ, with a harp at his heart.

The Eastern Orthodox Nicodemos from Mount Athos (1749–1809) tells us to guard the sense of hearing, because sounds impress themselves upon the imagination.[7] He cautions us not only about sound pollution, but about the deadly sounds which carry slander. Slander actually slays the life-formative forces in the soul that fill one with the warmth of enthusiasm. Nicodemos finally says that hearing is available to help us develop compassion and understanding. The former Benedictine monk Tom Moore extends the Nicodemian ideal and is even more explicit: "The soul becomes pregnant through what is heard. Words impregnate."[8]

The composer and musicologist Anny von Lange (1861–1925) understood the spiritual and sacramental dimensions of listening: "To listen is to make oneself selfless," she said.[9] For von Lange, hearing-listening as an inner activity creates the capacity for love in the soul, and a listening being is in constant readiness for self-sacrifice.

For me, in music, specifically in the experience of tone, one perceives the activity of the spirit penetrating matter, disclosing the spirit within matter. Hearing-listening is another way of describing the witnessing of spirit impregnating matter. A being becomes audible and in doing so, reveals spiritual activity. This can also explain why hearing-listening is so linked to the development of conscience. I am not suggesting that hearing-impaired people[10] are lacking in conscience. We may be hearing-impaired and still capable of profound reception, because this reception can occur through the opening of the heart, is extended over the surface of the skin, and is magnified in an inner attitude in which one welcomes the future. These subtleties are present throughout daily life as well as in at least three areas (in which I have intimate involvement): the educational processes devoted to the formation of contemplative musicians; activities and capacities required in the concert and recording world; and in the uses of prescriptive music in the palliative care of the dying. Having had the opportunity to work with and live in the *visionlieder* of Joa Bolendas has made all the above-mentioned and other teachings leap off the page. When one has the opportunity to experience these things directly, sound reintroduces beauty into the soul like a burning bush. Where there is spiritual fire, there is warmth and light in the music. This is the quality that makes music living and streaming; this is the content that must be poured into the music, transforming chilly laryngeal or fingertip perfection into something that is vivid and full of life.

It is possible to play or sing well-coordinated correct notes at reasonable tempi and with intelligent phrasing, and yet deliver "dead" music, music that doesn't move, affect, ennoble, or transform doers or receivers. Any repertoire can be reenacted, "played," but remain limp, lifeless, impotent. The question arises then about calling something back into existence. How is it done? What happens when we are working with the score for musical prayer? The score is merely a map, the repertoire is still a kind of vessel, and the sensitive musician continually asks: Can I find something in myself to pour into this container? How does one bring living, streaming music into the world? What is involved in bringing something from a mere indication on paper back into fully dimensional life? How does one sing living prayer? Authentic prayer?

Ultimately, to me, these questions revolve around the notion of *transubstantiation*, for living music can only occur at the threshold where matter and spirit meet, where spirit impregnates matter, and is then made audible, freely available to the hungry. In this perspective, the sacramental aspect of music is primary: in living, streaming music, the human, even the broken and wounded human, as either musical doer or musical receiver can experience the presence of the divine in multiple ways, in body, soul, and spirit. Such music can express joy and celebration or its opposite. I also feel that, ultimately, much authentic music becomes pure prayer in Simone Weil's sense of the word: rapt attention. To work with the *visionlieder* of Joa Bolendas is to understand music in its (Boethian) capacity as spiritual medicine, as a *materia medica* revealed to care for the body and cure the soul, and as a repertoire filled with life forces, streaming through the universe, connecting and bridging while healing.

Working with Sung Prayer, Working with Visionlieder

Life-in-music and *life-in-prayer* need not be understood as two separate and polarized activities of concentration and expansion. They
can flourish in the midst of a fully active life of work in the world and
feed the souls of the many when they exist as the warp and weft of
one singular fabric: *sung prayer*. Each point of intersection, each
place where music and prayer cross paths and become one, makes
room for a mysterious Third. It is in this selfless attitude of pure
readiness for the Word of God by which we open ourselves. This
soul-gesture asks us to become more chalice-like, and, in doing so,
we make room for the divine, the presence of the Third. Hans Urs
von Balthasar says, "Mysticism is a particular mission . . . a continual
and complete movement away from oneself, in self-forgetting and
virginal readiness for the Word of God." [11]

As singers working with the *visionlieder*, if we understand the Bolendas legacy in its mystical context, then the work of singing is sacramental. Here, our fleeting, temporal, and imperfect personalities
die many small deaths in order to make way for something far
greater, something eternal. This sacramental presence *shines
through* the music, and is intimately bound up with four interpene-
trating fields:

> 1) the spiritual practice of *listening,*
> 2) the intentional *fasting from sound* in the practice of *silence,*
> 3) the practice of *kenosis* or inner-emptiness,
> 4) followed by cultivating the burning desire for *communion.*

This communion takes place with the God of love, with the saints
and angels, with the communities of the living and the communities of the dead. Even when we shut the door and go into the privacy of our rooms to pray, we do not do so alone. The silence that
emerges out of the practice of *kenosis* (emptying ourselves of
attachments) is anything but a void. In this pulsating silence, music

and sung prayer can be met anew. The immediacy of sensing, knowing, and loving God in sung prayer affects both body and soul. We can describe this deepening process which grows over time as *contemplative musicianship*. This orientation is available to all, in solitude and in community.

The chanters' maxim *"to sing is to pray twice"* summarizes the potency of this direction. It is a line I have heard since youth. Can you imagine how startled and humbled I was then, one grace-filled day in a quiet Alpine mountain village, to receive the potentized version of this saying? The following brief account of a few moments of my initial meeting with Joa distills the urgency of her message: *storm heaven, renew prayer, pray for the unity of the churches, everyone's participation is needed.*

Lukewarm Is Not Acceptable

The only personal "assignment" Joa ever gave me was advice to read the *Book of Revelation* seriously and repeatedly. How troubling it was then for a person of so many failures to read and reread that the angel speaks to the community at Laodicea saying essentially, *"Lukewarm is not acceptable!"* Later, to the community at Ephesus, he says sadly, *"You have abandoned the love you had at first."* Maybe that angel comes to each of us, especially at mid-life, when most of us are lost in a darkened wood, when we are sorely tempted to coast along rather than deepen and renew. Living with the work of Joa Bolendas has taught me a great deal about fiery engagement, and she makes explicit that every moment counts.

It was a summer day; we were in the privacy of her home. Joa sat teaching about the manner in which she hears the songs of the angels: slowly, drawing near, approaching over the span of days, even a week. She asked me to sing a hymn of praise (*Lob*). She listened, wordlessly overlooked my lack of courage, corrected the tempo, addressed the importance of the rhythm of prayer (every seven hours). She raised one hand so that her palm faced me, moved it in a slow circle imitating a gesture the angels had taught her, and continued. She stresses an incarnational spirituality. She demonstrated how the hands of singers might quietly be left open if we want to make room for the fire of God's love to pass through us to others. She transformed the intensity and dimensionality of my rather clouded, introverted commitment with a manner of prayer that is available to and for people of every walk of life. I lost energy in worrying about forgetting some of the precious details, and knew that I was missing some things in translation. Then, with that kind of direct and penetrating lightning that is only available to those who speak the truth and to those who are on fire, she said:

> "To sing is to pray twice?
> *Yes . . . good.*
> But it is different now.
> Everything is quickened. . . .
> *Now*, to sing is to pray *tenfold*."

I had understood from Eastern Orthodox Christianity that light does not shine just to illuminate but also to transform. It would be difficult indeed for a musician to ignore that burning moment with Joa. It was a time of retuning, of burning away some older scale, and of returning to the next octave, where sound ignites both doer and receiver.

Joa is not the first to receive music from the angels in wide-awake consciousness. However, it is rare; she is exceptional, and has wrestled with this call, as a prophet. Lest readers assume that Joa might be an ethereal sort of feminine presence, let me dispel the image. She once described to me her frustration with the first songs the angels gave to her, banging her fist on the kitchen table. The songs were too difficult, and she let them know it!

The Visionlieder

Her visions are very clear, and the musical message is very strong. She speaks of a widened priesthood and discipleship. She is not naive; she does not advocate syncretism, yet affirms the primacy of both the Jewish Seder meal and of Christian Communion, of the spiritual healing available in prayer and in the Holy Eucharist. She also speaks of the unity of the churches, and of the call to joyful, radiant prayer. She faithfully learns and memorizes what is given to her in vision, and gives it away to all who, with hearing opened to the octave beyond, are ready to receive.

The songs are deceptively simple on the first read and might easily be overlooked by someone pressed for time, flipping through scores absentmindedly and distractedly and hungrily, the way every musician does at times. However, I know of no one who has *experienced* the *visionlieder* as sung prayer who remains untouched. There are over forty of them; most are monophonic, some are polyphonic. They have this in common with Gregorian chant—they require spiritual nakedness. You cannot hide behind them. Nor can they be used to display personal virtuosity. They purify and renew body and soul. Twelve of the *visionlieder* are published here in this volume. They are ones with which I have worked deeply over the years. They are a veritable world and spiritual *materia medica*.

Her songs of praise and reconciliation are brief, meditative, have very few words, employ pulsating images and echoes, can sustain repetition, and are meant to be lived with deeply, so that one forms a dynamic relationship with each piece over the passage of time. The lamentations are profound, earnest, and courageous. They do not avoid anguish; they acknowledge the dark violence in the world and the struggle of the Cross, though Joa never loses sight of the Resurrection. The *visionlieder* often concentrate on a single theme, such as honor, glory, praise, transforming light, or the name of Jesus. In describing the lives of mystics, Bernard McGinn has stated that language can be used informationally or transformationally.[12] Joa, like all the mystics, condenses language and uses it transformationally.

She hears the traditional Our Father as the most tender love song since Aquinas's *Adoro te devote*. Her *Vater* is filled with awe, leans into the vowels, and disables the paternalism which still troubles many modern women. Why not? Joa is a modern woman. She participated fully in a modern form, being married, giving birth to children, and even burying one of her sons.

In these hymns, the praying of the rosary is closely linked to the world of nature; the breathing becomes expansive, is aligned with the pounding of the waves of the sea, and is sung! She recently gave me a new piece, the voice of an infant singing from the other side, to console all grieving parents. The message? The most lyric, graceful, dancelike melody. It is cascading movement. In it, the child essentially sings, "Fear not, I sing and I praise!"

The most mystical songs employ no texts, but primarily vowels. Some are accompanied by angelic gestures; the act of beholding is critical. Somehow, in the Pentecost *lied* invoking light, she has seen the light actually radiating to the places of illness in the afflicted. In these light invocations, the physical heart as an organ of warmth can be pierced with tenderness, body and soul receiving beauty, intimacy, reverence. Still other hymns exist to assist heart disease, another for the relief of addictions. Singing these hymns, we can take up an important aspect of Eastern Orthodox Christianity. The entire human being can become something like a sacrament of light, and although time is replaced with eternity, the singers and the listeners remain grounded, in the body, now harmonized and more wholesomely tuned from being stretched and purified. Why? *This light is tempered and proportionate*. Physical bodies are irrigated with light, color, and tone, and are made more whole. The songs only help us to overcome our infirmities, not to disassociate from the pressing tasks at hand.

The Joa Bolendas Legacy Quenches Spiritual Thirst

At the Chalice of Repose Project, our sole focus is the care of the dying with prescriptive music. This contemplative practice is called music-thanatology and is a standard component of supportive care and palliative care in all the health care agencies in Missoula. Our graduates are now going out into the world and are working in hospitals and hospices across the country, and even as far away as Australia. With voice and harp, specially trained musician-clinicians attend to the needs of the dying 365 days of the year. The clinical basis for prescriptive music applications is based on a body-systems phenomenology. It far exceeds the scope of this article to describe the ways in which the *visionlieder* are employed and delivered in palliative care and in prescriptive music, but it is enough to let readers know that the thematic material (of some of the *visionlieder*) is incorporated into our work. The *visionlieder* are a source of inspiration and strength for some of our most difficult and mysterious hours attending the deathbed vigil. The patient response to this music has been remarkable.

To contrast *music-for-the-dying* with *music-for-the-living*, I have also included Joa's music in some way or other in all my solo concerts since 1988, European and American. There are even special occasions in which it has been appropriate and desirable to announce the evenings as occasions for sung prayer. One such example is a Pentecost Festival concert that occurred in Rotterdam (Netherlands) each year for eight years. In 1994, the Pentecost theme chosen by the organizers and which I developed in my repertoire concerned *the fire of the heart*. The music I chose began with Hildegard of Bingen and ended with Joa Bolendas. It wasn't a typical situation; after six consecutive years, the field had been very sensitively cultivated. The Dutch people joined me in sung prayer! They filled the church with the light streaming from their opened hands and hearts and sang Joa's song of Pentecost light. In her notebooks she wrote, "On Pentecost, when the breath of the Holy Spirit becomes more perceptible, I love to think of people when I am praying. And so it happened, that during prayer I heard the little song: *Jesus Christ, we implore You: through the power of the Holy Spirit, give us LIGHT!* As usual, I sang along, to learn it, and was astonished, how, in doing so, rays of light went out to people who were sick, and often quite unexpectedly to weak or sick places in their bodies."

A few days later, in a Franciscan chapel at de Voorde near Venlo, the Dutch people joined together for an ecumenical evening. Christians, Sufis, and Jews gathered together for sung prayer. I remembered the line from James Agee which Samuel Barber set to music: "Sure on this shining night, I weep for wonder. . . . all is healed, all is health!"[13] What happened? I played the harp and sang pieces from many traditions, but ended in Joa's Pentecost song. It is not that the people "dropped" or forgot their important religious intentions and identities. It must be that they lived a spiritual experience which transcended the definitions that separate us, and allowed them to bridge the differences, embody hope, and generate goodwill to all. They kept singing as if to drink in the light. Later, in silence, they simply would not leave the chapel, preferring to sit with eyes closed and hands still open. It was wondrous.

Visionlieder and Singing from the Future

I would like to say something about *singing from the future*. The isolated mechanics of vocal pedagogy do not move me, though they are important on one level, can prevent damage, and do fill important needs for singers at many stages. This might be understood as *vocal form*. What concerns me more than vocal form is *vocal content*. I am concerned with living, streaming music, as currents of warmth and light, not just repertoire. In order to address this, two areas will be discussed: bone-conduction singing, and a reimagination of the body in which the larynx is understood as an alchemical generative seat in the physical body.

There is one way of singing from a romantic past imbued with the mythos of the suffering artist. In this context, the uniqueness of the singer's vibrato impresses itself on each and every single note. I have always heard the vibrato as the fingerprint of the personality, made audible, rather than visible. When an artist has developed a great soul, the vibrato is used with extraordinary mastery. When this has not taken place, however, the excessive vibrato can cause us to shudder. Some voices are too tense, and this actually hurts and cramps the sensitive listener. It can shoot little slivers and arrows, or when the opposite is true, when the form is too slack, one passes over chasms and dips of the vibrato with a minor third.

Additionally and unfortunately, many teachers unconsciously employ the imagery of warfare when they teach students to project the human voice to fill the farthest corners of the concert hall. Let's be aware of that, and employ new imagery. Many a student singer and even some professionals project simple force or even false ego, rather than spiritual strength (a gesture of readiness), which is *selfless*. It is true that the projectile singing serves a particular purpose and does so very well when transformed and sculpted by a great artist. It can fulfill an established standard or custom, can scale lofty heights and agonizing depths, as in opera, where everything human is magnified and made larger than life. In this way, opera teaches us about our folly and our potential. The singers are very vulnerable because each note is wrung from the depths of their own bodies—the instruments that they "play" are within themselves. This places the singer in a completely different position from that of the cellist, harpist, or pianist, for example, each of whom plays on an instrument exterior to self. On the other hand, it is a great challenge for singers to shed narcissism regarding the voice. A singer in love with his or her own tonal color does not make room for the sacramental Third to shine through, which is to say, new life. This explains why a generation ago, many diva anecdotes were charitably published posthumously. They teach about our mistaken attachments and vanities.

There is yet another way of singing, however, outside the context of opera, where one actually sacrifices something of the volume and much of the vibrato, but nothing of clarity or tonal color. Here the singer sings in something slightly more silvery than pure tone, letting more of the longing for God fill the air, and redirects some of the tonal substance or sound stream back into the body. This is called bone-conduction singing, employing the skeleton as a soundboard. It creates a sweet ringing sound. This voice is not appropriate for all repertoire, but it is completely transformative in many settings and contexts.

I think that to sing from the future, something like Pentecost (*Whitsun*—White Sun) will occur internally, bodily. The skeleton will shimmer from within, and the singer's voice will ring in warm circles like the tones of a bell. As humans, we are meant to sing radiance. This radiance occurs, among other ways, when prayer and love become one in song.

If we image health as interior harmony or as numerous right relationships within the body, between the body and the soul, and between the soul and the spirit, it is then the human voice, in the activity of singing, that discloses our relationships or lack of them. The sacred singing schools of the past (*schola cantorae*) always sang the repertoire *a cappella*. Were these schools sacred because they sang music for specific liturgies? I don't think this explanation penetrates the depths nor allows for the presence of mystery.

A *cappella* hymnody requires spiritual transparency from all the singers. They must begin in silence, inhale, and, in doing so, breathe in oxygen, take something in. Physically, chemically, this colorless, odorless, and tasteless oxygen then travels from the nose and mouth, moves through the trachea and larynx, through the vocal folds, the vocal tract, and finally, we release the air, now stripped of something. It is exhaled as carbon dioxide, something that acts like a poison in the world. I would like to suggest that the larynx is an alchemical seat where we can transform coal and darkened lead into gold. There at the larynx, literally a threshold, the dead air can be transformed and spiritualized up one step higher; when this occurs, it is characterized by movement, sound is sculpted, and sensitive listeners can even perceive the flow forms in the various tones. We can transform the poisonous carbon dioxide to some degree, and the air can be released as song, love made audible. Because the larynx is a kind of altar, a holy ground in which some sacrifice is offered, spirit becomes audible, perceptible. Listeners can hear the air shimmer like gold or silver. *Logos-filled words*, whether spoken or sung, can be understood as a generative activity, for which we have responsibility. This larynx as altar is a second generative seat, a metamorphosis of the motherly womb. These creative, generative capacities and activities, however, are available to both men and women, and I am convinced that this was understood by monasticism in an earlier age. It magnifies the role of fire in truth-filled words and phrases.

To sing from the future then, implies that vocal pedagogy includes the spiritual practice of selflessness, and that the human body is reimagined and understood in a new way, with intensified responsibility. Singers involve themselves in a great meditative work in which they become increasingly more sensitive to the fact that spirit-filled tone emerging from within the depths of the transformed, reorganized human body can make love audible in the world. This makes the contemplative musician work with his or her repertoire in a manner that is always making room for the presence of the Third.

Conclusion

If it is the Spirit that prays in us, as St. Paul says, perhaps it must be the Spirit that sings in us too, if we are anointed singers. Joa Bolendas also is about the Spirit; her songs are spirit-filled. The *visionlieder* (as a genre) teach us that sung prayer is world work. Many of us have experienced the seeming acceleration of our personal and professional lessons, or "karma," so to speak. Thus, to sing in these days is to pray tenfold. But first, fast from sound; reserve times for silence, especially in nature, but even amidst the noise of the city, make yourself ready for the Word of God, the calm gesture toward welcoming the future. It is possible to hear the call of the seraph. Then, in singing the *visionlieder* from the future, we sing with our hands and hearts open. In this way, the tonal substance does not become invasive, and the purifying might of spiritual fire can fill the room of the living or the dying, transforming ordinary space into sanctuary space.

One final comment about Joa. A friend and I were once ready to leave her after a particularly vivid and powerful meeting. We were trying to calm the tears welling up in our eyes at the thought of leave-taking. We were down by the automobile, and she was up on a small balcony in her little mountainside chalet. She hobbled over to the rails, and raised her arms and hands over her head and crossed them, waving, smiling, shining, and blessing our departure. "*Not just for the dying*," she emphasized. For this and other reasons, I always stress the importance of both *music-for-the-living* and *music-for-the-dying*. We need them both. They serve different purposes. The *visionlieder* of Joa Bolendas serve both purposes.

The Gospel says, "*You shall know them by their fruits*" (Matt. 7:16). In this way, readers can practice discernment regarding their impressions and experiences. What are the fruits of the *visionlieder*? Dear reader, I hope you are both startled and strengthened. The world needs healing tenfold, to be sure. Gather together in twos and threes or more, making preparation for the Guest to arrive.

Start from silence. Sing! Sing prayer!

Sing from the future! Sing praise! Sing radiance!

You will become a chalice, serving the needs of the many who are broken or ailing.

> Chalice of Repose Project,
> Missoula, Montana
> Feast of the Immaculate Conception, 1996

NOTES

1. Jean Vanier, *From Brokenness to Community* (Mahwah, N.J.: Paulist Press, 1992).

2. See Paul Evdokimov, *The Art of the Icon: A Theology of Beauty* (Redondo Beach, Calif: Oakwood Publications, 1990); also, a monk of the Eastern Church, *Orthodox Spirituality: An Outline of the Orthodox Ascetical and Mystical Tradition* (Crestwood, N.Y.: St. Vladimir's Seminary Press, 1987).

3. See Tim Wilson, "Chant: The Healing Power of Voice and Ear—An Interview with Alfred Tomatis" in *Music Physician for Times to Come*, an anthology edited by Don Campbell (Wheaton, Ill.: Quest Books, 1991).

4. See David Wolpe, *In Speech and in Silence: The Jewish Quest for God* (New York: Henry Holt Publishing, 1992).

5. See Hans Urs von Balthasar, *Origen — Spirit and Fire: A Thematic Anthology of His Writings*, transl. Robert J. Daly (Washington, D.C. Catholic University of America Press, 1984).

6. See Barbara Newman, *Sister of Wisdom: St. Hildegard's Theology of the Feminine* (Berkeley: University of California Press, 1987); also Newman on *Saint Hildegard of Bingen: Symphonia* (Ithaca, N.Y.: Cornell University Press, 1988); also, the diplomatic facsimile by Prudentia Barth OSB, Immaculata Ritscher OSB, and Joseph Schmidt-Gurg, *Hildegard von Bingen: Lieder* (Salzburg: Otto Muller Verlag, 1969).

7. See Peters Chamberas's translation of *Nicodemos of the Holy Mountain: A Handbook of Spiritual Counsel* (Mahwah, N.J.: Paulist Press, 1989).

8. See "Annunciation" by Thomas Moore in Robert Sardello's anthology *The Angels* (Dallas: Dallas Institute Publications, 1994; also New York: Continuum, 1995).

9. See Anny von Lange, *Man, Music and Cosmos—A Goethean Study of Music*, trans. Florence Hough (London: Rudolf Steiner Press, 1992).

10. Sometimes it is just the opposite; furthermore, the formation of conscience may be closely linked to the ability to feel nuances and distinctions, and thus, to be able to experience personally the moral consequences of thoughts and actions. To cite the premiere example of a hearing-impaired person who is completely responsive and who demonstrates tha ability to feel and thus perceive extremely delicate nuances of sound, we can consider the international concert and recording artist Evelyn Glennie. She has established herself as a consummate musician and is recognized as the "First Lady" of solo percussion though she is profoundly deaf. This diagnosis does not mean that she does not hear, but rather, she says, that hearing is basically a specialized form of touch, and that the auditor *feels* vibration (as touch) as well as hears it. Deafness does not mean that you can't hear, she says, but it does mean that something is wrong with the ears. Still, "even someone who is totally deaf can still hear/feel sounds." Ms. Glennie tours through five continents, performs as a guest artist with the greatest symphonies in the world, and records exclusively for RCA/BMG. She will be releasing her eighth solo album in mid-1997.

11. See Hans Urs von Balthasar, *First Glance at Adrienne von Speyr* (San Francisco: Ignatius Press, 1981).

12. I am deeply indebted to Bernard McGinn—for his guidance, penetrating thought, endless scholarship, and generous humanity. See his *The Foundations of Mysticism: Origins to the Fifth Century*, Vol. I. in the series *The Presence of God: A History of Western Christian Mysticism* (New York, Crossroad, 1991).

13. James Agee, text from "Permit Me Voyage," Yale University Press, set to music by Samuel Barber in the composer's opus #13, no. 3.

Harpist Therese Schroeder-Sheker maintains dual careers in music and palliative medicine. She made her Carnegie Hall debut in 1980 and records frequently. She is currently the Academic Dean of the School of Music-Thanatology, Chalice of Repose Project, at St. Patrick's Hospital in Missoula, Montana.

ABOUT THESE VISIONS

I, *Joa Bolendas, received the following words from one who has risen from the dead:*
The words, the images——all that has been seen and heard——
are to be ordered metaphysically.

With visions, there is a difference between
clairvoyancy, premonition, psychic perception ——
and revelations from God's kingdom.

Many people can psychically perceive and foresee things, but
when God speaks to people,
then it is to people who have been chosen.

Examine all the spiritual gifts of human beings
with regard to truth——love——and their presence in God's creation.

Revelations have another wavelength.
The words, images, sounds (the hymns) come
over an extended period of time——with great intervals ——
which demands a lot of energy from those who receive them.
Devotion and concentration are needed.

Whenever someone receives revelations,
the brain works more quickly
and the heart beats more slowly.

When visions are passed on in writing,
it is good if the time intervals are graphically indicated —
as with dashes.
It is wrong when the words are dressed up,
to become profane sentences.
Their strength of expression will be taken away.
Additional explanation may be indicated graphically.

I wish to add that John Hill's translation provides the correct understanding of my visions. I withhold consent to any other translation into English of this book.

PART ONE

THE EARLY VISIONS

PREFACE TO PART ONE

These extracts from my journals are about what I personally experienced, through visions, concerning the unity of the churches. The extracts are only about visions on theology and theologians known to me from the Protestant, Catholic, and Orthodox Churches. They express a lot about the spiritual life of the church and what is necessary to live as a Christian in a Christian community. Other extracts will appear in a later work.

All this I experienced as a Protestant woman. I grew up in the Swiss Reformed Church, and I loved especially the great women of the Huguenots.

I was far from being a mystic. I loved life in all its healthy aspects — the beauty of nature, art, and music.

I never searched for visions and revelations. They were given by God.

Joa Bolendas
Autumn 1987

FROM MY JOURNALS

Spring 1957

Where shall I begin? As a child I did not have many experiences of God. I grew up just like every normal child. My mother used to say that I was always aware of any illness or accident in the family without anyone telling me. Later, whenever mother was ill, I would telephone knowing in some way that something was wrong. I remember once having returned home after school, just after a water diviner had visited us. Mother asked me to stretch out my hand and tell her where I felt a coldness in the room. I did so and became aware of a cold stream of water exactly where the diviner had said there was one. Without further discussion, I was allowed to go and play. I was happy that my parents never spoke about my gift and so I grew up in an uncomplicated way.

My confirmation was a great and powerful experience. Gradually I became aware that God was guiding me in greater and smaller ways. One of the more important experiences happened when I was sixteen years old. I dreamed: "In the middle of the night, men came walking on a stone path. They carried wooden poles, upon which were stone plates. On these plates was written: 'Keep watch and pray.'" I did not know what this dream could have meant. Without much reflection, I just put it into action. From then on, I prayed more, was more careful about myself and others, and perhaps became a quieter person.

In another dream, I saw the burial of my mother, a week before she actually died. Once she told us, shortly before her death, that soon she was going to return home. My mother and father believed in God in a deep way. After mother had left us, we all missed her very much. It was about two months after her death that she appeared to me in yet another dream. She spoke to me: "Do not mourn; look at me—I live again!"

It was during this spring of 1957 when I first began to see in vision dimensions of God's light in our church activities. These were beautiful experiences. I knew from many signs of God that God was with us Christians and that he was present in our community. I rejoiced when this awareness of God's intervening presence also came to my husband Otto, a pastor of the Swiss Reformed Church; to Pastor Werner and Pastor Eugen; and to Father Joseph, a Catholic priest. There were times when a great silence came over the people during divine service. Then I saw a fine, thin veil all through the length of the church lying over them. It appeared as a light grey mist—a transparent cloak—a spiritual substance that protected the people.

This LIGHT GREY MIST, in a Gothic form, was often to be seen in the office of Otto, when he was working. Once I saw it above Pastor Werner, just before he held evening service with my husband. Otto spoke first. Then Werner followed and he spoke on demons. While he spoke, I could see long snakelike arms come toward him. They came from the side windows of the apse, but they could not grasp him. I could also see this light grey mist whenever a pastor prayed for the forgiveness of sins of the community during service.

Easter 1957

On Holy Thursday at COMMUNION, while Otto was standing by the baptismal font at the front of the church, a great light in the form of a Gothic arch was to be seen. It reached down from the roof of the church to the floor and it was so large that Otto appeared to be very small beneath it.

After Werner's Easter sermon, I saw during Holy Communion something very beautiful that I had never seen before. As servers were standing at the baptismal font, a bright "mist" came down from above. It was lighter than mist, being white and soft and it covered the servers like a cloak. It was as if from another world. Of all those present, only Werner had a yellow light above his head. For a second time, I looked directly at him, and then it occurred to me that probably the light was there as a sign that he was a priest.

Ascension 1957

During the sermon on Ascension Day, a gleam of light in the form of a star suddenly appeared around Werner's head. Often while giving the sermon, Otto and Werner had light on their shoulders. This light fluttered as if moved by the wind.

Pentecost 1957

There was such emptiness during the week before Pentecost. This feast cannot pass by without our being aware of God's Spirit! On Friday, I found myself constantly having to swallow so as to avoid weeping. On Saturday, I went into the church to pray. My hands became limp and my lips were without movement. I saw in the apse two large, serious eyes turned in my direction. The entire apse was filled with darkness. It became clear to me that a certain pastor should not be allowed to give the sermon on Pentecost! I bowed down before God and asked him to help so that this pastor would not say anything stupid and, above all, so that he would not say anything against God's Holy Spirit. I did not go to the service of this pastor, but after it I felt the pressure give way. That evening I went again to the church. The apse was free from darkness, and it was filled with an atmosphere of goodness! I gave thanks to God and prayed for the Spirit of Pentecost, for the community and for the next sermon, which would be held on Pentecost Monday.

That night I went to sleep easily without any worries. Suddenly I heard a voice that called out:

You that have ears, listen to what the Spirit says to the churches. *(Revelation 3:13)*

I clearly saw the numbers shining in front of me. I quickly awoke and got up. It was five minutes past midnight. I went into the sitting room. There I prayed for the sermon that was to be held the next day and for the parish. I wrote the Bible reference down, went back to bed, and slept deeply until 7:30 in the morning.

On Pentecost Monday, I could see that God was with Werner, who gave the sermon, and indeed with us all. When Werner invited us to take Communion, he was enveloped in light; and when he took Communion himself, a light came upon his chest and face. My first thought was: Where does this light come from? Werner was not surrounded by light in the usual way but by a pure and strong beam that came from the baptismal font. IT CAME FROM THE BREAD that was on the font! Later the chalice shone with light and then everything became radiant. It was so strong that I couldn't understand why nobody had seen it.

July 1957

It was just before the holidays and again I felt something in the atmosphere. During this time I had the following dream:

A voice called out: Find a place of safety!
A 2,000-METER-HIGH MOUNTAIN WILL COLLAPSE!

Our family fled into the church and others were also there, including Werner's family. I didn't know any of the other people. We cooked, ate, and lived there. There was an atmosphere of peace, rest, and confidence. We also prayed. Suddenly there was a tremor. The church was shaken as the earth moved. Cracks appeared in all the church walls. When it was over, the sun shone. There was a bright light and the evil was gone.

Does this dream relate to our parish? Will there be a great crisis in the church? And the number 2,000—it is soon 2,000 years since Christ was born!

Toward the End of July

Mary has much more to say to us than we think. She means so much more to us than we are ready to realize!

I remember a service for the youth last spring. The whole evening was so enjoyable. When Werner spoke about Mary, the youth were covered by light; it was not the same light that God usually sends to pastors. The light for pastors appeared stronger and yellower. The light of Mary was white, pink, and bright blue, as when one looks through a crystal or broken glass. Mary's light did not envelop the pastors, but it surrounded the youth and others in the congregation.

August 9, 1957

Today I felt drawn toward the Glockenhof, a bookshop in Zürich. As an excuse to go there, I suggested to my sister that we could buy something for father's birthday. I went there with my children, bought a book for father, and went straight into the secondhand department. I was drawn there and yet felt sick as I came into this room. I pulled myself together and looked around for what could be there. The first thing that came into my hands was a folder with pictures in it. They were pictures of fifteenth-century stained-glass windows. My hands began to tremble as I saw these pictures. I felt as if I were going to faint while I looked at the last picture—a spiritual power almost knocked me down. I put the folder away, bought some small books, and went out into the fresh air.

August 13, 1957

My husband Otto had to give a cremation service in Zürich and I asked him if he would buy the folder for me. He went and looked at the pictures, but didn't like them as much as I had. So he did not bother about them.

August 14, 1957

The same spiritual presence was with me again, and a sense of greatness was in the atmosphere, so that my heart nearly stood still. That night I slept very little. Why did I not get up to pray?

August 15, 1957

Today this sense of greatness was so strong that I could hardly stay calm and I could not work. The Catholic church bells were ringing, and if I were away on holiday I would have gone to a Catholic church. I asked everyone what today's feast day was, but nobody knew. I discovered in a calendar it was the Feast of Mary's Assumption. Toward midday, this spiritual power left me. During the afternoon, Otto asked me to accompany him to Zürich. I was astonished, because he rarely goes there and does not even like going there. I went with him and asked if I could see the folder once more as I wanted to know what was special about those pictures. Otto said that if I liked them so much we would buy them. Once in the

Glockenhof, Otto took the folder into his hands and was curious to know what was special about the last picture. He read out:

> *No. 10, the Assumption of Mary.*
> *Second north window in the church of*
> *Our Lady of the Assumption of Romont.*

Otto bought the picture for me on that feast day of the Assumption. Give thanks! I have let myself be guided by God without even knowing it!

I would like to add that on this same day I went into our church and said to myself: "If I feel something of Mary here, then I will pray to her." But nothing was there. Nevertheless I tried to pray: "Holy Mary, mother of God . . . " This was empty and without strength. I felt no presence but, in prayer, I saw in the apse a kind smile and a gentle shaking of the head saying no. Then I knew that I had to give up. I prayed again to God and Jesus. The eyes in the apse were kind, full of love and affirmation.

December 1957

Looking out of our window, I saw a rider on a black horse in the heavens coming from the Albis hills. I shuddered at the sight of his face, which was grim and full of hatred. It was Krushchev, who was elected later.

As I later came to understand, everything that we see in visions has a significance, even though we don't immediately recognize it. For me, this vision was the first indication that I should pray for THE CHRISTIANS IN THE EAST. Thirty years later, I read in the Reformed Church newspaper about the great danger that Christians faced at that time:

In the fourth phase (1959–1964), Krushchev wanted to free the Soviet Union from all remnants of religion. He never achieved his purpose of "presenting the last Russian Christians on TV within a foreseeable period of time." But the church had to endure hard persecutions again. Many church buildings, monasteries, and several seminaries were closed; numerous church communities were dissolved and the clergy was reduced to half its number.

December 25, 1957

My heart leapt with joy as I read the following passage from Otto's Christmas sermon:

Let us go to the crib like the shepherds and wise men. You should know that the great things are not done in the public eye but in quiet places—in the light of a star of great promise. Let us turn away from the busy streets and give our attention to the still night of divine love. Let us fill our poor hands, and let our hearts be enlightened by the divine child. Let us see and hear what God has done for us.

When this part came in the service, I saw a cross radiating light in the apse. It was so strong and powerful! Nothing in the world is as beautiful and powerful as this light!

Passiontide, February 25, 1958

On the evening of the 24th, while I was writing, I saw a multitude of servile people. They were suffering and were not able to free themselves. They threw themselves down before God and lifted their arms up. They repented. They prayed to God, and I saw that he will forgive many! I saw the entire path of penance and the

length of time for penance. And in the end, Easter—pure and radiant! Easter is light—grace—joy. Easter is to be at peace with God.

And so I prayed: "Lord, you showed me yesterday evening that Passiontide has begun. So I ask you to cleanse our hearts. Make our souls pure that we may be ready to serve you. When we have made atonement and when we are prepared—use us as your instruments to help people who are searching for you at this time. Lord, behold the sea of people who are seeking you and who are making atonement. Be merciful and forgive us all."

As a Protestant, I did not know until then the significance of Lent. It was new for me to observe it and to know that it is a time of grace.

March 24, 1958

Today I met Pastor Eugen at the railway station. The "light grey mist" around his head was visible. I could see that there was a priestly power about him. This fills me with joy.

Tuesday of Holy Week, 1958

While praying for Pastor Eugen, I saw that he was surrounded by a spiritual strength during the entire Holy Week until Easter Mon-

day, even though he was so tired and exhausted. While praying for Pastor Werner, I saw that the heavens were dark and full of stars, and right through the center of the heavens was a bright path of seven golden stars. While praying for Otto and the community, I saw Christ. His body appeared to be almost black, like a silhouette, because behind him a bright light shone. His head was only outlined, for his whole face was radiant with light. With both hands he offered the bread—as if he were giving everything! This offering was holy!

Although he was ill, Eugen was helped and strengthened the whole week. Werner was made a dean. Would that explain the stars? Communion service was blessed as never before. More than 1,200 people took Communion in our church during that week. Light was around Otto during Communion and the sermon, and before the distribution of Communion a fine veil of light was around Werner.

April 20, 1958

I was resting in the church and looked from time to time toward the apse. There I saw three churches, two smaller ones and in the middle a larger one. Above them was a great cross. Does the large church have to do with ecumenism? I don't know what it could signify.

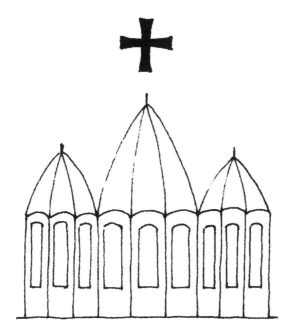

April 25, 1958

On the day of Mary's Assumption, I promised that I would follow the spiritual power that streams forth from Mary's presence, and this I would do regardless of doctrine. I would follow the spirit of Mary all the way and see what she wants to show me. That night I slept well. On Friday morning, Mary's strength was to be felt more and more. So I put on my coat and shoes, and with a quick and fervent prayer was on my way. Following this spiritual power, I was led to the Catholic church. No one was on the street: with throbbing heart, I entered the church and no one was there—God was gracious to me! As I went in, I felt Mary's presence no more. I prayed to God: "Help me—may your will be done." On the right, at the back of the church was a small ALTAR TO MARY, without flowers and without ornaments. I walked over there and was suddenly in the midst of a great spiritual strength coming from Mary. I prayed for a short time and went away. I looked around at the whole church. Nowhere else could I feel the presence of Mary, not even where there is a large statue of her with flowers and decorations at the front of the church. Everywhere else was empty. Only in the apse could the presence of Christ be felt.

Since I was already in this Catholic church, I knelt down before the apse, as I would in our church, to pray for the priests of this church and for all Catholics. After all, they are our brothers and sisters in the Lord. Then in the front part of the apse I saw Mary, young and full of love, reassuring me. She looked toward the small Mary altar at the back of the church—and smiled. She gave me courage and strength.

Afterward I saw Christ. He looked at the whole church and held out a book toward the community. It was the Bible. This image then disappeared.

I gave thanks to God. I went once again through the whole church and again to Mary's altar at the back. The greatness of her presence was still there, and I let it all flow through me. Mary was there as a messenger of God, but I felt that she wanted something from me.

Something in me was spiritually ready—but for what? What does Mary want from me? O God, I am ready, show me what I must do. I read something about "Help" written above Mary's altar, but I did not know what to do with that.

April 28, 1958

On the 26th of April, seven children were killed in an accident on Seestrasse. On Sunday, another child was killed in the middle of our village. In the community, several youths died during this time. Nearly every day we dug a grave. Accidents and heart failure were the cause of death. Children were in danger. Where was Mary? Shortly before these "woes," she was present and called me to her altar in the Catholic church. Her presence could still be felt today.

It has now been four days since I visited the altar of Mary, and since then I alone have carried around an awareness about these "woes" over the people. For four days I have known that Mary is with us when we ask God to give her as his messenger to help us. She was ready to help—and I had kept silent!

I remained silent because of my fear that the Reformed Church would not understand me. I knew that on that Friday at Mary's altar I should not just have been thinking, but I should have prayed and struggled until I received clarity. I should have accepted her help against these "woes." I should have been grateful that God showed to me and gave to us all the greatest messenger after Christ—Mary.

When one thing after another became clear to me, I spoke with Otto. We talked a long time, searching and praying. And so we were already two who were praying about these "woes."

So far I have already seen:

> Mary — who is present in the divine service for children.
> Mary — who showed me the day of the Assumption.
> Mary— as a heavenly messenger — as light — at Confirmation.
> Mary — who is present when evil strikes our community, as with accidents.
> Mary — who helps. (I remember on her altar in the Catholic church is written: "Mary of perpetual help.")

There have not been so many accidents in Switzerland for a long time. The newspapers are full of reports on accidents. In the *Zürichsee Zeitung* one can read that the accidents on Seestrasse seem endless! I can still feel the presence of Mary. What shall I do? Shall I ring up the Catholic parish? That is impossible! But what if our own children meet with accidents?

April 29, 1958

I had a dream:

A voice spoke: If you remain silent, you will be desolate, without life, and bleed to death. If you speak, you will live like this—and I saw a poor and simple pilgrim with a cloak thrown around him; a staff was in his hand and a light behind him—and that meant that God was with him.

I decided . . . and therefore I had to speak.

I asked Father Joseph, the Catholic priest, to visit me. I told him everything. He asked about all aspects of it. Above all, he promised to pray to Mary about the "woes." I then asked Pastor Eugen. He also promised to help and pray. So we were already four! Then Mr. F. helped too. Pastor Werner promised nothing, because it was about Mary. That hurt. He also gave me exact instructions about the Protestant Church and requested that I listen to its teachings: "Christ must increase, Mary must decrease."

I had a difficult time digesting Werner's message. It was, however, a joyful moment when eventually the "woes" went away. There was a decrease in the number of accidents, and for a long time there were no more deaths!

Our son Peter was astonished, and could not understand how his mother could say that the suffering was over and the terrible wave of accidents had ended.

After many days I went to Mary, bowed my head and spoke:

"Mary—you know my inner struggle—you know that I am, as a Protestant, not allowed to come! So I ask you to forgive me when I say to you that this is the last time I am here. Forgive me. I know it is not right, but I cannot!"

Then I heard above me one single word: "Betrayal!"

I will never forget that word—betrayal! Mary was right. She had revealed herself to me. She had given me so much—she was ready—and she helped. This word went through me like a sword. I wept and called out:

Mary, I will not betray you!
I will write down everything,
about your love, your light, and your greatness.
I will not betray my church.
I will betray no one.

I only want to serve.
Understand me — forgive me.
Do not withdraw from us.
Give me and all the others time.
I beg you — forgive me!

May 22, 1958

While I prayed in the church, I saw that Pastor Eugen will be further purified. He must go through a renewal and purification of his soul. His illness is part of it. Let us give thanks that God is working on the soul of Eugen! This is in preparation for some great task. Otto is at peace with himself and with all that surrounds him. God will be with him as he meets the people in his tasks on earth.

May 29, 1958

Again a terrible heaviness lay over the earth. And I was filled with sorrow that so many people have lost contact with the heavens, with God, with Christ, and with Mary. Are we Christians responsible? Do we have the courage to bear witness to the fullness, truth, and wholeness of Christianity?

I tore out page after page from my notebooks and rewrote them again. It is simply so difficult to put into words one's experiences with God. If only I could paint, maybe then I could pass on the visions in a better way—but that would be a never-ending task. I have taken so much out of the books about Mary and Holy Communion, but I can't leave out everything, when God wants me to write it.

Who is Mary? She was truly the mother of the Lord. God had chosen her to carry in her womb the most precious child. She nourished him and educated him—she also suffered with him. Christ returned to the Father, and later Mary was taken into heaven.

Mary is not just there as one who intercedes. In heaven she is queen, elevated far above the angels. Often I see her full of radiance and, around the edges of her cloak, a multitude of angels. Then I see her calm and full of love, often with the small, dark red-gold crown. Again I see her spiritually full of pain and suffering.

Whenever we pray to God for angels, a command goes from God to Mary—it is much more a "look" than a command. Even though I often see it, I can't explain it well with words. When I ask for angels, I myself pray to God. "Mary, I greet you," "Hail Mary," or "Mary, I give you thanks"—such prayers God and Mary accept. But does one pray to God alone or to Mary alone? I know that I pray wrongly when I bring everything to Mary! I am always searching for a prayer to Mary, but everything until now has not been right. How do the Catholics pray? I will search further—and wait.

Whoever encounters Mary must love her. I know for sure that Mary helps, protects, and watches over us, that Christ is present for spiritual matters and that God is above all else.

Some weeks later

Praying for Israel, I saw Mary radiant, full of light and with a great host of angels—a political crisis! Does Mary help with her angels when there is danger of war?

Pastor Eugen is stepping toward the light! How happy I am! At last!

In a vision, I saw Father Joseph in his room. He opened several books; some of them were very old. Then came a bright light through the window. It was so radiant. From it a voice spoke to Father Joseph:

Do not be afraid —

it is I, your Lord and your God!
Do not pay attention to the traditional laws of men,
but to me!
It is I, the living God, who meets you.

September 1958

In a vision, I saw an unknown Catholic priest, who disappeared and appeared again, advancing step by step. I saw how he struggled and did PENANCE again and again. I saw him kneeling down and waiting—waiting for a sign of God—for grace—for direction. He surrendered himself to God, so that all earthly concerns were gone; he stood alone as a human being before God.

Then, as this priest was praying, Christ appeared. He stood before him and looked seriously at the priest for a long time, examining him. I prayed and prayed and at last called out:

Oh Jesus Christ, have mercy on him!
Draw close to him —
I ask you to surround him with your light!
Have mercy on him.

Then Christ came a few steps closer. He raised his right hand and stretched out his thumb, forefinger, and middle finger. Both other fingers remained closed in his hand. He held these three fingers toward the priest. Christ did not say anything, but looked serious. Then I spoke: "Lord, I beg you, not like that! I believe the Catholics and the Eastern Orthodox Churches have this sign. Please give me another sign. What shall I do with this one? I do not understand the meaning of it. Send heavenly light, as you have always done. Approach him in goodness and love. Let your light shine upon him. Lord, be not so hard, for he is search-ing. Be merciful unto him — have mercy on us all."

At that Christ raised his head and looked at me with his searching eyes. He raised his three fingers again, holding them out toward the priest and then toward me. I then spoke: "Jesus Christ, I thank you!" I made the sign of the cross and continued: "Forgive me, I am such an ignorant and unimportant person. What is so vital is that you meet us and not how you meet us."

Late September 1958

Already on Monday, I was delighted with Otto's sermon for the coming Sunday. Early on Friday, I went to the church while Otto was preparing his sermon. And when I began to pray for him, I saw him standing in the pulpit preaching; and I saw the Spirit, appear-ing as a ray, come into him through his head — and out of his mouth. This sign brought me great joy.

"Bettag": The Swiss National Day of Repentance and Prayer

A strange spiritual struggle took place the week before this ser-vice. The right atmosphere was missing and I could not overcome it with prayer. Otto was working on his sermon, but a spiritual flame was missing. Again and again I went into the church and prayed and listened. On Tuesday in prayer, I saw Otto standing in front of a great wall that must be pierced with prayer. I asked Otto to STRUGGLE AND PRAY, and to do this in the church. He did not go. Nevertheless, I felt that he prayed to God in his room. What a relief!

On Wednesday morning, I prayed for a long time and asked God to be patient and merciful and to accept my struggle and prayers for Otto. When I came home from the church, Otto had already changed the text of his sermon. Then the organist of our church telephoned me and said, to my surprise: "That was a strange night—the ups and downs of a spiritual struggle—I changed all of the music for Sunday!"

Sensitive people simply feel whenever there are spiritual struggles—whenever heaven and earth meet each other.

As there was still no clear answer for the sermon, I began to pray for the people. Then I saw the "light grey mist" coming down over all the seats in the church. I knew then that the people would do penance and that they would be open toward God. Also, and this is important, God would draw near to them, forgive them, and have mercy on them.

On Friday morning, I saw a bright, fine light in the apse! I was grateful and full of joy over this sign. How good it is never to give up praying!

Never had a sermon of Otto received such a good response from the community as on this day. God had prepared the people and so many came that there was not enough space for them all.

It is about a year ago since I saw Christ during Holy Communion on our national day of prayer and repentance in 1957. Because these experiences were so powerful, I thought I would remain silent about them. I realize now that they were the starting point of my ENCOUNTERS WITH CHRIST.

Our day of prayer and repentance was never for me a feast day like Easter, Pentecost, or Christmas, but whenever possible I always take Communion. So on that Saturday evening before the feast day one year ago, I went to the service, altogether concentrating on Communion. And as always, I read in advance Jesus' last prayer for his Apostles and all believers (John 17). I sat quietly in the church in prayer waiting for the bread and the chalice. I had my eyes closed, which is unusual for me while praying. Then I saw the profile of Christ in color with the crown of thorns on his head. The thorns and twigs were fine and thin, fresh and partly green. They were not the thick thorns that one sees in paintings. It hurt me to see this. But I was much more shocked to see the expression on his face and the way he held his head. So much pain! I never saw any person with such an expression of pain and with so much spiritual suffering. I saw that his eyes were dark, that he had a short beard and dark hair. What was unforgettable was the nose. Forehead and nose were one straight long line — and there was hardly any bend between nose and forehead.

I only saw this image for a brief moment. I opened my eyes and closed them again. I felt stunned and had to recall where I was in reality.

Sometime later, I saw Christ without such suffering. Then I saw him without the crown of thorns and with his face looking upward. From above, much light, like gold, shone upon him. His hair became fair from the light and his eyes brown. As he looked upward, his eyes shone. All the suffering was gone; there was only eternal joy and unity with God.

This vision was hard for me. After I had seen so many heavenly things such as the pouring forth of divine energy or the way light descends upon the people, I had come to believe that if I ever should meet Christ, here or in the hereafter, he would be a great figure of light! What did I see? A young man — so young that no painter would dare to paint him like that. Here was a real human being! A man who suffered and after having suffered was flooded with God's light. At this moment I believed in all fullness that he became a man! It took me weeks to work through this. Up until then, I never really thought he was a human being.

It was just before Christmas 1957 when I saw Christ again — Christ on the cross.

The next time was before Easter when Christ appeared. He was not suffering. He appeared as one who gives and helps and often to people in need. He went to them, drawing close to them, and laid his hands on the heads of the sick; as Savior he was everywhere, giving, helping, and blessing.

I would like to add that Christ is invisible to many, but he is truly present—in his body—and this is not just a matter of theology. He is waiting for the people to meet him, so that they learn to pray to him and be united with him for a long time through prayer.

October 24, 1958

In my visions, I saw Pastor Eugen swimming through waves. The waves came and went, but not so high and deep as in other visions. It was a spiritual search. I also saw him bending down to the earth, praying to God. Christ drew close to him and covered him in radiant light with his hands.

Whenever Eugen approaches Christ in humility, he is guided and will become a great spiritual person—all this through Christ.

November 1958

ECUMENISM: As I was meditating in sadness and sorrow, during a concert in the church, I thought, where have I failed? Do I really pray too much? Do I speak too often for Mary's cause? Do I go to church too often? Are the accusations against me justified? Am I on the wrong path? As I thought about these things, I began to judge myself. I called to mind a "Catholic soul" in order to help me think clearly about the Catholic point of view. Then I looked toward Pastor Werner, who was singing in the concert, in order to remember the spiritual standpoint of the Protestants. I was trying to be clear and self-critical.

As I sat in the church, suddenly I saw a magnificent flower garden, full of the most beautiful flowers. Some single poppies, large and magnificent, were particularly noticeable. They were red and yellow in color. Around this garden was a very ancient wall made from square stones.

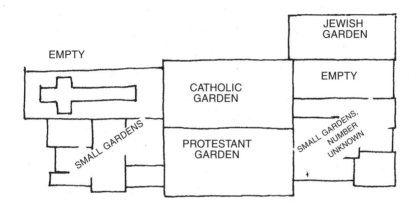

Something unseen raised me upward from the garden where I was standing. I saw other gardens with old stone walls joining them in places. All the gardens were linked to each other. And outside of these gardens was darkness—dark night. As I was raised up, I saw magnificent red and yellow flowers blossoming in those other gardens also. In the Catholic garden, the flowers were as large as in ours!

I was delighted with each flower and was grateful that the same flowers blossomed in the other gardens. I believe the garden to the right was the Jewish garden. A small stream with clear water gushed forth in that one. It also contained sand, desert plants, and bushes with fine thin thorns, like those in the crown of thorns for the head of Jesus. One garden was without flowers and that made me very sad. The sign of a long cross was formed on its sands. In it were a few dark, drooping cedar trees. No light and no sun fell on this garden—only a grey haze. Here and there were some foliage plants and grass which still lived but did not have the energy to unfold and grow. All were as if dead.

The garden is the faith. I recognized the Catholic faith, our faith, and the Jewish faith. I did not recognize the many small gardens, and I no longer remember what they looked like or how many there were, but I still see in front of me even today the great complex of gardens and particularly the larger ones in it.

The flowers are the faithful—even the grass—and how I rejoiced for every small leaf and every small blade of grass—and next to them great, magnificent flowers! There were so many flowers and so much grass and, above all, so much sun! And outside was darkness. This is the world without life, without sun, without Christ, without God.

For the time being, no one tore down the walls between the gardens. Every garden except one blossomed, and often a seed would be carried from one to another. Let us rejoice about that!

There were red, yellow, and white poppies! In the Holy Land, such poppies grow in the fields. It amazed me that there were so many of these flowers in the Protestant garden and even more in the Catholic one!

November 30, 1958

On Sunday afternoon, I was resting and felt happy about Advent, not only because of the sermon but also because it is such a beautiful time. God is so close to us! It is as if heaven and earth would then meet—a holy time close to God. It feels as if we are raised up. No! It is God who comes down to us.

As I was lying down and resting my body, I thought about the words I would use to explain to Otto WHAT PRAYER IS ABOUT and how, in the church, I go before God and pray. Then I saw a heavenly figure kneeling on the ground. He was clothed in a garment of bright yellow with wide sleeves. His arms were raised, and above his head was a white gleam of light. The eyes of this figure were raised upward to God, and just above his hands, hovering in the air, was a plate that had been brought there by angels. On it were seven red vessels. Flames ascended from them to God. The large plate was made from a rare dark wood, almost black, which is not to be found in our regions. The seven vessels were of the same red that radiates from Christ. Further above, a green-yellow light radiated in a curve—like the color of Mary's robe. Still further above, was a blue and yellow light—the risen Christ in union with God. Above everything else was a white, radiant light—God. The space between these appearances was filled with dark blue night.

THIS IS WORSHIP OF GOD!

December 1, 1958

Pastor Eugen telephoned and asked me to pray for his talk on ecumenism, because there will be difficulties from the Catholic side. During this conversation, I already saw a room, like a classroom, filled with light. This was the first sign that God would be present. As I had promised, I went into the church after eight o'clock. I knelt down and prayed. The contact between God and Pastor Eugen was still missing. So I called out to God: "Oh Lord, you have shown light! I take you at your word with all that you have said and shown. So I ask you once again, have mercy, Oh Lord!"

Then God showed me a figure standing on the left side of the apse. It was a man with a rough brown cloak thrown about him — with long hair — without socks — with rough sandals on his feet. He was simple, humble, and yet so full of spirit and strength. Was he John the Baptist?

Then I saw Christ on the cross. I grieved and said: "No, Lord! We are only asking for your help for this lecture — not for your suffering." Christ, in a yellow radiance, descended from the cross, stood before me, and looked at me searchingly. He blessed me with the sign of his three fingers. I called out: "Oh Lord, not for me, but for Eugen." His eyes became kind and he made the sign of the cross more or less in the direction of Zürich, where the talk was to be held. Then he stretched out his arms in the same direction, his cupped hands bringing an offering. I gave thanks and made the sign of the cross. All that was evil around Pastor Eugen disappeared!

Once more the man with the rough brown cloak became visible and again I saw Christ on the cross. This time he was not suffering but in light. People were coming and going, as on a stage, and each person stood quite consciously in front of the cross, as if wanting to say something. The man in the rough cloak was the first to do so. He remained a long time alone with Christ. Then he disappeared. After that a woman came to the left, and a man to the right of the cross. The man was a disciple who was tall and thin—John the Evangelist? This image—CHRIST, MARY, JOHN—lasted the longest. These three together were important. There followed a procession of men, women, nuns, monks, some Capuchins, Catholic priests, and Protestant pastors. Some were tall and thin and others were rather small and stout. There were people in gowns, people with white frills around their necks, many people in old-fashioned clothes. All were present—from the time of Jesus until today. They all came and placed themselves under the cross and continued on their way. They all belong to Christ—all who place themselves under the cross!

God showed me all this. Then I saw Jesus alone again—Jesus on the cross. Mary stood before him humbly; her eyes were turned toward him. She was wearing a wide blue gown.

THIS IS ECUMENISM!

[December 1987]

Today, thirty years after this last vision, Pastor Eugen is renewed and spiritually guided by Christ, and so has become a great spiritual[1] priest whom Christ needs for the Eastern Orthodox Church. This vision—CHRIST ON THE CROSS FOR ALL CHRISTIANS—came at that time for all important ecumenical work. Pastor Eugen has accomplished such work.]

December 20, 1958

For nearly an hour, I felt God's presence in the church! So I went into the church, and I had just begun to pray when I saw in the apse a mighty angel in a grey gown with white rays shining from him. His outstretched arms, together with the broad sleeves attached to the gown, went right around the wall of the apse, and in these open arms were many people: children with crutches, the infirm, the sick, old women, and old men—some with crutches and some with canes—the suffering, also those who suffer mentally; all these people were held in the safety and security of this angel.

What loving angels God has given for the sick and the distressed!

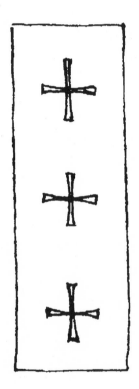

January 7, 1959

Today God's presence is over all things. He is there for us to encounter him. After my prayers for others, I made the sign of the cross and in addition I made the small sign of the cross on my forehead. I only do it when I feel a cold breath on my forehead, and on this day it happened after my prayers had been heard. As I made the small sign of the cross,[2] I saw a longish rectangle. In it, on a gold background, were three crosses: the first white, the second red and the third grey-blue. I am sure this means:

IN THE NAME OF THE FATHER, THE SON, AND THE HOLY SPIRIT.

January 29, 1959

I have overcome my doubts and again found peace in God. I will not listen to the voices of men. I will test myself and try to think clearly. This is easier said than done! What links me with God is not clear thinking or knowledge, but love. When God, Christ, Mary, a heavenly messenger, or only a breath of God's Spirit is present, then love burns within me and all earthly concerns disappear. Only the Holy is then present.

Today I found some Communion bread at our home. If possible I will take Communion from now until Easter. I will begin today because today I saw for the first time people who did penance and entered into THE SPIRIT OF LENT. I took grape juice instead of wine and I offered the bread and grape juice to God, asking him to bless them. I prayed, asked for the forgiveness of sins, and gave thanks. Then I saw how a messenger of God glided through the air. This messenger had something in his hand which he held out to my mouth. He was very close to me without touching me. Was this a purification of my spirit and soul?

After I had recovered and could breathe again, I ate the bread and wine. Something had changed within me. I then began to pray for others.

January 30, 1959

Filled with spiritual hunger, I went to church today to be with God and to take his bread. I began to pray, like yesterday, and felt God's Spirit strengthening me. I took the bread again in the palm of my hand and prayed that he would bless it and make it holy. Then I saw the eyes and part of the head of Jesus Christ. He was very serious and sad. I was shocked. "Lord, why are you so sad? What shall I do? I am ready. Speak! You know I can hardly bear your sadness!" Then I called out to God: "Please show me, what is Christ mourning about? I am ready to do everything that you ask of me." No answer. I did penance. Still no answer. "Lord, it tears me apart! Lord, help me!"

Standing to the right of the apse near the stairs, I saw in a vision a pastor of the Reformed Church. He offered me the bread and the chalice. Behind him was Christ—still sad and serious. I spoke: "Lord, how grateful I would be if every morning a pastor would be there to give me the meal. Now I have to offer it to you myself. I know it is strange, but I feel and see in your eyes that it is not a sin. You know my hunger. You know I have already searched for years. I can't go to Mass—and something about the Mass hurts me."

With all my words, the face of Christ became more sad. Christ looked at me for a long time. I cannot explain with words this inner relationship. There was silence. Afterward I spoke: "Oh, Lord, I understand. You have given us this meal, and we do not take it. The world does not want it; our pastors only give it rarely. The Catholics don't take Communion often, even though it is offered every day." At this, great pain came into the face of Christ, which intensified the sadness. "Lord, you gave us Communion. Lord, I want to receive it—in your way. Let your will be done. Stay with me and accompany me throughout the experience of Holy Communion. I give myself to you totally."

I made the sign of the cross and then saw again Christ on the cross, in his spiritual greatness, with the crown of thorns—a wreath of suffering around his head. I broke the bread and, as it broke in two, his hands were freed from the nails of the cross and his body lowered itself very slowly to the left. When I ate the bread, his body was so close to me—really alive in front of me! Blood was dripping everywhere from the body. Then it was a dead body. I shuddered and called out: "I do not want to eat this body or drink this blood. It sickens me." I knew this was a sin. "Lord, it is only you, in your spiritual strength, that I want to encounter in Holy Communion. Lord, have mercy on me. I cannot do it." But Christ remained firm, until I was able to win through—until I could accept his sacrifice. All this was so hard. I felt sick seeing the great suffering of Christ. In the end I took a deep breath and the image was gone.

After a while, I saw a great sphere—almost the width of one of the benches in the choir. It was a spiritual reality—God's Spirit—God's strength—full of a mighty, dynamic force, and in the midst of it was Christ, outlined delicately. He was no longer sad. Christ who had sacrificed himself was now present in all the spiritual strength of his Resurrection. I have often felt this spiritual strength of Christ in Holy Communion. I felt it with my whole being, and I live from it.

His body was dead!
The risen Christ lives!
He is present in Holy Communion!

This experience, and what was later explained to me about Holy Communion, is perhaps the most important vision that I ever had.

February 8, 1959

No doubt, I cannot yet pass on my experience of Holy Communion. Something still has to be added—but I don't know what it is. It must become a whole.

February 9, 1959

Strange, as I prayed for all priests, I received no answer. "Lord, what is happening today? I am tired. I can't pray anymore. Lord, protect all priests and be merciful. Whatever happens, do not abandon them."

During Communion, in a vision, I saw tall, burning candles on the benches around our baptismal font, just where the wine jugs usually are. Are they there for Christ—for his passion—or for Holy Communion?

February 10, 1959

Again no answer for the priests! I felt a seriousness in the air. Why was there no link with God? I did penance for a long time, until I received signs from God during my prayers for others.

February 11, 1959

The serious atmosphere was still there. Today Father Joseph was strengthened with the spiritual power for priests. But he was still not yet joyful and free. When I pleaded once more for the priests, I saw again Christ's large eyes—kind—smiling. "Lord, you know everything, every need, and you love all these priests. Your eyes tell me so. I give thanks!" With time, I saw the sadness of Christ lessen for several of them.

February 13, 1959

God's presence was powerful! The priests were again joyful and free, except for one priest I knew. Because of him, I still suffered with Christ but wanted to be joyful and free also. God's presence was powerful in Communion. While I was praying, the heavenly messenger came gliding along, as before. He again touched my mouth with something mysterious—without actually touching me. I prayed, praised, gave thanks, and made atonement with God, as I do every morning. Then something wonderful happened. Shall I try to put it into words? I know only too well what poor words I have. They are not very appealing; nevertheless, they give a hint about my visions.

This is what I experienced: first of all, God's presence—not God in person. God was there, yet not there. The core of his Spirit— the essence of his Spirit—his spiritual power—was present, and in front of it was a fine wall like a gentle and tender veil. God was present! After experiencing his holiness, I saw the heavens. To the left, high up, were the heavens in a deep golden light—like the background color of the three small crosses (vision of January 7, 1959). This I saw first: the kingdom of angels that never comes to earth, never reaches to us. These angels move in a circular pattern around God—giving praise and thanks. Then to the right, lower down, I saw the heavens with shining angels and with messengers in grey. Here is Mary—with the angels to serve her.

Afterward a grey, spiritual wall moved and obscured the heavens. A figure came through this wall. Slowly, consciously, it broke through—to the earth. It was Jesus Christ. He walked on the earth; he brought with him God's light and holy, spiritual strength. And wherever he walked, something of this light and strength remained behind. At the end of his work, he walked alone on a short path. He was a solitary figure. He only took with him the burden of sin. I saw his dying on the cross, his sacrifice, and then there was a silence. This is the forgiveness of sins—the wiping out of sin.

I ate the bread and raisins (instead of wine), and I saw and felt again the great, dynamic sphere of Spirit. It is Christ in the Communion—from there he shines forth. His light is pure and gentle.

February 27, 1959

Yesterday evening, when Otto read something about the Holy Land—where Christ often prayed the Our Father—suddenly my eyes were opened. The Our Father is indeed my Communion! The sacrifice of Christ, however, is not specifically mentioned, but it is certainly implied in "Give us this day our daily bread" and "Forgive us our trespasses."

OUR FATHER

in praise of God and the angels who circle around him and sing: the beginning of Holy Communion

WHO ART IN HEAVEN

the opening of the heavens

HALLOWED BE THY NAME

the worship of heavenly beings and of people on earth

THY KINGDOM COME

Jesus who comes to us on earth

THY WILL BE DONE ON EARTH AS IT IS IN HEAVEN

the mission of Jesus on earth

GIVE US THIS DAY OUR DAILY BREAD

Holy Communion

AND FORGIVE US OUR TRESPASSES AS WE FORGIVE THOSE

WHO TRESPASS AGAINST US

penance, forgiveness, Christ's sacrifice

AND LEAD US NOT INTO TEMPTATION BUT DELIVER US FROM EVIL,

FOR THINE IS THE KINGDOM, THE POWER, AND THE GLORY

FOREVER

God protecting us with his Holy Spirit,
Christ in the great sphere of Spirit

This and the blessing IN THE NAME OF THE FATHER, THE SON, AND THE HOLY SPIRIT are also my Holy Communion experience.

April 17, 1959

During Communion, I suddenly saw many sick and crippled people—those who suffer not only in the body but also in the soul. Christ went to one of these people, bent down to him, and light radiated from Christ to this unknown person. Christ placed his hands on the person's head, and then went to the others and enveloped them with his love. I was so happy about this experience—that today Christ is in this way among the sick. I began my work and often thought how indeed Jesus is everywhere.

After some time, the longer I listened the more I heard sick and oppressed people calling for help. I concentrated on other things but it was of no use. It was dreadful to hear thousands call out for help. I questioned myself and thought: "Lord, have mercy on them." But the voices increased and increased! I began to feel pain in my heart and my body became more and more miserable. I could no longer endure it and thought: "Now I will go to the church—God must help. He can no longer show me this world of suffering if he loves me at all!" It was no use to speak with the people. I felt: "God wants to say something with this. He wants me as his instrument." I knew that with my last bit of energy I should go into the church and stand before God.

I prayed a long time to God and to Jesus Christ for these poor people who were in such need. Often I said: "Oh Jesus, please go to all these people. I saw today how you were with the sick—how you went from one to the other. Come to these people! Send your light and your help! Don't you see how they implore, how they seek, how they struggle—don't you hear them calling and crying out? I can't help, but you, Oh Jesus Christ, can I ask you to have mercy on us!" Finally, I called out: "Oh Lord! Oh God! I know you are present! I know about this distress! Now I am ready! Show me what we poor human beings can do! What is your will?"

Then I saw people coming—all to one place, where the ground was bright. There were deciduous trees in lush green and rectangular stones placed in a row. The sun shone on everything. And now these people came with their sickness and their suffering souls. They came in crowds to the rectangular stones, knelt down in front of them, prayed, and waited. There was a fullness of life behind these stones. People appeared, and they were not Protestant or Catholic clergymen. They had a pure, white cloth wrapped around them, which certainly signified relatedness to God. In their hands, they held vessels with Communion bread in them. With a loving and compassionate movement, they took the hosts out of these vessels and gave them to the oppressed—into their mouths. Immediately afterward there came people, dressed in the same way, with jugs and cups who gave drink to the suffering. All this had so much light—so much love—peace and joy. Everybody, including the sick, was full of joy.

This image disappeared.

And I saw a field—a magnificent field, full of sunshine! Children came running. They danced joyfully, jumped, and played; children with crutches were also there, and they too had laughter full of sunshine on their faces. It was as if hosts were poured out from on high. The hosts fluttered and whirled around the children like butterflies.

I was amazed and said: "Jesus Christ, I thank you!" And afterward I continued: "I will write down and pass this on for all Christians and for all the sick, the dying, and those who suffer in their souls. Everybody should receive your Communion, which has been revealed to me. We want to help and serve you!"

Later I asked: "Is this THE ROYAL PRIESTHOOD?"[3] Christ answered: "Yes, learn from this!"

April 23, 1959

I often had the feeling from the last vision on the "hosts for the sick" that something more on Holy Communion would be added. On the 18th of this month, I was sitting at my writing desk to answer a letter, when I began to experience light—beams of joy—which came from God. I stopped writing, said a short prayer, and listened within myself. This light had something to do with Father Joseph. I prayed for him. Then I saw him in the confessional, praying. He had a lot of priestly strength and was close to God. I don't know how, but I was suddenly in the confessional next to him. My heart was beating and I said: "Oh God, forgive my sins." And then after a while, Father Joseph spoke: "Your sins are forgiven." This was all done in spirit—in vision. Later I telephoned Father Joseph and received the answer that he was in the confessional.

Early Sunday morning, before divine service, I wanted to go into the Protestant church and take Communion, but I overslept. So, in a quiet hour, I took it at home. As I took Communion, I saw Father Joseph in front of the Catholic church with a host in his hand. I had to pray a long time until I found a way to take the host from a Catholic priest. I began to pray the Our Father very very slowly so that spiritually there was place for Holy Communion in it. And then Father Joseph gave me the host, which I swallowed, as if it were real. And Father Joseph spoke: "Now part of your heart is in our church!" He said this joyfully.

After this I felt so exhausted that I could only pray: "Oh Jesus, you ask too much from me. All this is Catholic. It is beyond my physical strength and spiritual boundaries. You see that it is too much for me. It cuts right into my thinking, and I am afraid to speak about it." As I could only weep, I said: "Jesus, I am yours. I serve you here and, even if it is doing the impossible, I will do it! Show me clearly the path, so that I don't go astray, and, when my service on earth is done, take me unto you."

I could see that Jesus would do this and take me unto himself. This experience will always remain with me, and so all things are made easier.

[*Thirty years later:* I would like to add that over the past thirty years, I have participated in the Communion of the Catholic and Orthodox Churches in spirit and in vision only.]

May 7, 1959

The Johannine Church is being born! How incredible it is for me to be neither Protestant nor Catholic. Inwardly, I am no longer completely at home in any of the churches. I experience community with Christians, to be sure, but otherwise I am in the midst of a spiritual storm — in labor pains — in the new birth of the Johannine Church. I am glad that Christ and loving people are near.

May 16, 1959: Whitsun Eve

There was great joy in heaven. God was not angry or grave, only full of joy. The angels, in deep golden light, glided and circled around him, full of praise and worship. All around this deep golden heaven were dark red roses! Mary was also full of joy, and she wore on her head the beautiful small crown. The angels sang in Mary's heaven — if only I could convey this heavenly music.

Christ appeared. I could hardly see him, as he was so transfigured in Spirit. He paused a while with Mary. They looked at each other; then he came quickly, full of joy, toward the earth — and then it happened! Suddenly there was a radiant silver roof over the earth. It was certainly Spirit — but strong like steel. Nothing could break through it or destroy it.

I saw Christ no longer. In my prayers of intercession, I could see that Pastor Eugen was strongly linked to Communion, Otto had "tongued fire" above his head, Father Joseph maintained union with Christ in the Mass, and Pastor Werner had light in his ministry. I would like to add that, before I prayed, I had also seen those men from ancient times with "tongues of fire" above them.

June 15, 1959

During the Our Father, after asking that our trespasses be forgiven, I saw in a vision that Father Joseph put a drop of holy water on my forehead. This too I have taken into the Johannine Church.

I would like to add that, after this date, it took nearly thirty years before I could fully accept holy water.

June 24, 1959

Whatever happens, may your will be done, Jesus Christ. My life belongs to you in times of peace and silence but also in times of activity and turmoil.

Then I saw Jesus Christ appearing in the same way as on Tuesday before Easter, when he offered me the bread. Now his appearance was more powerful. Light was around his head, his hands were placed together with the palms facing upward and in them was the precious bread, shining with light.

I stood there a long time and did not know what to pray. Then I gave thanks that Jesus was present. I asked for the wine. There came no answer. I pleaded: "When you, Jesus, are so powerfully present and visible, surely you want to say something? Help me with the next step."

Suddenly I saw Jesus Christ standing in the midst of the universe, with the Holy Bread in his hands. I saw many priests standing in a wide circle around him. They were preaching throughout the world—bringing the message of the Gospels to humankind. They were guiding the people to Christ, with Christian love. It was wonderful to see how the people were coming from all parts of the world to Christ. They were wholly oriented toward Christ. They received from him the Holy Bread. Some received long pieces of bread in their hands, others, the majority, received small oval pieces of bread in their mouths. The bread never ran out. There was always more in the hands of Christ.

Then I saw a chalice filled with blood, directly in front of Christ, almost as large as Christ himself. All those who had eaten the bread drank from the chalice. Even a dove flew toward the chalice and dipped its beak in it. Those people who had come in their soul and spirit and taken of the precious meal, went back past the priests, back into their normal state of being. But they were different: more beautiful and noble, and filled with a love for Christ.

I was so happy when I saw that there was not just one type of priest who was doing this work. No, there were Catholic and Protestant priests, monks, several women, and missionaries. Here and there, a priest left the circle and went far out into the darkest corners of the world to preach God's Word.

July 1, 1959

There was exceedingly great joy today! Magnificent light shone forth from Christ toward the priests. Afterward they all came and took a drink of wine from a large chalice. What a sign for ecumenism! Imagine a giant chalice—even bigger than yourself—then Protestant, Catholic, and Orthodox priests and monks forming a ring around it, and all of them drinking from it—drinking the same blood.

Oh God—a great thing has happened!

July 7, 1959

Father Joseph held a sermon on the priesthood. In prayer, I asked: "Is a priest a second Christ? Is he Christlike?" I prayed for clarity. Then I saw Christ elevated, in a golden garment. He wore a crown; an orb of gold was in his left hand and a scepter in his right hand. JESUS CHRIST ABOVE ALL. The priests, their heads bowed down, were kneeling at his feet. They kissed the dust of the ground—not even his feet or the seam of his garment! Pope John himself was half a meter behind the first priests. He was humble and kissed the dust! None of the priests were in any way comparable to Christ—the almighty Son of God.

All lay at his feet!

July 20, 1959

Two days ago and again today, Christ appeared as if he had a gift for me—a gift that brings joy. I went to Mass at six o'clock in the morning, because it was a Mass that was going to be explained for a few interested Protestants. I had never yet been to Mass. Partly it agreed with what I had seen before in visions. It was important that Father Joseph, in the Mass, was completely open to Christ and thus came into contact with him. Later I recognized that the Mass I had experienced was the promised gift of that morning.

To this, Christ spoke: "Now join the Johannine Communion with the Mass and make them one!"

August 16, 1959

Today I went into church, already aware of the presence of Mary. I was not thinking of anything in particular but was just grateful that, after the summer holidays, I could again go into the church

I knew so well. What a shock I got! As I prayed to God that heaven might be opened—also the heaven of Mary so that the angels around her might be present—there she stood before me, not to the right as she usually does, but in the middle of the apse, elevated and radiating the light that she normally gives to humankind. Her garment was light blue and decorated with pink around the girdle of her waist. There were pink roses on her feet. Thus she stood in front of me and held out a rosary with her left hand. Anybody who knows me can imagine how I shouted no. I said: "Everything, but not that! Mary, why are you doing this to me? I can't!" But Mary remained there despite my weeping and denial. She looked at me lovingly, was not angry, and simply waited until I could say yes. It was not a joyful yes but a yes nonetheless, and I stretched out my right hand. Then Mary let fall the rosary into my palm.

For weeks now, I have been afraid of an encounter with the rosary because, in an earlier vision, I had already received one in my hands from Father Joseph. Since then I could hold only the cross of the rosary in my hands—my inward being was related to the cross—but the chain I left hanging.

August 17, 1959

Mary was in the same place in the apse as yesterday. She again held a rosary in her hand. It was a beautiful one, made of hand-carved, cornered beads from dark brown wood that was roughly hewn. Mary looked at me. With the rosary in her hands, she let bead after bead slip through her fingers. While she did this, she looked at me all the time, as if she wanted to show me all of it and explain it. In the end she took the cross in her hands and looked at it lovingly as if she were seeing Christ. Deep pain was in her face as she looked at the cross for a long time.

August 19, 1959

Today I was in the church twice. I have no peace of mind. I have
to decide what this is all about. I have to pray, fight, and struggle
through it, and not just remain in uncertainty and keep putting it
off! I would prefer a clear situation. When I have a clear attitude
to the teachings of faith, then my strength is free to work, struggle,
pray, and be related to God.

I saw Mary again, in the same blue garment, with the rosary. She
stood in the middle of the apse, and from behind came the figure
of a man who was only partly visible. What I first saw was a hand
with a rosary. The figure became more visible, and I recognized
and heard who it was: Nicholas von Flue![4] I breathed deeply, was
silent and looked at him—rather reproachfully. He was full of
peace. He held out his hand toward me with a rosary hanging
down from it and said: "My strength . . . came from it . . . " Deeply
moved, I looked at him and kept quiet.

Did Nicholas love the rosary? Is the rosary as old as he is? Does it
come from his time? What do I know? Very little—and nothing
about all that!

August 20, 1959

During prayer, Mary was again present with the rosary. Again
from behind came Nicholas with the rosary in his hand. He
looked at me. He showed me his rosary and spoke to me in a
pleading way:
Pray it.

I answered: Yes, but I still don't know the words.

Nicholas:
It gives you strength.

There was a silence.

Nicholas then said:
It is sufficient to live by.

I said: I give you thanks — I am beginning to rejoice.

Later I saw him praying the rosary. His innermost being was open to God, Christ, and Mary. A link with them was created. Perhaps I will never see him again, this Nicholas von Flue, who in such a short time, with so few words, came so near to me and revealed his innermost being. This I say because he spoke the words: "It is sufficient to live by."

Mary still remained there, full of love. She looked at me and knew that now inwardly and joyfully I really could say yes to the rosary. It was not just out of obedience.

Mary spoke:
Bring the rosary to the world!
Make the world love it again
(including the Catholics)!

I answered: Me? As a Protestant? I can't speak and I can't write.

Then Mary spoke:
The Lord is with you!

I said: Yes — so be it — give me time — with time I will do it.

But Mary shook her head at my final remark.

And so I said: Yes — I will serve you!

And Mary:
Don't serve me; serve God and Christ!

At the very end I asked if I could now go home, and she said:
Yes — go to your children!

September 25, 1959

As I was worshipping God, praying the Our Father in the Catholic church of Küsnacht, where an exposition of the Blessed Sacrament was being held, suddenly Christ appeared—severe—judging. His eyes were sad as he looked at the people.

The angel who was beside him spoke:
Write this down!

Then Christ spoke:
Who are my brothers? Who are my sisters?
Those who do the will of God.

And in a voice that was even more severe:
That is not faith! That is cult![5]

I said: Lord, have mercy! Look at those people who, with a pure heart, love you and seek you!

Christ:
I do not speak judgment over the faithful here —
but over the whole church.

And with these words, he looked over the whole earth.

October 6, 1959

Today, as I worshipped God, an entire wreath of blue stars was to be seen. When I prayed to God for Mary and her angels, I could not see Mary or her angels. God simply passed over this prayer! Instead, Brother Nicholas von Flue appeared in front of me. Behind him were many saints—men and women.

Brother Nicholas, pleading and serious:
Receive us!

I asked: How and in what way shall we receive you?

Brother Nicholas:
Pray that we may be with you!

Silence.

Brother Nicholas:
We do not serve like the angels ——
who guard, protect, and love all of you ——
bringing you holy joy.
We may help people in a very special way ——
and also give answers —— as messengers from eternity.

Do not reject us!
Do not worship us;
we are less than the angels —— and one does not worship them.

But receive us!

Silence.

Brother Nicholas:
Do not be sad,
when you still do not see who is above the saints.
You know that we are all placed under God.

At the right time, your eyes will be opened.
For the present, know that we are here —— to help humankind!

October 7, 1959

Brother Nicholas was standing there again —
more powerful than ever before!

I called out after a long silence: Brother Nicholas! Speak!

Then he spoke again, but more forcefully than the day before:
Pray that we may come!
The world, even the Catholic world, does not want us anymore!

I answered: Just simply come — without our asking —for the sake of
Christ's will! Simply love us!

There was a silence.

Brother Nicholas:
We cannot!
We are subject to divine law!
Mary is above her angels as well —— and God is above her.
So it is with us.
Pray! Then we can come!

Today I saw Brother Francis of Assisi, for the first time. He was suffering because many of his brothers—the Franciscans—do not
have the love of Christ within. I just saw him; there was no personal contact between us.

November 30, 1959

For me the visions could have stopped during Christmas of 1959,
because I was so deeply moved by all Jesus said. I could only pray
the Our Father over and over again. I did not do what Mary asked,
which was to light candles to the left and right of the altar during
Holy Night. Inwardly, I just could not find the way to inform the

Catholic Church about this. It pained my heart, because during Advent, as a woman, I am so close to Mary. It is, after all, the time just before Christ was born.

I started to pray the rosary, but spiritually something was different. Then I prayed for a long time the word "Mary." Only this word could come to my lips. All at once she stood there — Mary. As she was looking at me, she said:
Bring them the rosary ——

Silence

as it was.
In that way you will bring me great joy.

I asked: How was it, Mary?

For me, it then felt as if Mary embraced me completely with her eyes. She began to speak:
In the beginning was the Word!

Mary hesitated — entered into union with Christ — then continued quietly and slowly:
The Word from God —— to the people.
The Word and the Spirit entered into their souls ——
and from this, prayer to God came into being.
It was the strongest with Abraham, Moses, and the prophets.
Then God sent a part of his own "I" ——
first to the earth —— then elevated it, elevated Christ ——
and made him mediator between God and humankind.

He did not do it for the sake of himself or Christ.
He did it so that not just Moses and the prophets
could have a relationship with God ——
BUT ALL HUMAN BEINGS!

Christ stands between God and humankind;
through this all created beings can pray to God.
See the grass, see the flowers, and see
the entire earth in its fullness —— all things aspire to God.
See the murderers who struggle and pray!

*Here I interrupted: Should we not take Christians and priests
first?*

But Mary continued and spoke firmly:
See the murderers —— see the criminals ——
see those who suffer —— all are crying to God!
See the children —— with pure hearts ——
see the Christians —— see the priests ——
all are praying to God —— through Christ.
Only in this way is it possible to reach God.

And now let us continue.

Mary smiled:
As I was raised up into heaven —— I saw the world of angels.

Mary smiled again:
It is far greater and more magnificent than you have seen till now.
Later they will believe that you have seen so much of the Spirit,
the realms of angels, and powers that surround the people.
But rejoice!
Don't be annoyed —— when they don't believe you.
GOD GAVE ME A HEAVEN WITH ANGELS!

And now see the greatness of God.
First he himself spoke to the prophets ——
then he gave Christ, so that all the people might pray to God.
And, thirdly, he gave the angels and later the saints.

The angels and I — we come directly to you —
we are around you, we visit you, we make ready your souls.

Everything that we do — comes from God.
I tell you, it is glorious — wondrous —
to be able to serve God in this way.
We bring joy and peace from God.
We prepare the soul for the earthly tasks —
but also for eternity.

We — I and the angels who are subject to me —

carry the people through the realm of death into the hereafter,
AND SO THE ROSARY CAME INTO BEING,
that men and women may have a relationship
with me and the angels.

I am not an "intercessor,"
but I am in union with Christ — and with God.
God could not have given me
a greater and more beautiful place in heaven!
It was the voice of God
that gave this prayer — the rosary —
to a human being standing in a field.
This first prayer is the one that is most complete.

But you — should pray it in the way I taught it to you[6] —
and bring it to the world so that the world may love it.
Pray to Christ — for the saints.
You will come to love them all.

Much is new for you —

put everything together —

not one thing should stand alone!
God and Christ are one.
And we [Mary and her angels], we are they
who are from God, for God, and around God.

Amen.

After giving thanks, I asked: Oh Mary, why didn't you make this
prayer [the rosary] more magnificent?

Mary:
The rhythm must stay this way —
in this prayer everything is included!

Mary, severely:
You hurt God with your question.
Don't ask any more about it!
Pray to God for forgiveness!

December 5, 1959

As *I was praying for the priests, suddenly an angel stood there and*
spoke:
A priest is to take care of his rights.

I stared at him, as if I did not hear correctly. Behind him stood
Mary, so I took paper and pencil.

The angel:
A priest is to take care of his rights.
A priest is to love God alone,
and drawing on all that is godly
he should love his fellow human beings.

A priest is to be good to the poor — to those who suffer —
to those who hunger for the Spirit.
Nothing belongs to the priest; all *[earthly wealth]* belongs to God.

A priest is free to marry a woman who believes.
But it is better to live in purity,[7]
so that the love for his fellow human beings may be greater.
If a priest loves someone, he should marry.
All should be done in truth — before God.

In all that, may their sins be forgiven.
But woe unto the priest who misuses the sacraments!
Woe unto him when he rejects a repenting sinner!
Woe unto him when he does not forgive!
Woe unto him when he does not let one come to the Lord's table!
Woe unto him when he helps to cover up sins
because people are rich or influential.
A priest is to be true and authentic —
full of love — full of patience — and is to persevere in prayer.
He is to be an intercessor — a shepherd to his community,
he is never to forget his calling,
his responsibility and who has authority.
Let him purify himself daily through the Lord's Supper.

So will he receive the peace of God.
So is he able to carry burdens, and to give of the Spirit.
So is he able to relate to God,
and so can he worship, praise, and give thanks.

The angel spoke to all priests:
In this way, go into the world — among the people —
but seek also solitude,
so that you do not lose yourself in the world.

In great and holy silence, let your souls and spirits be filled,
that you may be rich enough to satisfy the hungry.

In this silence —— priests give themselves to God ——
they become holy.

Do not be discouraged!

Christ stood beside me and spoke:
I give the gifts
with which you all work.
May no one praise himself ——
but serve truly with the gifts he has received.
It is not the kind of gift that counts ——
but the love you have toward me.
Therefore, be brothers in the Lord!
You are all limbs of the church ——
and the Father is above all.
Rejoice! Rejoice!
And wherever a priest grieves,
encourage him and set him on his feet again,
so that he too may rejoice!

December 9, 1959

Christ looking across the earth:
I worked miracles ——
I carried for all of you the crown of thorns ——
I let myself be nailed to the cross ——
I descended into the realm of death.
For you I have risen from the dead ——
and met with you again ——
and ascended into heaven ——

and have sent you the Holy Spirit.
I gave you Mary and the angels ——
I am with you in Holy Communion ——
I offer myself up for you
and suffer pain for you, even today,
every time, with the forgiveness of sins.

I give you my body and my blood.
Whenever you seek and serve me,
I will give you the Holy Spirit,
so that strength and joy may dwell within you.

I gave you the sun, the moon, and the stars.

I love you.

Christ looked around at the mad scramble of Christmas and said:
What am I to you?
Leave everything and follow me!
So, in truth, shall Christmas be in your hearts.
Come before the altar!
Worship —— so that your joy may be great!

December 14, 1959

Yesterday Mary appeared in all her magnificence at her altar in the Catholic church. I was full of joy—full of the joy of Christmas. I went to the church and, just as I began to pray, what did I see? Jesus with the crown of thorns! His head was powerful—full of the strength of Christ who sacrifices himself. This was in the midst of Advent, just before Christmas. What I saw—what Christ said—shook me to my innermost depths.

Christ with the crown of thorns spoke:

I came to help all of you.
Rejoice that I was born.
Rejoice even more
that I am here for you —
that I can help you,
because God has descended to you.
God has not descended to other worlds
by giving of his beloved Son — by giving of himself.
God gave me to you.
Beyond all the suns, moons, and stars —
HE SENT ME TO YOU!

He chose you —
to give you the gift of his love —
so that you may become divine.
He sent to you the Holy Spirit, the host of angels, and the Word,
so that you may not be just flesh and blood,
but the living breath may be in you.

The breath of God touched you —
you are marked.
Not only human beings — but all creatures
have been touched by the breath of God —
that distinguishes your world from other worlds.
Therefore, don't be exalted above others
when you encounter them —
for it is God's love — his work —
that has made you what you are.
From him you have wisdom and knowledge.
If God takes his hand away from you,
then you are like the other beings.
Your wisdom is lost.

You have never fully understood what it means
that God created the human being[8]
in his own image and likeness.
God created us —— in his own image and likeness.

I was amazed—I gave worship—I bowed before God, the
Almighty. From all the millions of suns, God has chosen ours. He
has chosen us human beings here on this planet to be his children.
Although he has done this, I wish to become the dust of the
earth—to be nothing—in the presence of Christ, in the presence
of God. I wish this because of my shame that we do not love and
serve him more.

Then Christ continued to speak:
I came as an infant.
I am in your midst
as the crucified and resurrected Christ,
so that you may not be lost in sin and poverty.
It is I who feed you with Holy Fire.
It is I who have made you God's children
through my body and blood.
It is I who forgive.
It is I who have all world events ——
here on the earth —— under my command.
Mine is the earth and all that is within it.
You princes and potentates —— bend your knees ——
so that I shall be with you.
I delight in the development and unfolding of all beings.
I chastise and punish.
I am the Lord.
I came as a child —— and yet I am your Lord.
I came out of love —— and yet I correct you.

A father and a mother also love and correct.
How much more, then, do the Son of God
and the Father in heaven.
He and I — are one.

Whoever encounters the love of God in Communion
remains in the Father, and the Father remains in him.
That is the great miracle.
Remain in it — keep the Eucharist.

Fear not — I speak for all peoples,
so they may know that all things are mine —
that I am above them all.
Fear not, all of you, who bow before God.
Come to me, all of you,
so that your joy may be complete!
Stay in this love.

Love one another, as I love you.
May one carry the burden of the other —
in that way the glow within your hearts
will never be extinguished!
Be on fire — a fire for God!
And so you will be enflamed with love
for your brothers and sisters!

Amen.

For Christmas 1959

All my private concerns melted away as Christ, the all-powerful,
stood before me. I was not even a grain of sand on the shore.
Mary went to the sick and the oppressed, to all those who are

always close to me. But everything was brief. Mary did not wish to communicate with me. She did not even accept the "Ave," because Christ stood behind her—waiting. I went before God, asked for preparation for my soul and made confession. I wanted to do this in advance, because I saw the spiritual strength of Christ. Then I prayed to Christ, but there came no answer. Thus I became quiet, and only looked at him and waited.

From this great peace, stillness, and freedom from earthly
concerns, Christ spoke:
I came into the world ——
and the world did not receive me.
I call once again:
Come to me, all of you!
And then will come the day of Judgment.

Christians! Go forth!
Gird your loins!
Go into all the streets
and call the people back
into the UNIFIED CHURCH.
Give them my body —— and my blood.
Give them my love ——
so that they may find their way home
to the Father and to me.
ALL OF YOU WHO HAVE RECEIVED KNOWLEDGE FROM ME —
BUILD MY CHURCH!

Woe when you do not want to hear my call!

I am with you all!

Amen.

Postscript, December 1987

The preceding documents are extracts from the first two years of my journals. Some years later, I stopped writing a journal and started to gather together testimonies on certain specific themes. I have selected some of these themes and placed them in part two of this volume, for example: "The Grail Legend," "Icons," "Treasures of the Faith," "Ten Messages of Wisdom," "Risen from the Dead," and "The Peoples of the Earth." A book of hymns and tapes belonging to it will be published separately. They all belong to the path that leads to the unity of the churches.

I will summarize what Christ asked over and over again: that we may become ONE ROCK—that Christians may be one—so that we are not weakened but remain in spiritual strength. Otherwise there will be great cracks in the walls of the churches. There will be earthquakes and wars. Blood will fall on the earth. Persecutions, fear, distress, hunger, and death will follow. There will be radioactive dust, and the ozone belt will be torn, leaving a hole in the stratosphere. This was already shown to me in 1965. Storms will follow, and there will be outbreaks of water and fire. Mountains will fall and valleys will be filled.

Many of these prophecies have already come to pass. There has been a war in Vietnam with millions of dead. There have also been wars in Cambodia, Angola, and Ethiopia. We have witnessed hunger in the world, the radioactive pollution of Chernobyl, floods, forest fires, and earthquakes. The hole in the ozone belt, in the meantime, has become a frightening reality and seems to be getting larger. We pray that the angels will weave so that this hole may be closed. May God prevent the sun from burning everything! We also pray that God will not let all these things happen! Many people have prayed with me.

To be honest, I must state that all those who prayed with me remained in their own communities and their own churches. Worldwide ecumenical movements are evident, but a lot more is needed before the main churches recognize or even accept anything from one another and are prepared to change their theological positions. According to the words that I received on John's Revelation, much more will happen before we are brothers and sisters in Christ!

PART TWO

FOR THE UNITY OF THE CHURCHES,
FOR THE PEOPLES OF THE WORLD

*W*ith *the powerful visions of Christ in the preceding section, we bring to a close the excerpts of Joa Bolendas's journals. In part two the messages and visions appear no longer in a chronological order but have been arranged in a thematic way. They are to be understood from an ecumenical perspective. They contain transconfessional statements about important theological themes and the essentials of sacramental life. The prophesied unity of the churches bears the promise of peace for the peoples of the earth. All the churches and nations of the world, according to the messages contained in this book, can participate in this unity.*

THE GRAIL LEGEND

A *messenger appeared in my vision. He spoke:*
In the tenth century
a saint saw in a vision that went back in time:
Christ on the cross —— Christ's suffering —— Christ's death ——
how Christ was pierced in the side,
and how cloth was laid on his wounds.

When Christ was being taken from the cross,
a man was to be seen.
He was Joseph of Arimathea.

He, Joseph, took a cup of blood
from under the cloth near Christ's wounded side.
He held the cup in his hand, and the cup radiated a strong light.

The messenger continued:
What the saint saw in his vision
and then passed on to others was the first Holy Communion
[after the death of Jesus].

In truth,
Joseph of Arimathea received primal light,
the light of creation from the risen Christ.
He received it from Christ, the man of light,
who has primal light from God.

He received it from Christ, who can pass on primal light.[9]

The reality and life of Christ
brought to humanity the truth of creation.

Whoever discerns the truth receives primal light.
The saint saw and experienced how, with the cup,
Christ passed on God's light and life to Joseph of Arimathea.

Joseph of Arimathea passed on this light to others —— to Lazarus ——
who then handed it on spiritually in John's Gospel.

The Grail legend is Celtic, Christian, and holy.
Whoever finds John will find the cup!
[*This refers to the quest for the truth of the holy vessel.*]
Whoever has found the Johannine Church has found this chalice!
[*The primal light of creation that becomes present in Holy Commu-
nion is the keystone of the Johannine teaching.*]
In order to do this, the sword is needed.

Later a messenger spoke:
Everything that was added later is legend and saga.
King Arthur did guard that place
[*the grave of Joseph of Arimathea at Glastonbury*],
in a state of mental illness.

In the tales of King Arthur,
that place became the Grail kingdom,
around which so many legends have grown.

*It was nearly a year later when a saint spoke again on the Grail
legend:*
Put together what you have received about the Grail legend
with what you have read.

Regarding the truth, the ways parted further
when the legend became more mythical.

Joseph of Arimathea was in England as Christ's witness.
He had the cup with him.
It was placed in his grave when he died.
What you have read about the chapel touches on the truth.[10]

Joseph of Arimathea, a saint who was pure,
took Christ down from the cross,
washed him, laid him in the grave
and experienced his Resurrection.

Thorn and chalice
accompanied Joseph of Arimathea throughout his life.
Whomever he loved, he initiated by showing them the cup.

And again a year later, Mary Magdalene and a saint spoke:
I am Mary Magdalene.

I am Joseph of Arimathea.
Do not be afraid!
On my flight I took the cup of Christ's blood with me —
the blood that I saved when Christ was brought down from the cross.
Wherever my travels led me, I was a witness to Christ.

I died in England.

And Mary Magdalene spoke:
I testify to this.
I was present at the burial of Christ.

Joseph and I took with us twigs from the crown of thorns
wherever we traveled.
What you have written about the Grail legend is true!

Seek out the hill in England.
Purify it with prayer and water —
this place where truth became legend and saga.

This I did in vision. An angel now stands in this place.
Light radiates across the hill and the fields.

An angel spoke:
Victory!

So legend will pass; what remains is the truth about the cup of
Joseph of Arimathea.

Joseph of Arimathea

THE ROSARY

I *pass on the rosary in song form, received in vision. Its words correspond to the older, simpler form of the rosary practiced in Medieval times.*

A Garland of Roses

People can participate in the life of Jesus by reading the Bible or by contemplating icons. The same may occur through praying or meditating the rosary. It is a very ancient prayer given by God to all people.

For many, the rosary has become a prayer of intercession. Jesus lived, suffered, carried the cross, died, resurrected, and ascended into heaven for us all. The rosary can be understood as a prayer of help for an individual person in the light of these mysteries. Mary and the saints in heaven may also be active and work for this person.

I was deeply impressed by the way the people of Ireland prayed the rosary long ago. Whether individually or in community, men and women prayed it following the rhythm of the waves. Their souls were at one with the mighty roaring, rushing sea that lay around them. By placing themselves in this unity of nature, man, and God, they contemplated the life of Jesus.

I have grown to love the rosary in song form given to me through visions. It is not important how often one repeats the Our Father and Hail Mary, or if it is sung or spoken. Often the Irish only prayed a few of the mysteries, but then with their whole strength.

The Rosary in Song Form[11]

THE FIRST HYMN OF PRAISE

Praise, praise we bring to you,
to the King of heaven and earth,
to the Father and the Son
and the Holy Spirit.
Praise, praise we bring to you.

THE OUR FATHER IN SONG FORM

Father, Father, Our Father
who art in the heavens,
hallowed be thy name.
Thy kingdom come.
Thy will be done on earth,
as it is in heaven.
Give us this day our daily bread.
Forgive us our trespasses,
as we forgive those who trespass against us.
Lead us not into temptation;
deliver us from evil.

Amen!

THE AVE MARIA IN SONG FORM

Hail Mary,
full of grace,
the Lord is with thee;

Blessed art thou among women,
and blessed is the fruit of thy womb, Jesus.

THE FIVE JOYFUL MYSTERIES

Whom you, maid of light,[12] from the Holy Spirit have received.
Whom you, maid of light, to Elisabeth have carried.
To whom you, maid of light, have given birth.
Whom you, maid of light, in the temple have offered.
Whom you, maid of light, in the temple have found.
Amen.

THE FIVE SORROWFUL MYSTERIES

Who for us has sweated blood.
Who for us at the pillar was beaten.
Who for us with thorns was crowned.
Who for us carried the heavy cross.
Who for us was crucified.

THE FIVE GLORIOUS MYSTERIES

Who from the dead has risen.
Who into heaven has ascended.
Who has sent us the Holy Spirit.
Who has taken you, maid of light, into heaven.
Who has crowned you, maid of light, in heaven.
Amen.

THE CONCLUDING PRAYER:
THE OUR FATHER IN SONG FORM

October 5, 1959

Mary's eyes were full of love. She spoke to me:
Shall we continue our work with the rosary?
I will help you.

You know about the light in the hands of the angels.
You have seen it often.
Through the rhythm of the rosary, I give this light to the people.

Through devotion and repetition, but not prattling,
this light is kindled becoming stronger and stronger.
In the beginning it is weak, then gets brighter and brighter.
THIS LIGHT IS ETERNAL HOLY JOY
AND ETERNAL HOLY PEACE.

Through the joyful mysteries,
eternal joy will resound in all your services on earth.

Through the sorrowful mysteries,
every pain or wound may be healed.

You may receive the light of the glorious mysteries
also through praying the sorrowful ones.
But then you will only have understood a part
of what lies in the glorious mysteries.
For this light has such width, depth, and magnitude
that you are not yet able to measure it.

> Here I saw dying people who were praying; the glorious
> mysteries of the rosary were upon their lips. They were
> filled with joy as they were carried into the next world.
> Those who were close to the dying prayed with them and
> thus were less sad about death. They too entered the joy of
> Resurrection.

Mary continued:
The intensity and abundance of light
that you have seen is not everything.
Didn't you feel the warmth of its radiance?
You do not yet understand
the strength that lies in these rays of light.

This is a path — not the only one —
to pass through death and enter the hereafter.
There is another path, but this one is magnificent
and so simple, a great help, a great gift!
The rosary — all the rosaries —
are like the movement of waves.
The summits of the waves are its mysteries.
The troughs of the waves are the Aves.

In the Ave, the angels and I carry and support the people
from summit to summit — ever nearer to God.
The Our Father and the Glory Be are the flames between.

So dying becomes a joy for those who are close to death
and also for the bereaved who remain on earth.
Mourning can be changed to joy!

Through this rhythm, people come closer to eternity
and so will be raised up on high.

Tell this to everyone.

ICONS

Preface

The main purpose of this work is to reveal something of the spiritual and religious value of icons and, by doing so, bring them closer to humankind. In the spirit of ecumenism, this book may also serve as an aid to a better understanding of Christians in the Orthodox Church. The visions themselves present the full testimony of an early Russian saint. "I am Nicholas of Russia, an early saint of the Eastern Church." This was the way he presented himself to me. There are other icons that were proclaimed holy in my visions, but to make them all known would lie outside the scope of this work.

I would like to add that Saint Nicholas spoke very slowly and often paused. This has been indicated in some places with dashes and in the arrangement of sentences.

We searched in Ireland for some of the icons illustrated in this book, following a vision. We found them there in Glenstal Abbey, a Benedictine monastery.

Joa Bolendas, 1979

Our Lady of Feodor

In *this vision an unknown saint appeared to me. He wore a gray cape with a double hood. I looked at him questioningly. He spoke:*
I am Nicholas of Russia,
an early saint of the Eastern Church.

I remained silent.

He continued:
You shall write about icons.
Be careful about how you write.
What you have seen in vision is not just interesting; it is true.

An Orthodox Christian of the East lives in spirit with the icons
and receives strength from them.

They are not paintings;
they are icons painted according to biblical laws!

Sitting down, Nicholas the saint held an image in his hand. I saw that it was the brown icon "Mary with the Child," which we had found in Ireland. Nicholas said to me:
Behold this mother with the infant!
She is a woman, feminine, bearing the love of a young mother
for an infant, for a helpless being.
She loves the child. The child is safe with its mother.
This mother is true, authentic, and just,
without any falseness or wickedness.

Whoever looks at this image,
knowing that it was painted as the mother of Jesus,
will see the pure and holy.
Love and trust in Mary will be in that person!
Aggression will recede!

Our Lady of Feodor
19th century, 14.5 x 17.5 cm., in Ireland

The spirit of that person
will be open to the kingdom of heaven
and able to pray to the risen Mary.
The soul and spirit together with the intellect
of that person will be open — open to Mary.
The icon works in this way.
It is most sacred.

The Mother of God of Kursk

Nicholas the saint:
Look at this blue icon.
[It is "The Mother of God of Kursk."]

Mary looks out in a sincere and searching way,
as though she sees through us and the church.

The child is turned toward us
and not pressed close to its mother.
Mary releases the Spirit of the child to us!

You can only be honest and sincere in front of this icon.
Mary reveals the full truth by holding out the child Jesus to us.

Mary, with the saints, looks at the living and active church,
which is there before her.
She also looks at each member of the church
and to everyone who is a Christian.
Mary tests and searches.
The truth is Jesus, whom she reveals to us.

Thus she tests the church in the way it serves.
She tests each individual person.

The Eastern Church lives with the truth of this icon.

The Mother of God of Kursk
Mahopac/ New York
At regular intervals, this sacred object
is brought to the communities of exiled
Russians dispersed throughout the world.
Photographed on
September 24, 1975,
in Zurich, Switzerland.

Jesus Christ–Blessing

Nicholas the saint:
This icon of Christ, painted from a vision,
is most sacred —— with a rare power of expression.
It is the icon of the church for every kind of sick person!

From the visions, you know about God's light of creation
passing to Christ, to humankind.
Song and prayer bring about a joining with this light.
And light shall be given!

The painter has succeeded
in moving the senses and quickening the spirit
in those of you who contemplate this icon,
so that you may receive.

Anyone contemplating this icon
begins to be oriented spiritually toward Christ and his light.

Thus you receive light and spiritual strength.
What happens then is most holy.

By this experience, not every sick person will be healed;
but they will begin to become holy.

This icon must not be lost!
It is most sacred!

Jesus Christ — Blessing
North Russian, Wologda, 17th century,
26.5 x 23 cm., in Ireland

The Crucifix

Nicholas the saint:
From the earliest times,
man recognized and understood the vertical and the horizontal:
the Spirit being received and the earth containing it.
From this understanding came the sign of the cross.

A new sign of the cross came with the crucifixion of Christ:
the cross that joins, joins us with Christ, God, and the Holy Spirit.

An Orthodox cross of the Eastern Church must bring about this union.
Whether cut in wood or painted, it carries this spiritual heritage.
It brings union and healing.
It is holy.

I asked: In a previous vision was it not said to evoke a blessing?

Nicholas:
Blessed be those who welcome this unity.
You need UNION WITH GOD, the Father and Creator,
WITH CHRIST, the Son of primal light —
he who receives the light of creation —
AND WITH THE POWER OF THE HOLY SPIRIT,
which is subordinate to the primal source, that is, to God.

You are blessed if so united.

In the church this union is visible
when making the sign of the cross in prayer,
and when contemplating the visible cross,
whether done alone or with the community.
The sign of the cross is ancient.
It is in us, as is the circle, the symbol of fulfillment.

The Crucifix
Carved in lime-wood, polychrome
Russian, 16th century, 25.5 x 13.5 cm.,
in Ireland

Mary's Death

Saint Nicholas became thoughtful and serious. A tinge of sadness
was to be felt. He held in his hands the icon of Mary's death. He
spoke slowly:
As he was dying on the cross,
Jesus turned to his disciple John: "This is your mother!"
Then he turned to Mary: "This is your son!"

For forty years Mary was the mother of the disciples,
and for forty years they were her sons, until Mary's death.

Mary was not alone in life, nor in death.
Together they experienced all the love and strength
that is in life and the suffering that is in death.
Joy was in their hearts as they celebrated together,
knowing about the Resurrection.

Wherever Christians live truly and authentically,
they should support each other and experience
a common sharing of life, of death, and of the Resurrection.

Love this icon!

*The next icon, the Ascension of Elijah, is closely connected to
this one!*

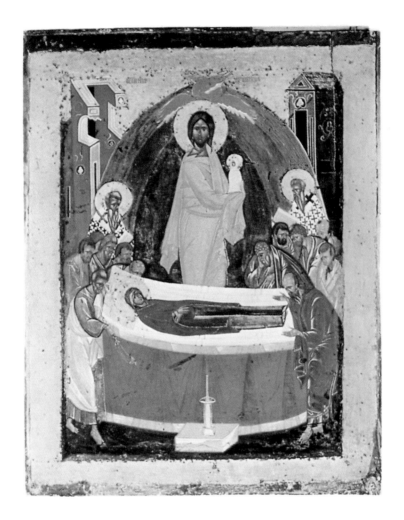

Mary's death
Moscow, 14th century

The Ascension of Elijah

Nicholas the saint:
This icon relieves the stiffness of death!

[The saint means it frees one's thoughts from physical death and turns them toward the Resurrection of life.]

The ball of fire releases movement.
It does not roll over the earth.
It rolls away from the earth.
Angels guide the way.

The Ascension of Elijah
Russian, 16th century,
in the collection of
George R. Hann,
U.S.A.

Virgin and Child

Nicholas the saint, with great joy:
Painted by a saint,
this icon shows
Mary with the three holy kings.

Look at them.
Look at the truth and simplicity of Mary and the child
together with the three holy and wise kings.
Look at them in this way
and thus this icon becomes an icon of humility.

Virgin and Child
— lateral panels — Saints Triptych
Greek, 18th century, 29.5 x 18 cm. (closed),
in Ireland

The Presentation

Nicholas showed the icon in which Mary and Joseph bring the child to the temple. It was the icon of the Presentation.

Nicholas:
Every icon with this theme awakens in the soul
the offering of oneself to God.

A child belongs to its parents.
The greater the soul and spirit of the parents,
the more they will understand
that they should offer their child to God.
This submission to God frees them from
possessing the child for themselves.
And then, together with their child, they are open to contact
with their fellow human beings.

The Orthodox Christian of the East
loves the offering of a child to God,
as with Jesus — as with their own children.

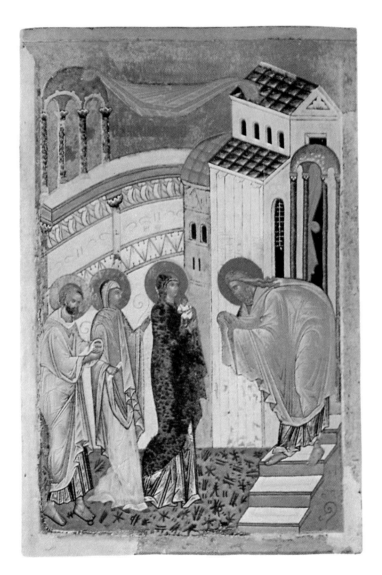

The Presentation
Novgorod, 15th century

The Mother of God of Philothéou

Saint Nicholas:
Take the icon from Athos in your hand.

The child is out of the artist's imagination.
Look at Mary.
SHE REALLY WAS LIKE THIS.
You know her from the visions.

It is Mary from the stem of Judah,
with a lean, youthful, and spiritually formed countenance ——
the nose long and fine,
the features austere and beautiful.
This is her true countenance.

Cover everything except the face.
It becomes the face of Jesus.
It is Jesus —— until shortly before his death.
He was young and had the features of his mother.

This is the holiest icon of the world.

The Mother of God
Icon from Philotéou, Athos

Saint Basil, Saint Gregory, and Saint John Chrysostom

Nicholas the saint:
Rejoice and be glad!
You will recognize the saints on icons by their foreheads.
They are not caved in, but arched.
Thus the painters showed the farsighted thoughts of the saints.
For Orthodox Christians this signifies
wisdom — purity — truthfulness.
That kind of representation
is not so deeply rooted for you in the West.

Look at the saints on the icon,
and you will understand.

Saint Basil, Saint Gregory, Saint John Chrysostom
15th century, 19.75 x 24 cm.,
in Ireland

Saint Cyrill of Beloozero

Nicholas the saint spoke with love:
In your prayer,
send greetings from me to this little great saint.

He was a wise starets[13] from the Eastern Church
who lived in the Middle Ages
and loved neither power nor reputation.

His spiritual strength and wisdom influence even today
Christians in the East and throughout the entire world.

Pray to him ——
when you are in need of true understanding.
This strengthens those people
who have a great responsibility and stand before God.
It also strengthens those who have the gifts of a starets.

Be wise and full of love in contemplating this icon.

Saint Cyrill of Beloozero, 1337–1427
painted by the ascetic Dionysij.
Cyrill was abbot of a rich monastery in Moscow.
He gave up this high office, so that he could
practice a hard asceticism. He left his monastery
and went to the desolate woods of Beloozero.

The Greek and Russian Fathers

Nicholas the saint:
Those who serve are royal figures of strength!
They are spiritual, exalted, and healthy.
Their greatness lies in their humility.

Humility and service are not weak.
There is strength in them!
These serving people know whom they serve!
And so they are free!

The two panel icons
show service to God in the church, very beautifully.

Lateral panels of Deisis
(*middle panel missing*)
Novgorod school, 16th century,
25 x 18 cm., in Ireland
Left panel: Constantine and the Greek fathers
Right panel: Vladimir and the Russian fathers

Saint Zossima and Saint Mary the Egyptian

Nicholas the saint:

Saint Mary the Egyptian[14] and Saint Zossima[15] were also servants.

Saint Zossima and Saint Mary the Egyptian
Northern school, Usting, 17th century,
30.5 x 24 cm., in Ireland

The Crucified Seraph

Nicholas the saint spoke about the icon of the covered body of
Christ:
Hang this icon up
so that it may visibly remind you all of this:

Don't cover up Christ!
Don't cover him over ——
not theologically, nor philosophically, nor psychologically!

The Bible and the testimony of the saints
are and remain the truth ——
from the birth of Jesus, to his Resurrection, to Pentecost,
to the present day.

Stay true and authentic, faithful and firm!
In this way you will participate in building God's kingdom.
In this way you will be God's servants.

The Crucified Seraph
Russian, 16th century, school of Moscow

The Virgin and Child with Three Saints

Nicholas the saint:
This icon, given to you, is the icon for all of those
who fight with a pure heart, without theological quarrel,
for God and the earth.
It shows to us Mary, the child, a disciple
and two warriors on horses.

Two horses will come:
the red horse —— blood and war,
and the black horse —— destruction, hunger, illness, and death.

Horses symbolize the possession of fighting power.
This is the language of signs, which one should learn.
It helps to express many things in few words.

Two horses are coming: a red and a black one.

You all will receive two horses from God
[so as to fight against the red and black ones].
They are fast horses, for time is hastening by!
Be strong and full of wisdom.
Remember shelter
[in case of nuclear war],
food, supplies, and medical care.
You need "the horses with warriors."
This means outside help in order to survive.

Love this icon ——
the icon with Mary, the child, and the disciple!
Give thanks for the horses, and do not forget them.
Christ rides the white horse. *(Revelation 19:11–13)*

The Virgin and Child
with Three Saints
Bulgarian, 17th century,
48 x 27 cm., in Ireland

And once again Nicholas spoke:
Love the icons and their language ——
love the language of the people
of the East ——
and you will understand each other.

TEN MESSAGES OF WISDOM

This book is about wisdom which has been lost and given again. May that be a sign that people of today need it once more. These messages refer to the time of the Christian origins in Ireland and the Church of the East. The first, seventh, and tenth messages of wisdom may be new for us. Nevertheless, after reading them many times, I believe they can be understood by everybody. The language of these messages is unusual, short, and decisive. "Mary" in the text always refers to the mother of the Lord. The visions, seen and heard in prayer, were experienced in a state of normal consciousness. I received them in 1980.

The Messages of Wisdom

Mary spoke:
It is important to make known
the origins of Christianity in Ireland,
and the parallels in the Church of the East.
This is the great spiritual understanding of the early church.

These early Christians knew about spiritual strength
and the relationship between God and the human being.

The primary form and realization of this kind of strength
was a strong faith that could move mountains.

The first Christians in Ireland and the Church of the East
understood the wisdom of the faith.

You shall receive ten truths from that time.
Put them together and pass them on to humankind.

Understand these truths;
they were lost in the Churches of the East and the West.

The First Message of Wisdom: Asking for the Holy Spirit

Mary:
It was through the concentrated strength of the Holy Spirit
that these Christians, their churches, and even their lands
were preserved and kept safe.

Abbots, kings, priests, and the laity
prayed for this great spiritual strength
when they broke bread at the Lord's Supper.

Mary continued:
When they spoke the words
"and he took bread, gave thanks, and broke it,"
they entered into silence
IN ORDER TO ASK FOR THE HOLY SPIRIT,
for light and for the power of God.
They did this also when praying for others.
Then they ate the bread.
THEY PRACTICED RECEIVING THE HOLY SPIRIT

and received the Holy Spirit when the words of the Bible
"and he took the chalice" were spoken.

Practice asking for the Holy Spirit
at the breaking of the bread in the Lord's Supper!

Practice receiving the Holy Spirit,
light, and the power of God at the taking of the chalice!

It is a prayer of the greatest strength.

At the Lord's Supper,
heaven is opened and union with God is close at hand.

The Second Message of Wisdom:
While in Prayer

Mary:
A center is located in the middle of the cerebrum
under the crown of the head.
It passes on signals to the source of life, to God.

During prayer
this center must be well supplied with blood
if it is to be spiritually active.
Relax the neck and the cervical vertebrae
so that blood can circulate freely.

During a longer prayer,
pay attention to regular breathing,
warm foot-joints and hand-joints, and a warm neck.

Meditation in a motionless sitting position is not right.
The principles given here
enable an active and open communication in prayer.

The Third Message of Wisdom:
Water for Life

Mary:
It is the wisdom about water and earth.
God created heaven and earth.
Water is a combination of chemical elements
for the preservation of the earth, human beings, and all creatures.

Hear!
Water is pierced with vibrations.
WATER LIVES FROM THESE VIBRATIONS.
This is a primal law of creation
by which living water is and remains around the earth.

These vibrations can be influenced
and brought to life through the spirit.

Through prayer,
send vibrations to the atmosphere around the earth!

The formation of water is only possible
where traces of moisture are found.

Mary gave a prayer for water:
Kneel down,
and make the sign of the cross over the earth.
Rise up,
make the sign of the cross towards the sky and say:

"In the name of Jesus Christ,
I ask you, God, to move fire toward the sky
and let rain fall!"

Do not forget this in case of a nuclear war. Then the air is dry.

It will save millions of human beings and living creatures.

After this prayer,
wash yourself from head to foot. Oil your forehead.
Go forth upon the earth again. It is healthy to do this.

The Fourth Message of Wisdom:
At One with God and Creation

A *saint from Ireland stood before me and said:*
I am Patrick, a saint known in Ireland.[17]
I lived there, united through light with Christ.

The fourth message of wisdom is about
the earth in the universe and the wonder of creation.

WE, THE ORTHODOX EARLY CHRISTIANS, LIVED ON THE EARTH
WITH THE SUN, THE WATER, THE AIR, AND THE STARS.
In spirit, we were united with these elements
and were aware of this unity.

Silent — knowing — contemplating,
WE CONTINUALLY SEARCHED FOR THIS UNITY,
living spiritually within creation, as if in the axis of a wheel.

From our understanding of this unity
came prayer to the primal source, to God.

The human, as the highest developed creature,
received life — healthy, vital, effervescent spiritual life!

The entire universe belongs to God, who is primal.
Whoever lives in the fullness of creation has strength within.

Knowledge is not life.

You cannot grasp the entire universe with science alone.

You can learn to live in the universe
through your own personal searching,
and by being centered in the axis of life.

To be at one with God and the entire creation,
and in this way to receive strength and light,
can only be experienced individually.

Separate this from communal prayer, song, and sacrament.

The Fifth Message of Wisdom:
God between You and Your Neighbor

Mary:
The understanding of truth lies within the heart.
There is pure science, but in addition to that is wisdom.

In the early church,
wisdom was to have a sense of God's justice.
WISDOM LIES IN THE DISCERNMENT OF GOD'S WILL.

A wise person is one who knows the soul of man and woman.
Philosophy is not meant,
but the perception of how and where our neighbor lives.

You have different laws according to times and countries.
Yet the wisdom to live according to the justice and will of God
has been lost.

Seek to be just in your dealings with other people.

Be wise and recognize
what God wills for any person whom you meet.

Look at the person with whom you speak.
Love that person who stands before you.

Look on that person as if God were there between you.
Thus hate, antipathy, or exaggerated reverence will recede.

Then justice will prevail!

The Sixth Message of Wisdom:
On Time

Mary spoke:
Look toward the East.
The early Christians spent time in God's presence.
They had time for God.

As in a sphere of light,
the human being and God were one — one light.

With this light, they lived for God.
Miracles occurred.

The first Irish monks acquired this being in God
from the Church of the East
and lived with it.

The light —
in which this island, Ireland, is bathed, came from that time.

[In vision, I could see this light even today.]

Light through the sacraments, prayer, and song
is still given today in the West and in the East.

BUT THE TIMELESS UNITY WITH GOD BECAME LOST.

Great joy in the heart is a sign that your prayers
have become one with God, and thus part of God's creation.

The Seventh Message of Wisdom:
Binding and Releasing

An Orthodox saint with a double cowl spoke:
Today "binding" and "releasing"
are understood as the absolving of sin. Confession.

In truth it is a struggle,
and in this work you are assisted by the Holy Spirit.
Only people with spiritual strength
can stand in this way before God and Christ, without fear or hesitancy.

We know the laws:
what is good and what is evil,
what is light and what is darkness,
and what is embraced in God's love for all creation.

With this understanding go before God!
Do it wholeheartedly!
With strength! And not out of pity!
Practice it! It is strong and effective.

Do it alone, not in a community.
This is a dedication of one's strength,
and yields a direct relationship of light
to the altar, to Christ, and to the saints.
Miracles will happen.

I asked if it had to happen by way of the altar.

The saint:
Whenever you pray in this way,
remember the Lord's table, even if you are far away.
Christ gives life through the bread and wine.
Think about the light at the Lord's Supper;
then you are near to Christ — joined to the light.

And then say:
"Light before us, light in us,
we ask you, Jesus Christ,
to release this person from wrongdoing and sin."
Or,
"We ask you, Jesus Christ,
to bind this person back from doing wrong and sin."

RELEASE AND BIND UNTIL EVIL IS OVERCOME
and light is given! [*Here prayer is struggle.*]
Do not be afraid to do this.

John the Baptist appeared and spoke to me for the first time:
I lived before Christ,
and so, as one risen from the dead,
I know what the words
in Matthew *(16:19),* "releasing and binding,"
and in John *(20:23),* "forgiveness of sins," mean.

Releasing and binding
requires a full commitment in prayer.
Few have this strength.

A Christian who has learned the faith
and has discernment can forgive.

And the difference?
RELEASING AND BINDING is a struggle before God.
FORGIVENESS means creating a bond of light
between God and the human being
which shines through, overcomes, and heals darkness.
It is good to fulfill this forgiveness of wrongdoing
together with a brother or sister,
this in a talk with a fellow Christian.
You called it confession.
We call it not holding on to guilt and wrongdoing:
a healing, a new beginning.
This is becoming a
new person in Christ.

See the Epistle of James (5:16–20).

The Eighth Message of Wisdom:
The Bread of Life

Mary:
The human, as a living creature,
NEEDS ALL OF CREATION FOR HIS OR HER NOURISHMENT.

Wheat —— whole wheat —— is the most perfect food.
Water is necessary for life.

There is enough protein in good grain.
When necessary, complete this
with fish, chicken, quail, duck, and sheep.
Roast the meat and fish!

Grapes and grape juice (*red*) lengthen one's life.
A small quantity of wine is permitted.

Remember, water is essential.
Bake bread with yeast.

Apples, nuts, and fruits of the fields enrich the table —
but are not indispensable.
After grapes and figs, the best fruit is the blueberry.
The best nut is the coconut.

The Ninth Message of Wisdom:
The Death and Resurrection of Jesus

Saint Patrick:
CHRIST DIED AND YET LIVED ON.
We know this from a true source — from the Holy Book *(Luke 23:43)*.
The thief who was crucified with Jesus also died
AND LIVED ON THE SAME DAY.

Therefore we believe
that the people of light — those who are close to God —
die and live again on the same day, in the kingdom of heaven.

We lived in the truth,
with this understanding and discernment.
We lived, united with the saints *[those risen from the dead]*,
in prayer and meditation.
Thus we were joyful.

Spontaneous prayer is
a true dialogue
with the risen people of light.

This is a great message of wisdom.

The Tenth Message of Wisdom:
Primal Light

What happens at the Lord's Supper?
Does not the bread remain bread and the wine wine?

A *saint:*
At the Lord's Supper,
you may dare to accept light directly from Christ.

In confession and the eucharistic meal,
forgiveness happens through words and prayers
to the risen Christ in heaven.

Becoming a new person through light happens directly
when you knowingly take and eat.
There is no closer union of light with Christ.
IT IS THE PRIMAL NUCLEUS OF CREATION!

Take and eat from the Lord's Supper!

The priest is not essential; he is the servant.
What must be
is a direct relationship between Christ and the individual!
In the eucharistic meal,
the servants must work with concentration.

Whoever eats and drinks,
may he or she think only of Christ and his light —
and he or she will receive primal light.

This is the tenth message of wisdom,
truth that has been lost.

Later the saint spoke:
The great and wonderful mystery
in the creation of the human cell
is the same mystery in the risen
body of light.
The same primal energy is in both.

> *Today scientists know a great deal about the human cell.*
> *Do they know that the energy that divides the cell is the*
> *same primal energy which makes life within it possible in*
> *the first place?*

Listen!
The human is born with body, soul, and spirit,
AND DEVELOPS TO BECOME A BEING OF LIGHT.

How far he or she develops
to become a person of light
lies within the freedom that men and women have,
here on earth or later in heaven.

We taught that you become a person of light
through the commandments of God,
which are contained in the Bible,
and through the sacraments
such as baptism and Holy Communion.

There are many spiritual values on earth,
yet the true values lie in Christian understanding.

> *My responsibility to pass on this wisdom was so great that*
> *I went once again to the church. I prayed that I might*
> *hear what the contents of this tenth truth were. I have not*

often seen Christ in my visions. Now I was grateful that
he stood there and spoke:

Go on the straight path!
Do not turn aside from the words that you have heard.

I, the Son of God, have risen from the dead
to receive light from the source.

I pray for the Spirit —
a force proceeding from God —
which can work and be active, also without me.

In Holy Communion,
you stand in front of the table to receive my body and blood.

What happens?

You stretch your hands out to receive.
Light radiates through you.
This is the cleansing of spirit and soul.

You take bread and wine.

What are they?

The Orthodox and Catholic priests pray beforehand,
so that the bread and wine become flesh and blood.

As Christ spoke these words, I saw him covered in a deep golden
light. It was the risen Christ, and he said:
Not flesh and blood but life —
life from my life as the risen one.

The Eucharist gives you that primal energy of life
which brought the living cell into existence.

You renew within yourselves the energy of life
and, with that, the mystery of the cell's creation
each time you take Communion.

Listen well!
I live!
I give life —— life that has strength and spirit!
Whoever is in me —— is in God.

This means
that the human being can participate in creation by working with it.
He thus lives on earth with strength
by receiving the primal energy of life.

Pass on this life in Holy Communion!

An angel:
Read Luke 24:13-35 *(Emmaus).*
Christ broke the bread consciously.
He did it knowingly.
He gave the bread as the bread of the Eucharist.
He united the disciples with the source.
"Fire" burnt within them.

The great mystery: you know it.

TREASURES OF THE FAITH

Many people have asked me to pass on the following records about Pentecost, baptism, penance, prayer, the laws of the Old Testament, and ecumenism. These visions date from 1984. I include also "Eureka"—answers to questions about the Holy Spirit and Holy Communion. Much of this material has been elaborated in my works on the Old and New Testaments.

Pentecost

A *messenger read from an open book:*
Listen to the Word of the Lord!

The Holy Spirit is active and works
through the resurrected Son of God — through Jesus Christ.
Therefore we pray
in the name of the Father, of the Son, and of the Holy Spirit.

We receive the Spirit as light — through Christ.

All of creation is from God —
God who is primal and alive in Christ.
God's light is in Christ.
God's Spirit comes through Christ — to the earth — to humankind.

Do you understand this?

Pentecost happened and is still happening today.
Pentecost is given wherever people turn to God!

I asked: What happened before Pentecost? Were there no workings of
the Holy Spirit then?

Silence.

The messenger:
There was a rushing of wind.
God guided several figures with the Holy Spirit.

Try to see this as an instrument, which you all have received
through the presence of Jesus Christ here on earth.
Christ's life, death, and Resurrection
brought you all a new understanding — including that of Pentecost.

Hear!
Since Pentecost, every human being is entitled to turn to God.
They are entitled to ask Christ for the gifts of the Holy Spirit!

All that happens through the workings of the Holy Spirit —
is in God's creation, thus is good.

God's Spirit encounters the human's spirit.
God's Spirit purifies, opens ways,
changes human beings, and changes situations,
even in the order of creation.

You may continue to do everything
in the name of the Trinity,
but since Pentecost
you are entitled to ask directly for God's Spirit.
Amen.

Baptism

Saint Peter appeared and said:
I am Peter.

Baptism *[for children and adults]* is the affirmation of becoming Christian.
The first link to God comes through this sacrament.

I, Peter, confirm that baptism creates a link to God.
Christians, let yourselves be baptized!
Baptism means when you take in Christ's light
you belong to God's people.

You belong to those people
who have accepted Christ's teachings.
They are carriers of light.

Forty days after baptism
it is good to ask for the Holy Spirit.

Mary Magdalene adds to this:
The Lord is resurrected — and is with us!
He is with you — with me — with anyone who is baptized
in the name of Jesus Christ, the Son of God.

Baptize in the name of the Father, of the Son, and of the Holy Spirit.
This should be done in spirit — water can be added.

If you baptize with water,
then you should bless it beforehand.
Amen.

Repentance and Reconciliation

Mary Magdalene:
You know about repentance and reconciliation
from the "ten messages of wisdom."

It is important that the evil of wrongdoings
be wiped out and healed before God!

Pray to Christ
that you may become pure, true, and authentic
in your spiritual life.

First comes discernment, then healing.
A new beginning leads to love.

Speak about your guilt and wrongdoing
with a brother or sister in the Lord — with a fellow Christian.
May he or she then pray for forgiveness.

You question this ?

After your talk, may your brother or sister pray to Christ,
and then say the words: "May the Lord forgive you,"
or "May God forgive you."
Amen.

Mary Magdalene continued:
Don't forget the communal practice
of repentance and reconciliation in the liturgy.

If in public with a priest
or in private within your own heart,
these words are spoken:
"Lord forgive me, for I have sinned,"
then Christ will forgive.

There is no collective guilt for the individual,
only personal guilt —— even in war.

Self-defense is permitted. You know this already.[16]

I asked: Must repentance come before baptism?

Mary Magdalene:
You become Christian,
according to your understanding of Christ.

With this discernment
there follows in natural continuity:
putting one's house in order, purifying oneself, baptism.

Don't make laws about what comes first and what comes last.
Faith must live, not become sterile.
It must not die!

There are people
who travel on a long solitary path of repentance,
who have never spoken about it with any fellow human being,
who are far away from the churches ——
and nevertheless are close to Christ.

There are people who, in spirit,
place themselves wholly under Christ
and have never been baptized.
Spiritually, they assimilate baptism within themselves,
not even knowing what they have won in the presence of Christ!
All this I say
so that you may not be small-minded but open and generous.

Amen.

Prayer

Mary *spoke:*
Pray:
Father, we have sinned.
We humans carry a heavy responsibility and are guilty:
for the politics that have created so many wars
over thousands of years.

We are responsible and guilty:
for the distress of many peoples.

We are responsible and guilty:
for the destruction of the earth ——
its soil, water, air, protecting ozone belt, its flora, and its fauna ——
and for the destruction of human culture.

We are responsible and guilty:
for our wrongdoing toward the religions of the world.

Father, you see the earth, which you created,
torn apart and in danger.

Mary, thoughtfully:
Weep, Israel!
Weep, O Israel, so magnificent!
You have suffered as the people of God.

There, at that time,
God gave to me the child Jesus.
Something new happened:

Light came to earth and a new era began.
This light and the coming of the Holy Spirit at Pentecost
brought about a new bond with God, the Creator.

God's light
shone over the whole earth
through Jesus Christ, the Son of God.

The Holy Spirit was active and worked
where people opened themselves to meet God.
People let themselves be baptized
and became followers of Christ —
became men and women of light.
Heaven and earth became one.

The rich shared their bread with the poor.
Grace was bestowed on the people.
They loved the animals and plants.
They loved the earth and the cosmos.

Mary, very seriously:
Why have you turned away?
Why have you undone the bond
with Christ, with God, and with creation?

Weep, Israel!

Build the new city on the mountain!

After I prayed the Our Father, an angel spoke:
Pray:
Oh God, so great, you are active in all; in you is life.

Father and Creator, to you we bring all things,
so that the light of your creation
will make whole all that has begun here, on this earth.
We bring before you
        our children,

our families,
our friends,
our fellow humans,
the animals and plants,
the rising and setting of the sun,
our earth and the stars.

We bring everything before you and ask you to make it whole.

May Christ and the active presence of the Holy Spirit
stay with us.

Amen.

The Laws

A *saint:*
Hear the Word of the Lord!

The laws in the Old Testament
were important for human spiritual development.

Much has developed further,
so that only a few of the laws of the Old Testament
have remained important.

—   Through Jesus Christ,
        primal light was given
        in Holy Communion.

—   The asking for the Holy Spirit
        and receiving the Holy Spirit
        guide and form a person
        throughout his or her life.

— The prayer of the Lord, the Our Father,
annuls all the laws.
It is very important to know this.
Add to these words
the Our Father and your commentary.

The Ten Commandments remain.

Amen.

Ecumenism

The pope has visited Switzerland. Ecumenical discussions have taken place. What separates us still? The problem most mentioned was: the pope as vicar of Christ. And added to that: the Catholic priest as a representative of Christ. There was much discussion in the Catholic Church and in the other churches. This is why today, after an impressive celebration of the Mass, I asked Mary: Does the priest represent Christ?

Mary:
He is worthy to give the Eucharist.
He is worthy to break the bread and drink the wine
and to pass them on to the faithful.

Again I asked: Not as a representative?

Mary:
No.
He is trained and undergoes a process of formation.
He should be at one with Christ

and at one with the Christian teaching.
No personal matters should separate him from Christ.

Mary, slowly:
Words, many words,
stand in the way and separate.
Bring the truth —— and the words will fall away.

Living with your whole being before God
is more than any learnedness!

A Francis of Assisi is more than a bishop,
an abbot, a cardinal, or even a pope.

The ordination of a priest as it is today will be simplified.
This will bear many fruits —— wonderful fruits.

Priests will be taken into the church as servants of Christ.

The pope will be:
Father of the churches and not vicar of Christ.
He can change his office. By doing this
he will become a greater, not a lesser person.

Understand, whoever can understand this!

Later, Mary added:
You have asked severe questions!

The Catholics
believe that Christ is present in Holy Communion,
and that they participate in the body of Christ!
This is an essential part of their faith.

Acknowledge it!

Eureka!

What is the Holy Spirit?
What is the body and blood in Holy Communion?

For nearly thirty years, I have tried to explain these questions to friends and acquaintances. I have tried to do this in some of the books I published about my visions. Have my words been understood? Hardly; otherwise their hearts would burn. Even in discussions, I felt that the Holy Spirit and Holy Communion remained for many something strange and foreign. Perhaps the problem lies with me, since I am not a good speaker. I don't have the words to explain all these things. Nevertheless, today I dared to ask in prayer once again: You know about the many discussions we had concerning the teachings of the Orthodox, Catholic, and Protestant Churches.

Understanding the Holy Spirit and Holy Communion is important not only for theologians and the churches, but for every human being!

I have received many words in visions, and for all of them I give thanks!

At the Last Supper Jesus did not eat, nor did he give his body and blood.

Today I ask that you tell me, if it is possible, in simple, human language:
WHAT IS THE HOLY SPIRIT?
WHAT IS THE BODY AND BLOOD IN HOLY
COMMUNION?

Christ answered:
The Holy Spirit is a power
proceeding from God and from me, God's Son.
Through the Holy Spirit come:
messages, discernment,
a strengthening of the spirit, a lessening of temptation.

Through the Holy Spirit,
your adversary will be guided, led, or held back.

Through the Holy Spirit,
messages and information are given to people,
also to the plants and animals,
to the wind and the clouds,
to life in the water and on the earth, even to the stones.

The angels bring messages —
and bring back answers to those messages.

Angels are created beings in human form
who serve, sing, praise, and glorify!

The Holy Spirit is a power
arising out of God and me, the Son of God.

The Holy Spirit does not sing,
does not worship, and does not praise
as the angels do when in contact with human beings.
The Holy Spirit works directly on the human spirit,
strengthening it — changing it.

A saint:
Therefore, pray
in the name of the Father, the creator,

in the name of the Son, who links us with the light of creation,
in the name of the Holy Spirit, who is active in us.

The saint:
You have it!

Thus will be the worship of God and his Son.
Thus will be the asking for the Holy Spirit
and readiness to let God's Spirit work.

> *Again I asked: What is Holy Communion? What is the*
> *body and blood in Communion? Then in vision I saw*
> *saints and angels. A saint spoke:*

If you received from Hannes or any other person
a toe, a finger, or a piece of his body,
would that be life?

> *I answered: No. It would just be a dead piece of flesh but*
> *not the life of that person."*

The saint:
If you received blood from someone,
would it be the life of that person?

> *I answered: No. But I received life from my husband and*
> *could give life to a child.*

The saint:
No.
That is something different;
that belongs to the order of creation.

Now look carefully.

Yesterday you had a visitor. You talked with Hannes.

Open your eyes!

> *And I "saw" the same Hannes as yesterday except that his*
> *body — his arms, legs, and head — was full of small rays*
> *of light, like small lines of light. The trunk of his body was*
> *darker than the other parts. I "saw" an aura around his*
> *body consisting of thin, short, intensive rays of silver. And*
> *when Hannes spoke, all this light was in movement —*
> *like active energy.*

The saint:
THIS IS LIFE.
When you speak with Hannes or he with you,
he gives of his life.
This energy renews itself in him.
You passed on life to him in this
discussion, too.

Every human has this life within himself;
otherwise he would be dead.
Some have more, others less.
Those who are strong in spirit
radiate and pass on an abundance of life.

The saint:
And now about Christ in Communion:
He, Christ, did not give of his own blood or of his own flesh
to his disciples at the Last Supper.
HE GAVE AND GIVES HIS LIFE —
from his light,
from his energy,
from his spiritual body,
from his own true life.

We receive Christ's life in Communion.

Christ, in the form of man and as a figure of light, gives us life:
life from his own life — from primal light —
from the light of God's creation.

I asked again: Why do you say from his body and blood?

The saint:
Body and blood is the ancient understanding
for the whole body — for the whole being.
This way of understanding was lost.

It is not simply energy that is present,
but energy of a formed being —
Christ who came forth from God.

Do you understand?
Do you discern that Communion is
light, spirit, and life from the whole being of Christ.
It is not simply from a field of energy,
but from God's Son in human form!

This unity of the whole body and being of Christ
gives energy — gives life!

> *Ashamed before the greatness of all this, astonished by
> what I had received, I stared at the saints and angels.
> Then: joy, joy, joy! I called out loud: Eureka! And I
> banged with my fists on the table!*

Mary Magdalene added:
Rejoice!
You have received so much.

Tell all the people
what you have seen and what you have heard!

Do not be afraid.
Build the church with the real life of Christ!

Love Advent
and the feast of Christ's birth!

These words were said in the first week of Advent 1985.

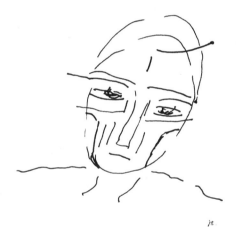

Grief

RISEN FROM THE DEAD

Preface

In my work on the universe, I wrote: "God is in this creation —
in the expanse of the universe" and "Those who are redeemed live
near the earth in a field of light with Christ and the angels."[18] The
following visions are about the risen human being.

Since the beginning of time, humankind has searched for a meaning
to life and with that the possibility of survival after death. We humans
have always questioned what it really means to have risen from the
dead. In this book I pass on answers received through visions.

At present a large number of books are on the market that deal with
this topic, and much has been said about it in the mass media. The
search for life beyond death continues to be of worldwide interest.

Two modern scientists, Jean Charon and Teilhard de Chardin,
have addressed the topic from their respective viewpoints. Both
adopt a scientific approach to the question of the human soul and
its survival after death.

Charon, in his book *The Unknown Spirit*,[19] introduces survival after
death as his central theme and investigates the possibility of spirit
in matter — more specifically, spirit in the most elementary particles of matter. From his observation of the electron, with its capacity

to store and increase information, its subjugation to cyclic rather than linear time, and its ability to communicate with other electrons, Charon concludes that this complex behavior of elementary particles reveals a dimension of spirit. "Spirit is indeed at the centre of the universal adventure, but this Spirit is not the privilege of man alone. Man does not process all the available potential of Spirit just for himself. And the cosmic adventure is not a tale told for man alone."[20]

Perhaps the works of Teilhard de Chardin approximate more closely what I have received in visions. He attributes a spiritual and material aspect to all matter. "The time has come to realize that an interpretation of the universe—even a positivist one— remains unsatisfying unless it covers the interior as well as the exterior of things: mind as well as matter. The true physics is that which will, one day, achieve the inclusion of man in his wholeness in a coherent picture of the world."[21]

According to Teilhard, in its beginnings, the universe presents itself as an incredible organized whole. All matter is in a state of genesis. Elementary consciousness is already imprisoned in matter so that the increase both of spirit and of the complexity of matter is one and the same phenomenon. This upthrust of evolution continues through the biosphere, and only the postulation of an inner spiritual principle can explain the sharpness of direction that marks the process of irreversible advance to higher and more complex organisms. In human beings, evolution becomes conscious of itself. In the individual consciousness, an extension of one single organism over the entire earth takes place. The human mind is in the process of discovering the furthest star and the smallest particle of matter.

Finally, according to Teilhard, a further ascent of consciousness indicates the course of evolution towards an Omega point. Omega, another name for God, is the supreme fulfillment of the entire evolutionary process. Omega is the principle that explains love, which is understood as the inner affinity that unites beings with one another. It is also the principle that wards off the threat of disappearance, incompatible with reflective activity. For Teilhard, the overcoming of death is the irreversible thrust of the whole evolutionary process. Through this process, all beings achieve their spiritualization and immortality as they move toward God. "When, in the universe in movement to which we have just awakened, we look at the temporal and spatial series diverging and amplifying themselves around and behind us like the laminae of a cone, we are perhaps engaging in pure science. But when we turn towards the summit, towards the totality and the future, we cannot help engaging in religion. Religion and science are the two conjugated faces or phases of one and the same complete act of knowledge — the only one which can embrace the past and future of evolution so as to contemplate, measure and fulfill them."[22]

In this little book, I cannot profess to answer or even understand all the questions raised by these scientists. I am simply surprised that a natural scientist and an anthropologist have attempted to explain the spiritual dimension of the universe and the possibility of survival after death on a scientific basis. It is my hope that the answers received in the following visions will further clarify questions about life beyond death and the imperishability of the human soul. In my next work, I intend to publish messages received directly from individuals who died and have risen from the dead.

Joa Bolendas et al.

The First Answer

What is the substance of one risen from the dead?

This was my question, and a saint answered:
It is a spiritual substance of energy.[23]
It is of light, unchangeable light, which is the same as energy.
The risen human remains a created being
linked with God's Spirit.

The flesh, the earthly covering and clothing, falls away.

You can say this with other words:
The soul and spirit of the human, together with God's light,
come into existence, evolve, and develop
within the earthly clothing made for all human beings.
They develop into an image and likeness of God —
a human being
united with God's Spirit!

Don't you see that when the earthly clothing falls away,
the risen being lives on!

Risen humans exist according to the primal laws of
LIVING, GIVING, AND RECEIVING.

> _This means they live, they give of their love, and they
> receive God's light and strength and the Holy Spirit, as
> they did when they lived on earth._

The Second Answer

The development of the human being of light.

The saint:
The semen is given to the ovum.
During the last months of pregnancy,
the vessel of the soul forms itself.
The development of the human spirit
coincides with the growth of the brain.

All this was created by the primal source —
by God.

At birth the child, God's creation,
comes into contact with life on earth.

Once the human is born and lives the fullness of his life,
then his or her development into a being of light will begin.
Thus body, soul, and spirit receive God's Spirit.

The image and likeness of God consists of
the human body, soul, and spirit
completed with God's Spirit and light.

When the earthly clothing falls away,
eternal light in human form remains.

This body of light lives!
God's Spirit is in it.

The people of light are noble and fulfilled
when integrated into God's kingdom.

Whoever does not develop on earth

into the image and likeness of God
will be a weaker figure of light in the kingdom of heaven,
eventually will evolve to become a person full of light —
all according to God's primal law.

The Third Answer
On God, the risen Christ, angels, the risen human, death, and
Mary.

Mary, the mother of the Lord:
The greatness of the Lord Jesus Christ is his light
— unchanging, eternal light — primal light.

At birth he received primal light.
When he was twelve years old, he received primal light.
At the baptism in the Jordan, he received primal light.
He received primal light
in order to live and work as the Son of God until his death.

The light that he received on earth, in his human life,
made him, Jesus Christ,
into THE FIGURE OF LIGHT for this earth.
He is this, through his death, as the risen one,
and as the mediator between God and humankind.

Christ was brought forth from God's own being,
and God gave him to humankind (*John 1:18*).

Thus light came to the earth, to human beings —
light from God to humankind.

This is the greatness of the Lord!
Blessed be those who believe, love, and receive light.

As an example of a human being risen from the dead,
Mary showed me my son Peter, who died when he was
twenty-three years old. Mary spoke to me:

Peter is a man of light.
He was surrounded by prayer
as he developed in his mother's womb and in his youth.
He loved God.
He was related to Christ.
He is now a holy man of light linked with Christ.

Learn from this:
There is God, who is the primal source.
There is Christ, who was brought forth from God,[24]
and who is called the Son of God
because the magnitude of light received by him from God
is the same as that of God, the primal source!

The angels are created by God as beings of light ——
not with the same light as humans.

Risen men and women are people of light
without the clothing of earth.

My son Peter was shown as an example.

Many people grow to become people of light
in the kingdom of heaven.
Their levels of being are different.

Few become extinguished.
They burn out to nothing.

That is real death.

I still asked Mary: What are you, Mary, as one risen from the dead?

Mary answered full of joy:
I am risen!
I may serve Jesus ——
I was created to serve.

The Fourth Answer

Mary *summarized everything once more:*
The risen body is a spiritual substance of energy.
Men and women are born with body, soul, and spirit.
They develop in order that they may be linked with God.
You call it religion and faith.
Light comes into existence
through contact with Christ and God.
This light in men and women is imperishable.

Thus the life of the new human will be soul, spirit, and light.
The light of those risen from the dead has human form.
The earthly covering falls away at physical death.

Do you understand this?
Give life —— eternal life —— to others,
so that you all may move towards becoming people of light!

Hold on to this:
The new church, the unified church,
is all that makes men and women into people of light!
Holy Scripture and the truth of the Old and New Testaments
will remain.

The church that has grown and developed will remain.
Repentance and reconciliation, baptism and the eucharistic meal,
will remain.

Love is the sign and testimony of the Christian faith.

To be left open
are the ways in which different types of people develop.
Love the men and women of the East *(the Eastern Church),*
of the North *(the Protestant Church),*
and of the South *(the Catholic Church).*
Do not be small-minded; be open and generous!
You will discern all things through love!

Death

PEOPLES OF THE EARTH

1984 – 1986

Mary, *the mother of the Lord:*
There will be peace
when the peoples of the earth understand each other.

A Sioux Spoke

I *saw a ray of light moving toward North America, where
an old Sioux Indian was standing. He looked toward
Africa and then spoke to me:*

When a friend —— a brother or a sister —— is in need,
then pray together:

"Jesus Christ, forgive my friend and me
for all wrongdoing which
has cast a shadow over life.

We ask you to remove this shadow,
and let us have light before us again. Amen."

The Sioux added:
These are the words of an African soul.

*The ray of light moved from Europe to North America,
over to Africa, and then back to Europe. It was the first
time that I saw in vision a spiritual contact between the
white, red, and black peoples of the three continents.*

The Ages

An angel of great brightness spoke:
THE FIRST AGE
is the age of the stars
and of God's creation of the universe.

THE SECOND AGE
is the age of God's creation of the sun
over a long period of time.
The right measure of light for life on earth
is given by means of the solstice
and the coming and going of day and night.

THE THIRD AGE
is the age of life.
God created the human being —
his coming into existence and his passing away.
God created the plants and the animals.

THE FOURTH AGE
is the age of the spiritual unfolding of life.
Peoples of the earth,
you will come to understand about giving new life to others:
"to be born of the Spirit and enter God's kingdom." *(John 3:5–6)*

This passing on of life occurs naturally through conception and birth.
A further unfolding of this process is the passing on of the spirit —

the transmission of cultural and spiritual understanding
to other humans, which happens through

— formation and development of communal life;

— advances in communication, from whistle signals to language;

— capacity to formulate thought and share it with others;

— spiritual encounters: it took a long time before one could give
of one's life to another, this being done in spirit;

— placing one's being in God and serving one's fellow human being,
which is the highest level of evolution.

Thus the passing on of life occurs through conception and birth,
and through the growth of the spirit
in the family, the village, the school, the city, and the living of the faith.
You will discover the strongest form
of the passing on of life in religion,
which is a living in God for others.

THE FIFTH AGE
is the age of eternal life which is primal and created by God.
It remains forever.

THESE ARE THE AGES.
Live!
Grow and develop!
Become a person of light!
And so you will live in all that is primal — in God and with God!

The angel spoke slowly:
The wheel of life turns
and the spirit of love is in its axis
—at the very core of life.

Christ came from the primal source and lived the spirit of love.

The Stone Age

Mary, the mother of the Lord:
The stone age
was a period of beauty and happiness.

The people of this age possessed a profound sensitivity,
which was not disturbed by power and technology
as it is today.

Their sensitivity was experienced
in one-to-one relationships between individuals ——
in love, work, and even in strife!

The Age of the Planters

In the age of the planters[25]
men became intoxicated
with their own possibilities.
They sowed.
They reaped.
Through their intelligence,
they experienced growth and prosperity.

This was an important step
in human cultural development.

The Age of the Astronomers

The study of the heavens
gave humans a rich understanding.

It bestowed on them
a nobility above all other beings.

Their eyes were no longer fixed on their immediate surroundings.
They began to relate to distant objects.

Their way of thinking
expanded into new dimensions
as they sought what transcends this world.

The spiritual development of human beings advanced rapidly
with the emergence of a religious sensitivity.

This is the reason
why the first astronomers were the first wise people:
they could point to the greatness of the cosmos
and to a world beyond the earth.

The Beginnings in the Old and New Testaments

The migrations of the peoples of the earth
started in the Mediterranean region.
They migrated to the East, the South, the North, and the West.

The history of the peoples of the earth
began with Noah. (Genesis 6–10)

Moses brought together and formed the people of Israel.
They will continue to survive as a people,
and their story will be the oldest
among the peoples of the world,
as they find unity with Christians.

The people of Israel are described in the Old Testament.
A new light came to mankind through Christ.
A new human being evolved.
All this has been written down in the New Testament.

The People of Africa

The African people
received a thin but strong aura of light
around their whole body.

[This aura appeared to be about five centimeters in thickness.]

It protects them
from a development that would be too fast.

It protects them from becoming brutal.
As a people they remain
self-disciplined, kind, and good-natured.

The rhythm and movement of these people
continue to be good.
Do not destroy them!

The length of time that is necessary
for a people to develop
is connected with their music and rhythm.

Pay attention
to the ways of life and the crafts of Africa.

In three thousand years,
their appreciation and composition of music
will be more beautiful than that of Europe —
more beautiful than Bach, Mozart, Schubert, or Liszt.

The appeal of their paintings
will be in their magnificent perspectives —
perspectives converging toward light.

In their community life
there will be monogamy, with many children,
together with a strong feeling
of belonging to one people —— the African people.
All this will come through a new, well-grounded
Christian understanding of life, creation, and God.

The People of China

An angel spoke:
Write down:
China is a holy land!
Its people are a holy people!

China will continue
on its long path of spiritual evolution.
In five to seven thousand years,
the Chinese people will be capable
of a powerful, inner, spiritual relationship
with God through Jesus Christ.
Thus they will live with God's Spirit.

The rhythm of Chinese music will change and develop,
which will be important.

God created the soul and spirit of these people
so as to evolve in this way.
It is different from training intelligence
and the physical body.

Living in God
will be the fulfillment of these people.

Love them!
Watch over them!
Pray for their fulfillment,
which will take place over thousands of years.

When the time comes
that an oriental and a black person
will be able to meet without experiencing
a barrier in soul or spirit,
then the soul will be open and free
and a spiritual life in God
will have been accomplished.

The first unity in soul and spirit
between two races of the earth
will be achieved between these two peoples.

I asked about the origins of the Chinese people.

A saint answered:
A human of fair complexion was created.[26]
The sons of Noah and their sons
peopled the whole earth. *(Genesis 9–10)*
Their bodies changed
through the influence of plants and climate:
thus the black people of Africa,
the oriental people of China,
and the indigenous people of North America.

Boundaries were created between the peoples
so that the great races of the earth
preserved their identity.

Later a saint spoke about China:
China, like Africa, is evolving
over thousands of years.
Each race evolves in its own way.

The Indian People of North America

The Indian people
experienced a great cultural development.

I saw in vision Indian people standing on high plateaus opening
themselves to the Great Spirit.

As a people, they lived in kinship
with the earth, the sun, the moon, and the stars,
and in this way evolved to a people of high degree.

A linking
of their powerful sensitivity to this way of living on earth
with the Christian faith
would be of great value for their development.
Thus Christ will enable a further opening
to the primal light of creation.

After six hundred years
of their own authentic Christian development,
an inner encounter with Jews and Christians will be possible —
an encounter from soul to soul, without barriers.

From then on
the Indian's way of living in God will evolve rapidly,
and so also their contact with white people.

When you have finished writing down your records,
place them in the hands of an Indian chief.

He will read your words.
As one risen from the dead and with light from eternity,
he will let them grow in the hearts of his people
over a thousand years!

Later a saint added:
The Indian people of North America are the blossoms of a tree!

They reached the highest level of natural human dignity,
even without the influence of the Old and New Testaments.

When the spiritual discernment
contained in the Old and New Testaments
is added to their way of life,
they will mature and have great spiritual leaders.
They will bring forth men and women of great spirit
for the benefit of humankind.
They will become a people of great spiritual wisdom.

Let them mature!
Do not exterminate them!
Otherwise a limb in the body of humanity will be missing.

The Indian people of America
possessed a great peace of mind
to live with the earth and the cosmos.

India

India —— a rich land that has fallen and crumbles!
The flowering period of magnificent craftsmanship
and the goodness of a Gandhi,

manifesting in different people at different times,
are no longer there.

A strong hand to awaken and lead the people is missing.

It was a rich land that is now decaying.
Its culture is passing away.
The richness of its soul has been weakened —
extinguished in the Ganges.

Later a saint:
India has become lost in its own mythology.
The continuation of a religious thinking,
where faith in God as the Creator is no longer present,
weakens the spirit of a people.

I prayed for India.
Others too prayed for this land.

Israel

Israel lives from the faith.
Israel lives with the faith.

Christ came out of Judah's stem.
He was a Jew.

He could pass on life.

A son of Israel
passed on and still passes on light — God's light.

He testified to God.
Expanding the faith of the fathers,
he brought Christianity to mankind.

The Age of the Celts

The Celts were a people of great spirit
made up of many warlike tribes.

They loved beauty and artistic creativity.

Knowledge about them differs.
The people of the Celtic period
were divided into different classes:
— a few spiritually creative individuals;
— gifted artists;
— the warriors and heroes of the myths;
— the masses.
The people were poorly educated!
If it had been otherwise,
the Celts of Ireland would have achieved
a higher level of development.

> *I would like to add that after Saint Patrick brought the Gospels (and with them the Latin alphabet) to Ireland, a great blossoming of learning began.*

Europe

The Romans and Etruscans
laid the foundations of Europe.

The Etruscans were great thinkers.
God's light reached their minds
and a development was granted,
through God's will in the unfolding of creation.

An Etruscan

Their language, music, and song
were noble, beautiful, and rhythmic.

The Etruscans were a great people —
a pillar of light among the peoples of the earth.

The Romans
took over the knowledge and culture of the Etruscans.
The decline and fall of the Romans was due to their arrogance.

Arrogance and presumption weaken a people until they fall.
Learn from this.

The Etruscans and Romans were important
for the entire cultural development of Europe.

The Franks and Hungarians
heard the rushing of the winds as they rode their horses!
Europe needed both types of people.
They learned from the rhythm of their horses,
and their influence prevailed in music and dance.

The Goths and Vikings carried a cross of light.
Their understanding of the earth and the spirit of heaven
was embodied in the horizontal and vertical beams of the cross.
Consciously they brought together
life on earth with the life of the spirit.

The Goths and Vikings were a holy people.
They integrated within themselves
spiritual guidance from the heavens.
They were warriors according to the times,
but in their soul they were a good people.

Europe needed the Goths and the Vikings
so that the law might be fulfilled.

Europe needed the Goths, the Vikings,
the Greeks, the Romans, and the Etruscans
so that soul and body might be formed
to embrace the Old and New Testament.

This process of formation
leading to the birth of Christianity in Europe
stimulated the Germanic people!
They were caught in the tensions that ravished Europe —
between the impact of the invading tribes
and the ancient cultures of the South.
They learned to be critical.
In their spirit, they struggled to reach

a true understanding of the new faith
during the age of migrations.

This powerful inner struggle
still influences the German people today.

Luther too searched for the truth.

The United States and Canada

The United States and Canada:
A new land without the old traditions of Europe,
but a culture rich in what has been newly discovered,
through the influence
of books, schools, music, various cultures, and religions.

Delighting in what is new,
the American people have developed in leaps and bounds.

Unlike Europe,
the people of America are not burdened with the past.

Think about the wars, struggles, and slaughters
between the kings, nations, and religions of Europe.

These sins and wrongdoings,
even up to the last great war
and the blind and brutal conflicts of today,
have been neither atoned for nor healed.
Thus they remain a burden, whether conscious or unconscious.

America has much of what is primitive in humankind,
but it does not have to carry the heavy burdens of the past.

It must not forget the wrong done to Native Americans
and should continue to hold these people in high esteem.

For America,
a rich period of blossoming and maturity lies ahead,
which will be linked to the Christian way of life.

Let Us Repent

A *saint:*
Pray and ask
for forgiveness of the wrongdoings of Russia.
I prayed.

Pray for forgiveness of France,
from the time of the Franks to the present day.
I prayed.

Pray for forgiveness of the wrongdoings of the Huns.
I prayed.

Pray for forgiveness of the Goths —
the Ostrogoths and the Visigoths.
I prayed.

Pray for forgiveness of the Vikings and Warangians.
I prayed.

You have already struggled and done penance for the Celts.

In vision I saw a youth in a white robe. He said:
I am Conall.
The Christian people of Ireland
have already repented of their wrongdoings.

The saint continued:
Pray for forgiveness of the Etruscans.
I prayed.

Pray for forgiveness of the wrongdoings of Italy,
of the Romans and of Pilate.
He decided on the death of Christ.
I prayed.

Pray for forgiveness of the wrongdoings of the Germans.
I prayed.

Pray for forgiveness of the wrongdoings of England.
The English ruled in many parts of the world;
much blood clings to them.
I prayed.

Pray for forgiveness
of all Africa,
of all South America,
of all North America,
of Asia,
of Australia,
and of Europe.
I prayed.

There are small pockets of evil power
in the middle of Africa.

Pray and struggle so that they may be overcome!

A lot of work in prayer
must be done for the Indo-Germanic peoples.
Worship and do not be afraid!

Japan too possessed a great empire that did evil.
Pray and ask for forgiveness
and the healing of its wrongdoings.

It is a great spiritual task,
but also one of the most dangerous ones,
to struggle in spirit and to overcome the past.
All this be done through God and for one's fellow human.
I prayed.

In the name of the Father, the Son, and the Holy Spirit.

Christ appeared and spoke:
A new beginning!

*Some years later (1989) a saint of the Eastern Church spoke about
"Peoples of the Earth":*

With the beginning of the Johannine age,
light pierced through the dark centers of power,
which still existed.

Light penetrated
and overcame darkness upon the earth,
through God's will in the unfolding of creation.

Dark spiritual influences from
the time of the Pharaohs *[from Israel's captivity in Egypt]*,
the time of the Celts,

the time of the Mongols,
the Hitler period,
and the small centers of power in Africa,
have been conquered —— overcome through prayer.

The wall in Berlin has fallen
and with it, the power of the Soviet Union.
The Jews in Russia are free!

The saint spoke seriously:
Prayers, many prayers are needed to influence the power of Islam.
Ask for the Holy Spirit.
Ask that the rays of God's light work and renew,
so that shadows give way and new life will begin!

Amen.

GOD

In profound silence before God, I dared to ask: Who is God?

An angel of great brightness appeared. He looked at me searchingly, for a long time, and then spoke:

GOD IS LIGHT —
eternal, unchanging light.
God's form is similar to the form of a human being.

GOD IS SPIRIT.
God's Spirit is in light, of light, around light.

GOD GIVES LIFE.
He has life within himself.
Only God can bestow life.

God created all things —— also the cosmos ——
you cannot comprehend this.

All of creation is evolving
with light, Spirit, and life.
Without God's life, everything would be dead.

JESUS CHRIST
can pass on life as the Son of God.

*Whenever I have prayed in the name of the Father, the
Son, and the Holy Spirit, I tried to concentrate on God's
life, light, and the Holy Spirit. At such moments, I often
saw in vision the three main churches. They were made
out of wood and were filled with a pure, radiant light.
These churches of wood are symbols of the living church.*

Some months later an angel spoke:
Hear the Word of the Lord!

God is life.
God gives life.
God is light, imperishable light.
God is Spirit.

When you pray to God,
you enter the realm of life.

When you pray to Christ,
you enter the realm of light.

When you pray to God and Christ,
and ask that the Holy Spirit be active in you,
then you will enter the realm of the Holy Spirit.

The angel spoke with a firm voice:
God is the primal source,
and all being and life in the cosmos and on earth
are of God.

Live as Christians!
Open yourselves to God, Christ, and the Holy Spirit!
Love the Eucharist!

Love the scriptures!
Love community with your brother and sister!
Live the spirit of love,
for love comes from God!

Amen.

The angel continued:
In this way,
the three main churches will be filled with light!
THIS IS THE CHURCH WHICH WILL BE ONE.
It will live with God's life, light, and Spirit.

You, Joa Bolendas,
are to enter the realm of life,
light, and into the expanse of the Spirit
from time to time, when you pray.

These words were given to me in Advent 1990.

Silence

PART THREE
ON THE OLD AND
NEW TESTAMENTS

The last part of this volume contains visions and
messages which Joa Bolendas received over a period of
several years (1980–1987). She was given the heavy task
to work through the Bible. The visions presented here bear
witness to the source of truth contained in Holy Scripture.
They are also to be understood from the perspective of the
coming Johannine Church.

PREFACE TO PART THREE

If you are someone who is critical, seeks the truth, and is eager for knowledge, I will ask you what you would have done if a saint, an angel, or Mary had stood before you and said:

"Write —— take the Bible —— read section after section —— we are going to work through these books."

Would you have said yes? Would you have written everything down?

I needed time to say yes, and then I began to work. I read the Bible, as much as I could survey at a time, section after section. Then I went into the church — prayed — and started to write.

First I received the words on the universe, then on the Old Testament, the New Testament, and later on John's Revelation. The words received on John the Evangelist focus on the question of why we need religion to attain full development of our being.

Read the words critically — seeking the truth — and you will be enriched.

Joa Bolendas
Autumn 1987

THE UNIVERSE

One risen from the dead:
Blessed be Christ, who joins earth with heaven.
Love the churches: they serve God's love.

Slowly:
The universe is the creation of the
one primal source; it belongs to God's creation.

The saint continued.
His words described the unfolding of the universe:
—— SPACE WITHOUT AIR.
—— GASES —— were created and came into being.
—— CONSOLIDATION —— of the same gases over millions of years.
—— FIELDS OF TENSION, MAGNETIC FIELDS.
—— RAYS —— from God —— rays of creation.
—— CHEMICAL PROCESSES —— over a long period ——
    preparation for the unfolding of life.
—— EARTH VIBRATIONS —— the rotating of the earth,
    the sun, the moon, the stars ——
    the coming of day and night ——
    as in all life, given by God.
—— LIFE BEGAN ON THE PLANET EARTH —— microcosmically.
    Millions of years were necessary,
    in order to complete this creation.

— Finally God created
THE HUMAN BEING — WITH A SOUL —
and gave to him the realm of spirit.
The human — as a spiritual being — was created.

Humans need space on the earth, and beyond the earth,
so as to live the lesser *[earthly]* as also the greater *[spiritual]* life.

All had to be created —
for the one made in the image and likeness of God —
for the human being.
— Come and see the garden of Eden.
Wood, jungle, land, and bush are visible, in the midst of them:
A man — a woman — not the first ones!
BUT THOSE WHO RECEIVED POWERS OF DISCERNMENT.
The human developed to become one who discerns:
a stage of evolution.

— LOVE ALL CHURCHES; LOVE THE EARTH,
LOVE THE GREATNESS OF CREATION.

— After millions of years other earths will evolve —
AND ALWAYS THE HUMAN BEING SHALL BE AND REMAIN
THE GREATEST CREATION.

You have seen and perceived great things.
No eye has seen and no ear has heard these things.
— THE LINK BETWEEN MAN AND GOD
shall always be the crown of creation.

Every earth will receive — when it is ready — a mediator
as the highest spiritual link.

For union with God,

the human being must be in the image and likeness of God.
No ideology may change that!

God will punish and correct again and again —

when man turns away from God or destroys the image of God —
as human history shows, and as will happen again.

— GOD IS IN THIS CREATION — in the expanse of the planets.
Creation is expanding through the universe.
It is still in process.

The first, great, completed creation is the earth.
It shall not perish before the coming of the Lord, Jesus Christ.

Those who are redeemed, the dead, live near the earth
in a field of light with Christ and the angels.

They influence the earth — part of the order of creation.
That is why the resurrected are near
and yet in the kingdom of God.

On two moons there are beings —
yet they are not as developed as the human.

Signs in the heavens [*like flying saucers*]
originate from the human mind on earth —
mainly in the Caucasus,
where there are descendants of the Atlanteans.

In the time of Atlantis
there was a flowering of the spirit and of knowledge.
They saw into the mysteries of nature
and could apply this knowledge to practical life.
Signs and traces remain until today.
Descendants from the Atlanteans

live in the Caucasus, in Asia, and the Mediterranean.
They are unknowingly carriers of inherited brain functions
up to the present day.

Your spiritual understanding of nature
through science and technology
has not yet caught up with the Atlantean period.
Three centuries are necessary
to reach again that flowering of knowledge.
When excavators come across traces of the Atlanteans,
the world will be astonished.

Mary, the mother of the Lord:
From the human perspective you have seen in visions:

THE SOURCE.
BEING.
BEAUTY.
GOODNESS.

Pass it on!
Complete the books —
You, all of you, live with them!

Joy be in you!
Praise be to the Lord!
Amen.

THE OLD TESTAMENT

These visions are better understood if the corresponding text of the Bible has been read in advance.

Genesis

The saint:
God created the heavens, the stars, the moons, the suns.
He created the earth.

God's Spirit moved the earth —— and life came upon it.

He created the human being
in image and likeness —— in his own image and likeness.

This was the first day.

He gave to human beings fields —— to cultivate.
He made the earth subject to them ——
with all things that live upon it.

He gave to them wisdom and knowledge ——
He made "their eyes open" to see and to hear.
He made their souls strong!
And God encountered them.

This was the second day.

He gave names to them,
and guided them over the earth:

from the Mediterranean — to the East,
over thousands of years,

from the Mediterranean — to the South,
over thousands of years,

from the Mediterranean — to the North,

from the Mediterranean — to the West,
all over hundreds of thousands
of years.

He gave them language.
He formed the soul — according to each land:
East — South — North — West.

He gave them color.

He gave them song — the movement of soul, spirit, body.
Through music and song, dance and rhythm,
the human being became ennobled.

On the third day, humans opened their souls:
to receive vibrations from God.

The beginning of the fourth day:

Strong souls grew in spirit.
The light — encountered them!
And God's Spirit could touch their souls:
a Moses! An Abraham! An Isaac!
There were many of them — until the time of Christ.

David too — with such a strong soul of light!
A strong spirit — dwelt within him;
open, true, he lived according to God's primal law.

Read through the Old Testament — we shall work!

The saint:
Listen!
The first book of Moses is symbolic — and yet true.

At the time of Adam *[at the time of the account of Adam and Eve]*
there were many races.

Cain slew Abel, but many robbed — killed — as did Cain.
It was so at that time.
By the time of Adam, humankind was already five thousand and one years old!
[A symbolic number; the story of Adam and Eve belongs to the oldest
history of humankind.]

The story of Adam and Eve — is not a legend. It is symbolic!
A story that was told over and over again — from tribe to tribe;
they, the tribes, eventually turning it into their own Hebraic history.
Therefore it is both true and symbolic.

God created the human being as he is — still today.
He, the first human being, was very primitive —
and yet he had power over the earth *[animals, and so forth]*.

His legs were curved, curved thighs, rounded kneecaps,
curved lower legs.
His toes were curved, gripping.
In a short time he conquered distances far and high.

His eyes were slit — very good eyes! Farseeing!
Strong cheekbones, strong pelvic bones.

Very good ears, a sharp sense of smell.
Whistle signals! Later sounds.

First God created a woman;
God breathed into her; she gave birth to a man!
God breathed into her —— and she gave birth to a woman!
It was —— so! *[not "Adam and Eve"]*

On Genesis 4:17–22

The saint:
Those people —— dwelling in tents, raising cattle,
making music, harp and pipe, forging brass and iron —— did exist.
It is true!

On Genesis 4:25–26

The saint:
SETH came from the North into the land of Cain.
His clan had nothing to do with the descendants of Cain.

But he was said to be the son of Adam!
He came from a high-ranking clan —— of repute!
It was the tribe of Jit that became the tribe of Judah.

> *In vision I saw them as a tall, thin people. I was uncertain*
> *about the tribe of Jit and later asked: Were these people the*
> *Jebusites?*

A saint answered:
The Jit were an ancient tribe —— you do not know these people.
It is not important to dispute this.
What do you know about those times!

On Genesis 6:4

The saint:
"The sons of God" were ancient giants.
This is not so significant.

On Genesis 6:8–22

The saint:
NOAH —— was obedient; that was important.

NOAH —— had a cerebrum larger than that of any other human of that time.
A blossom of creation —— was given to him.

The saint:
Tomorrow we will begin with Abraham.

I still asked: Did the Flood, at the time of Noah, cover the whole earth?

The saint:
No:
It happened in the Mediterranean area ——
where there were human beings and,
considering evolution, many species of animals.
All were submerged.

On Genesis 10:1–32

My question: Did the sons of Noah's sons go farther in all directions — to Greece, Cyprus, Spain, Egypt, and other places?

The saint:
Yes. It was the beginning,

where God began to guide the people over the earth toward
the East, the South, the North, and the West.

I asked the saint: Where does your knowledge come from?

The saint:
You ask that?
It is knowledge from the source of life.
An angel brought the message.

Earnest, commanding:
Recognize the greatness of the message!

I asked: And the tower of Babel?

There was no answer.

On Genesis 11:26–32 and Genesis 12

An angel:
ABRAHAM —— was a figure of light, full of the Holy Spirit!
His life was decisive for humankind —— for the people of God!
A great soul, a great spirit!
Abraham still is active in the hereafter —— as a figure of light.
Give to him great glory!

Angels sang for me so that I heard the hymn:
LIGHT —— LIGHT OVER THE SUN ABRAM! [27]

Light —— light —— over the sun Abram,
over the sun Abram, over the sun Abram!

Abram's Hymn

Isaac

On Genesis 21:1–21

A saint:
God touched Isaac and gave him a sword of light to fight with!

An angel:
Abraham had from Sarah two sons: Isaac and Ebanel.

My question: Why is it important to mention the second son of Sarah?

An angel:
Isaac was the one with the sword of light —— to fight for God.

I asked: And his brother?

An angel:
His half-brother Ishmael was blessed ——
a figure of light in the third heaven; bow before him.
His real brother, Ebanel, was killed in a fight.

Later in prayer, I asked: What happened to Abraham's second son, Ebanel?

The saint:
He was killed while still a youth. No one saw him anymore.
Shepherds tell of a cry —— of a fight.
God took him unto himself, for he had a soul of light.
He was not loved.
He was not beautiful in form and appearance ——
with disheveled hair, unsteady eyes.
His place is in the seventh heaven.

I know him; he serves God and the Jewish people.
Let us go further.

On Genesis 12:10–20 and Genesis 20:1–18

*I asked: When he was in danger, Abraham spoke repeatedly of Sarah
as his sister — why?*

The saint:
Listen!
Sarah was a half-sister; it was not a great love.
Remember the times —— the customs —— the traditions of those days.

The greatness of God was revealed!
The procreation of Isaac, through Abraham and Sarah, had to be.
Only in that way could there be an Isaac
with holy fire —— and great knowledge.

On Genesis 19:30–38

*My question: And Lot's tribe — conceived through his daughters?
I saw in vision that light was with the pregnancy of both daughters.*

An angel:
Lot was worthy to have his blood live on.
It was not a question of lust, only of conception,
so that his tribe should live. Do you understand?

I asked: Does Lot's tribe also have a meaning up to the present time?

An angel:
Yes.
Tablets, stone or clay, came through them.
Spiritual, high-standing people of wisdom were among them.

They provided knowledge and laws on tablets.
That was right for the development of the human spirit.
Lot's wife and sons-in-law bear the guilt that the conception had to be so.
God blessed Lot and his daughters.
Write this down!

Lot was a great man; love him as one risen from the dead.

Isaac was the chosen one, and is even today a great light ——
that reaches the earth! Bow before him.

A saint:
Read the life of Isaac in the Old Testament
and Psalm 8 by tomorrow. It is his, Isaac's, psalm.

Isaac's Sons Esau and Jacob

On Genesis 25:19–34

An angel:
ESAU, Isaac's son, was a figure of light!

He sought the ways of God.

JACOB, the twin brother, was the blessed one!
Learn from this!

Learn: REBECCA, the mother of Esau and Jacob, had four sons ——
and she recognized that Jacob was the best-born of the four sons!

ISAAC was great —— Isaac is great.
Love Isaac with the great light that touches the earth even today.

REBECCA was beautiful, good-natured, noble, a pure light.

She was wise, and in old age no shadow was upon her.

A WOMAN WAS CHOSEN
TO RECOGNIZE WHO WAS TO LEAD JUDAH'S TRIBE
TO BECOME ISRAEL.

Pay honor to her — Rebecca!
GOD placed her on the same level — as Isaac!
THE WOMAN LIKE THE MAN IN RIGHTS — IN RESPONSIBILITIES!

GOD MADE THE WOMAN ON EQUAL TERMS
IN THE IMAGE AND LIKENESS OF GOD.
It was a development of the spirit of man and woman!

From then on God gave the woman to the man
and the man to the woman — to recognize God's will!

The saint:
Rejoice and jubilate over what has been received.
The Lord is good, to have let you recognize so much.

Mary:
Let us go further.

An angel:
From Jacob — Israel came into being;
with Israel came the foundation of "the city on the mountain"
that was, that is, that will come: the city on the mountain!
It is the people of God who were gathered together.
"The city on the mountain" began with Israel — with Jacob.

An angel said to me:
With him, Jacob, the angels ascended and descended.
They brought tidings — heaven was open;
never forget that.

I asked: Why was there no second blessing for Esau? Today one can
bless all children.

An angel:
Until the time of Isaac, all rights went to the firstborn son.
With this severity, this discipline, this education,
it was possible to raise up a people — a tribe —
a chosen people whose spirits were strong.

It was the will of God!
The people, the number of human beings, increased —
and from then on everyone who sought God was blessed.

Esau became a blessing in that he sought and found God.
(*Genesis 28:6–9 and Genesis 36*)
Later, others became a blessing:
Jacob's Joseph — a David — a Mary, mother of the Lord.

A MEMBER *of the family* PASSES ON THE BLESSING —
this is Jewish.

AN INDIVIDUAL PASSES ON THE LIGHT —
this is Christian.

My question: Is there a difference between the Jewish faith that
passes on the blessing and the Christian that passes on the light?

The saint:
— Yes —
The Jewish people pass on the promise of human development
— which is the blessing.
The Christians bring the light — the rays of primal creation.

The promise, which is Jewish, is the spiritual force
that forms human beings.

Whole clans, tribes, peoples became spiritually educated.

When the full basis of creation is present in the human spirit,
then the light of God's primal creation is added.

Without light — humankind would decay,
would move toward death over thousands of years.

May humankind live!

Light from the primal source must be!
Vibrations from Christ!

The saint in earnest:
A single person
who opens himself or herself honestly to Christ brings about vibrations.
That means light — for thousands of people —
through his or her living in prayer.

Open your eyes to creation!
Open your eyes to the development of the human!
Be in the image and likeness of God!

*My question: Before I read further, I asked: What about the sacrifice
of Isaac? (Genesis 22:1–19) In vision nothing was said about it.*

The saint:
God said: "Put an end to human sacrifice."
This is partly known to theologians.

*I asked:Does the circumcision at the time of Abraham have a mean-
ing? (Genesis 17:10–14)*

The saint:
ONLY a sign! Nothing more!

It was abolished — no longer a sign: abolished with Christ.
Read the first book of Moses to the end.

Joseph, Son of Jacob and Rachel

On Genesis 30:23 up to the end

Mary:

JOSEPH — LIVED TRUE TO HIMSELF AND GOD — EVEN AS A CHILD!
He could have withheld his dreams!
He loved his father, his brothers;
he was true and authentic in the way he loved.

His deliverance from the house of Potiphar
came from his life with God *[incident with Potiphar's wife]*.

Joseph suffered in prison — and yet was spiritually exalted!
Even there he did not turn away from God. He lived truly!

On Genesis 50:20–26

His responsibility was to preserve the life of a great people
[Israel, the famine].

He — Joseph — saw the greatness of God, the love of God.
He — Joseph — let himself be guided, and said yes to his life's task.

HIS WHOLE SPIRITUAL LIFE WAS — FROM BIRTH TO DEATH —
PURE, IN GOD!

Until Christ, no other human being lived the full truth in God
in the purity of Joseph, son of Jacob!

Joseph the Dreamer

On checking this again:
A saint:
What you have seen about Joseph is true.
Joseph was pure. He was true to himself and God.
He lived the visions in which God spoke to him.
HE SPOKE ABOUT THEM OPENLY AND TRUTHFULLY, without fear.

HIS LIFE WAS WHOLE AND PURE, IN THE PRIMAL CREATION
OF GOD.
There are few people who dare —— have the courage —— to live like him!

The Second Book of Moses

I *read Exodus 1.*

A saint:
The Spirit of God moved over Moses.
Thus he could become a servant of God.

On Exodus 1–2 and 13:22

The saint:
Moses, with the people of Israel, left Egypt.
The story is true. It lasted over years.

I asked: What is true in the story?

The saint:
During the journey out of Egypt, many died —— of exhaustion.
MOSES — WAS A LEADER,
BECAUSE THE POWER OF GOD LIVED WITHIN HIM.

I read up to the crossing of the Red Sea.

The saint:
THE PASSOVER MEAL — IS FOR SPIRITUAL STRENGTHENING!
He who is of the Jewish faith,
receives strength in God, becomes self-assured.

It is very important to live this consciously as a people!
Accept the Passover feast in the faith, as:
God has done great things!
He —— God —— lives even now!

WE LIVE IN THIS STRENGTH!
WE LIVE IN GOD!

Celebrate it — the Passover —
in the language of today, with the Jews!
[It is to be part of the one unifying church.]

Put it into practice!
You can celebrate it spiritually and through fasting.
Or you can eat unleavened bread, roasted lamb,
and drink wine, grape juice, water.

I received, for the Passover, the song "Sing, Sing." [28]

Sing, sing.

Sing, sing,
praise the Lord;
sing, sing,
praise the Lord;
praise and glorify the Lord!

Sing, sing.
Drums deep and clear,
praise the Lord!

Cymbals and flutes,
praise the Lord!
Praise the Lord!
Praise the Lord!
Praise the Lord!
Sing, sing.

Sing, Sing

From Exodus 16:14–15:
"There lay a small round thing, as small as the hoar frost on the ground. And when the children of Israel saw it, they said to one another, It is manna. . . ."
My question: What was that?

An angel:
The flour of seeds, moistened.
It swelled up from the clouds and the dew.

I asked if it is right to eat "manna," i.e., bread and corn, in the morning and meat in the evening.

The angel:
Yes.

The Ten Commandments

On *Exodus 20:1–17 and Deuteronomy 5:6–21*

An angel:
The laws are fulfilled by anyone —— who lives in the light,
who lives in Christ,
who lives in the new laws of Christ.

Where there is light —— there is no sin.
Whoever is in the light —— shall not carve images
or fashion anything in the
likeness of God.
Whoever is in the light —— does not kill.
Whoever is in the light —— is not thoughtless or
without love [as in marriage].
Whoever is in the light —— does not steal.

Whoever is in the light	—	does not lie
		but speaks the truth.
Whoever is in the light	—	loves humankind,
		all living creatures,
		the whole of creation.

My question: And what about the killing in war?

An angel:
Let one make the enemy a prisoner.

I asked: And when one must fight?

An angel:
Then only in defense.

I asked: And killing in self-defense?

An angel:
That is defense.
There is a difference between murder and defense!

> *I inquired about Jethro's proposal (Exodus 18:22) which was about referring lesser matters to the judges and graver matters to Moses, who asks God.*

The saint:
Only prophets can receive direct answers, as you do.

My question on Exodus 20: 25:
"To use any tool in the making of it [a stone] is to profane it."

The saint:
Stone against stone   — a clap.

Stone against wood   —— a thump.
Iron against stone   —— a shudder, a vibrating;
                               it loosens the core of the rock.
                               In its innermost being
                               it is no longer a stone.
                               This belongs to the laws of creation!

My question on Exodus 21: 6:
"He will bore his ear through with an awl."

The saint:
This was without significance —— only a sign.

The Laws

An *angel:*
These laws are not necessary for those who live in God's light.
And where no light is there should be wise judges
to protect the people and creation.
May they, the judges, be wise, strong and not weak in love!
May their laws take into account the land and the times.
The judges should be true and authentic before God.

On Exodus 23:14:

"... three times a year, you shall keep a feast in my name ..."

My question: What feasts for the present day?

An angel:
These are right:
THE FEAST OF UNLEAVENED BREAD *[Passover]*,
THE FEAST OF LIGHT *[Christmas]*,

THE DEATH OF JESUS,
THE RESURRECTION,
THE FEAST OF THE SPIRIT *[Pentecost]*.

On these days bear in mind the Lord, and go before him.

Whenever you have corn and wine, and the fruits of the fields,
GIVE THANKS *[harvest festival]*.

On Exodus 25:29–30

An angel:
THIS IS THE TABERNACLE OF TODAY.
May Christians place the bread of the Lord in it!

Sternly:
Remember!
The unleavened bread should be well guarded and carefully preserved.

It is worthy and right that one does this.
Neither silver nor gold is important!
To those who are hungry, do not merely display bread for show.
Nourish them until they have eaten their fill!
When they seek to renew soul and spirit,
when they demand spiritual strength ——
then give them THE BREAD OF THE LORD!

On Exodus 25:31:

"In the case of ... the lampstands with stems, branches, flowers."

An angel:
Signs of that time.

On Exodus 27:1–19

An angel:
It is unimportant.

On Exodus 27:20–21:
"Oil ... for the lamps ... in the holy tent."

An angel:
IMPORTANT as a sign.
They, the oil lamps, should burn day and night.

On Exodus 28:2:
"... holy vestments ..."

An angel:
NOT necessary.

On Exodus 28:3

An angel:
A priest is one who loves God,
who lives in the light and in the laws of creation
[according to earlier visions]!

My question: Are all the words concerning these vestments from the Lord?

An angel:
No. Words added by human beings.

I asked: Those about the temple likewise?

An angel:
Likewise!

On Exodus 28:36–38:
"Cord from the miter"

An angel:
Wrong.

On Exodus 28:40:
"... miters, to their honor and adornment ..."

An angel:
Wrong.

My question: Are they the miters of bishops?

There was no answer.

Exodus 29:7:
"... anointment with oil ..."

An angel:
May he, the priest, be true and authentic.
May his yes be a yes. That is sufficient!

On Exodus 29:8–37 and Exodus 30

An angel:
Not necessary! Christ lives for us!
A stone —— as an altar —— with a light upon it is enough.

The light is not absolutely required.
The relationship to God in spirit is important! It is life!

On checking this in prayer:

An angel:
The words are true;
a new age of the spirit came through Christ.
Moses needed the temple, altars, offerings,
vestments, oil, myrrh, and incense.

Following their own inclinations
they added gold, silver, precious stones.
Leave it all behind —— and move with the times ——
with the development of humankind.
BLESSED WATER and LIGHT ON THE ALTAR HAVE REMAINED.
Holy water can also be blessed by anyone
with the sign of the cross, according to the circumstances.

A light —— is a symbol. It is usually possible to have one,
but it is not a law that you must have one.

On Exodus 31:12–17:
"Six days of work, the seventh is the Sabbath. A day of rest."

An angel:
One of the laws of creation: a law of rhythm.
Six days to work for the earth, but
ON THE SEVENTH DAY SOUL AND SPIRIT SHOULD
WORK, RECOVER, AND DEVELOP.
That means six days for the earth,
one day [*the seventh*] for union with God.

An angel continued:
I should bring you a new commandment from the Lord;
it will give you a new understanding:
The human being can develop more quickly,
receive strength more intensively,
through this second stage of the primal law of creation.
For six hours, the eyes turned to the earth ——
the seventh hour for prayer and being with God.
In the night, rest,

for example:

4.30 —— 5.30 A.M.	prayer
5.30 —— 11.30 A.M.	for living on the earth
	[including eating and everything
	else that belongs to life]
11.30 —— 12.30 P.M.	prayer
12.30 —— 18.30 P.M.	for living on the earth
18.30 —— 19.30 P.M.	prayer
19.30 —— until rest	for earthly life.

My question: Why not one hour in the presence of God just before sleep?

An angel:
Learn from this:
For recovery, it is better to pass over into sleep
having your eyes on earthly matters.

[This refers to active and intense prayer and not one's peace with God, as witnessed in the many forms of night prayers.]

When you pray, be awake! and receive strength!
for example: three hours, earthly matters ——

one hour, prayer;
six hours, earthly matters ——
one hour prayer;
then work for a short while.

Read further.

The Adoration of the Golden Calf

On Exodus 32

I asked: What about the golden calf?

An angel:
You have seen in visions that when they wore ornaments
God did not punish them!
The sin was to amass wealth,
and then for the leader of the church ——
here it was Aaron, the first priest —— to say:
SEE! THIS IS THE CHURCH!
The church with wealth and power!
[This is the adoration of the golden calf.]
Moses crushed the gold and gave it to them to drink with water.
Seen from the spirit,
God crushes the wealth and the power of the church.
HE BREAKS IT.
HE DISPERSES IT.
HE TAKES AWAY THE EARTHLY POWER OF THE CHURCH ——
from time to time. Today also.
It brings about development of the church's spiritual life!
A way of sacrifice —— even without bloodshed!

[The breaking and distribution of wealth and power is also a path of suffering.]

On Exodus 32:21

An angel continued:
EVERY PRIEST CARRIES GREAT RESPONSIBILITY.

On Exodus 32:30

An angel:
EVERY CHRISTIAN IS WITH CHRIST AN ADULT
AND CARRIES WITH OTHERS FULL RESPONSIBILITY.

May the church be neither power nor possessions!
May the church be an opening of the path to God —
a serving church!

On Exodus 33:17

A saint:
THE LORD SPOKE WITH MOSES.
Moses passed on the basic laws
and thus established a relationship with the source.
In this way, grace was bestowed.

On Exodus 33:20

The saint:
No person can behold the source, the source of all energy.
But build for yourselves
A ROCK.

What you have just seen in the visions is true;
BUILD YOURSELVES A ROCK.

PLACE YOURSELVES
—— IN A CLEFT OF THE ROCK *(Exodus 33:21–22)*
—— IN A CHURCH
   WHERE GOD IS NEAR YOU. *(Exodus 33:23)*

Grace —— to whom he is gracious.
Mercy —— to whom he is merciful. *(Exodus 33:19)*

On Exodus 34

An angel:
Chapter 34 is not important for the present time.

On Exodus 34:7:

"... the sons must make amends for the father's guilt,
to the third and fourth generation ..."

An angel:
Today one understands that as heredity, also psychological damage.
Psychological damage heals more or less quickly
depending on the environment and the bonding
between various types of human beings.
Do not try to read too much into these words.

On Exodus 35

An angel:
The accounts are so old that they repeat themselves.

On Exodus 36

An angel:
Moses hungered for beauty — but not for power.
He did not need wealth; he was a man of the spirit
[not a man of power like Aaron].

On Exodus 34–40

An angel:
These chapters have been handed down from the traditions,
and belong to the history of those times.
DO NOT INCLUDE them as an article of faith.

The Third Book of Moses

On Leviticus 1:
"The burnt offering" [meat]

An angel:
That was in the olden days.

On Leviticus 2:
"The bloodless offering" [flour, corn]

An angel:
Early Christian times.
[Such offerings were made until early Christian times.]

On Leviticus 3:
"The peace offering"

An angel:
A great error, a sad error in the way it was enacted.

On Leviticus 4:
"The sin offering"

An angel:
Spiritual repentance is right.

On Leviticus 5 and Leviticus 6

An angel:
Repetitions.

On Leviticus 7:
"The trespass offering"

An angel:
All repentance should take place spiritually before God.

On Leviticus 8

An angel:
How a priest should be has already been said.

On Leviticus 9

An angel:
AARON'S FIRST OFFERING!

A priest is to give the sacraments with clean hands,
that is, with a soul that is open, spiritually related to God.
Do not ask more about it!

On Leviticus 10

An angel:
Likewise [as Leviticus 9].

On Leviticus 11

An angel:
ALL ANIMALS ARE CREATURES OF GOD!

Men made them into fabled beings.
Not all meat is edible —— there are also poisonous animals ——
TAKE HEED!

On Leviticus 12:
"Woman after childbirth"

An angel:
Today's medical understanding is right.

On Leviticus 13

An angel:
For the whole chapter, today's medicine is correct.

On Leviticus 14

An angel:
Today's understanding.

On Leviticus 15

An angel:
Today's medical understanding.

On Leviticus 16:1–2
[with reference to Leviticus 10:1–3 and 8–9]

My question: What really caused the death of Aaron's sons?

An angel:
They presented a large incense offering;
they offered it in ignorance,
and poisoned themselves with poisonous scents [smoke inhalation].
The alcohol of the wine paralyzed their thinking.

On the rest of Leviticus 16

An angel:
It belongs to old historical material.

On Leviticus 17:12:
"No one may consume blood ..."

An angel:
The time of blood is over.
Whoever brought blood to the altar
avoided blood feuds among the people.
That is the wisdom of the blood prohibition.
Blood awakens feelings of revenge.

A new commandment came through Christ —
the commandment about human dignity: to love!
Whoever loves will not need to avenge blood.

Digesting a lot of blood is injurious to the health of the stomach.
Therefore, white meat is healthier.

On Leviticus 18:
"*Marriage and blood relations ...*"

An angel in earnest:
Chapter 18 is right.
It is a standard still valid today — and will remain so.

On Leviticus 19:19:
"*Do not mate any beast of thine with one of another sort, or sow thy field with a mixed crop, or wear garments woven of two different fabrics. . . .*"

An angel:
Today this has no more significance.
They dwelt on particulars
in order to preserve the purity of God's people.

On Leviticus 19:23–25:
"*When you reach your own country and plant fruit trees there, you will regard their fruits as uncircumcised ... until the fifth year ... nor shall you eat of it.*"

An angel:
Laws handed down from distant times,
which you — in this country — cannot recognize.
Years went by until the emanations
from the blossoms and fruits of the trees
were no longer "foreign" to the people.
In this unity between the fruits of nature and human beings,
they lived — and were healthy people!

On Leviticus 21:14:

" ... must not marry a divorced woman ... or a harlot ..."

An angel:
Out of date.
With the love that Christ preached about,
the soul becomes great ——
so as to love people who have made a fresh start
and have returned to the path.

On Leviticus 21:17–20:

"... no one who has infirmities, no one who is castrated ... shall come forward and sacrifice to the Lord ..."

An angel:
Only the soul and spirit count before God.
[Physical infirmities are no hindrance to being a priest].

On Leviticus 21:20

An angel:
This is right
[in the case of injury to the sexual organs or castration]
ONLY when his soul is not balanced.

On Leviticus 22:27:

"... a lamb when it is newly born must be allowed to suck for a whole week; only on the eighth day ... may it be offered to the Lord ..."

An angel:
The first seven days belong to the GROWING OF MAN
and the ANIMALS —— to the unity of mother and child.
Show respect for life! This is a law of nature.

On Leviticus 23:
"... The festival laws ..."

An angel:
The feast days have already been given.

My question: Passover, Good Friday, Easter — how can I combine them all?

The angel took a book and read from it, as an answer:
The Passover feast is possible for Christians
at the beginning of the year.
In the twenty-first century it will be right.

I asked: And until then?

An angel:
Let time "weave" it. Let us move on.

A saint:
Write everything down! Go quickly through the books of Moses.
The prophets are important!

On Leviticus 24:9:
"... the showbread ... Aaron and his sons are to eat it on holy ground ..."

An angel:
This belongs to olden times.
The New Testament has become the guide.

On Leviticus 24:10–23:
"... a man ... blasphemed the Lord's name ... and the whole people put him to death by stoning ..."

An angel:
At that time, this was given by God
so that God might be glorified.

Christ — died — on the cross.
Christ sees the human being if he truly stands before God,
and Christ forgives by taking the guilt upon himself.
He forgives EVERYONE who loves God — who has found a way to him.

As to the rest of The Third Book of Moses, nothing more was said.
Not even in answer to questions.

The Fourth Book of Moses

On *Numbers 1:49–50:*
"*... Do not count the tribe of Levi ... but*
give them charge of the tabernacle that bears record of me ..."

An angel:
They were a spiritual and intellectual people, a sensitive people.
This is of no account for Christians.

Concerning the question about Numbers 2–5 on the encampments
to the East, South, West and North, there was no answer.

On *Numbers 3:12–13:*
"*... I have singled out the Levites to be my own in place of the first-*
born ... all first-born things belong to me ..."

An angel:
Their own laws — not from God.
[Part of their religious and cultural unfolding, but not laws from God.]

On Numbers 5:

"... infidelity in marriage ..."

An angel:
Guilt is only to be healed through Christ,
a new beginning through Christ.

On Numbers 6:1–3:

*"... taking the vows ... abstaining from wine, grapes,
and dried grapes ..."*

An angel:
An old law —— to be annulled as law.
Acidity in wine and grapes stimulates; they wanted peace of mind.

On Numbers 6:24–26:

*"... The Lord bless you and keep you ...
the Lord turn his regard towards you ..."*

An angel:
The blessing does not heal!
It strengthens —— gives spiritual strength —— protects.

On Numbers 7:

"... the anointing of the altar, the offerings of the tribes ..."

An angel:
May the people build the church! The rock!
The church should not be rich for the purposes of power.

On Numbers 9:15–23:

"... Setting out in the Sinai, the guiding cloud ..."

An angel:
They were then still able to see the signs;
they lived according to the primal laws!
This belongs to historical research,
to human change and development.

On Numbers 11:3:
"... Taberah ..."

An angel:
Learn from this:
Where there is spiritual chaos, there Taberah can happen.

On Numbers 11:17:
"I will come down and converse with you there, taking away some of the spirit which rests upon you and giving it to them instead, so that they may share with you the charge over the people ..."

An angel:
This would be in the new church laws of the Johannine Church.
Weep, that these gifts were lost!
The people, the startsi, hermits, saints, strong spiritual people,
are responsible for their loss.

On Numbers 12:6–8:
"... To one I appear in a vision, to another I reveal my thoughts in a dream ..."

An angel:
Visions —— dreams —— remain.
Study them sincerely; seek the holy in them.
Work only with what is genuine.

The Holy Spirit brings messages to thousands of people through them.
Learn from them!

There are few to whom God speaks.
[He speaks not only in visions and dreams.]

These few —— are moved;
they have tasks —— special messages —— to fulfill.

They can be —— a vessel —— a center —— a field of light.
God needs them as part of the primal law.

On Numbers 12:10–15:
"... Miriam was taken back ..."

An angel:
That was love.

On Numbers 13

An angel:
It is history.

On Numbers 14

An angel:
It belongs to history.

On Numbers 15:17–21:
*"... When you have reached the land I mean to give you, you must
not eat the bread its harvest yields without assigning to the Lord first
fruits from your table ..."*

An angel:
God was honored.
Today it would be a prayer, a thanksgiving to God.
Give praise and thanks to God!

On Numbers 15:32–36

An angel:
The old laws.
The breaking of the laws of rhythm is not sin.
Whoever does not hold to the rhythm of life ——
daily or hourly rhythm —— does not develop fully,
especially spiritually.

On Numbers 16

An angel, reading from an open book:
If power is in the church, men and women
who are in a process of development rebel.
Aaron became obsessed with power.

The angel passed over a few pages and read further:
This chapter shows
THAT THERE IS ONLY ONE GOD.
GOD SPOKE TO MOSES.
One who lives according to the primal laws —— is near to God.
[Also those without claim to the office of priesthood.]

On Numbers 16

An angel:
Neither power nor cunning
enables one to claim religious rights —— the priesthood.

Aaron used power; as a result, resistance followed.
The "band of Korah" *(Numbers 16:1)*
presumed unduly on their religious rights.

On checking this:
An angel:
Moses was a man of the spirit.
Aaron loved power —
which led to opposition among humans
who were changing and in a process of development.
Moses had the right to appeal to God.

The Old Testament had laws first of all concerning
        — the covenant,
        — all things held to be most holy,
        — the servants.

The angel:
Later God expanded the gifts of the spirit,
in accord with human development.

These laws were annulled in the New Testament.

Whoever is pure — man, woman, or child —
may move in the holy places, in the churches,
always and everywhere.
Whoever is pure — may serve;
whoever is pure — may receive
all that can come from God to the human being.
Everyone who is pure may receive
light — prayer — bread and wine.
Everyone who gives should be in the light.

Church rules are good.

The angel closed the book.

On Numbers 17:
"... The sprouting staff of Aaron ..."

An angel:
The story is not true.

On Numbers 18

An angel:
For historical research —— not more.

On Numbers 19

An angel:
For historical research.

On Numbers 20:7–11:
"... Water flows from the rock ..."

An angel:
Nothing exceptional.
A shaking in the rock loosened it and let water flow.
It was a gift from God.

On Numbers 22:
"... The seer Balaam ..."

An angel:
He was a seer, not a prophet.
Note the difference. A seer is also obedient to God.

On Numbers 25:
"... Idolatry and its punishment ..."

An angel:
A time of disobedience.
To live in the spirit needs discipline!
To meet the Spirit of God, the source,
requires people who have undergone a process of formation.

On Numbers 27:1–11

An angel:
Antiquity.

On Numbers 27:15–23:
"... The appointment of Joshua, a man in whom is the Spirit ..."

An angel:
It was important that this was noted.

On Numbers 28

An angel:
Antiquity.

On Numbers 29

The angel:
The same.

On Numbers 30

The angel:
Laws of old.

On Numbers 31

The angel:
History.

On Numbers 32

The angel:
History.

On Numbers 33

The angel:
History; it is true.

On Numbers 33:50

The angel:
Laws of old.

On Numbers 34:1–15:
"... The boundaries of the new Israel ..."

An angel opened a book and read:
These are the boundaries of Israel, of the Jewish state.
They are valid forever! This land is holy.

Later I saw in vision the land of Israel covered with light.
An old Israeli, one risen from the dead, spoke severely:
Leave the words as they are! You may add to them:
The good news of God's encounter with the people of Israel
was received upon this holy ground.
Here God encountered human beings
—— God was seen and heard ——

and he descended to them
and gave them the name of God's people.
Christ too was in the land of Israel.
He lived there and surrendered his life for the people.

This is the homeland for all Jews and Christians.
Others may be guests.

> *Some years later I prayed for the peoples of the Near East*
> *and was concerned about the future of the Palestinians*
> *and Israelis. Christ was present and spoke:*

Pray twelve Our Fathers so that the Holy Spirit
may descend upon the Israelis and the Palestinians
in order that peace will reign.

> *Here Christ implied that we have to pray the Our Father*
> *slowly and consciously, keeping in mind that so much is*
> *contained within this prayer: the praise of God, the asking*
> *that his will be done, the coming of Christ, the forgiving*
> *and avoiding of wrongdoing, and that God together with*
> *the Holy Spirit may protect us from evil.*
>
> *Christ looked at me a long time and I started to reflect on*
> *all that I had read in the Old Testament. There were two*
> *brothers who buried their father in peace: Ishmael, the out-*
> *cast, who became an archer and lived in the desert and*
> *from whom the Arabs are descended, and Isaac who became*
> *Israel. Then I asked if that meant that the Arabs and Jews*
> *are brothers. Are they to divide the land and the city?*

An angel answered:
Yes, but according to their gifts.
Ishmael owned principalities and lived in the desert,
as was promised.

Isaac received a spiritual life in God
so as to become the people of Israel,
as was promised.

Both brothers were reconciled in accepting the difference —
in respecting the different gifts, which God had given them.
Honor, respect, goodness, which are all an expression of love,
were the outcome.

Recognizing the different types of human beings
is the key to peace.
This does not mean that each type has to remain the same;
rather they are to be given the possibility to develop in freedom,
in their own way.

An angel:
Let us go further.

*Nothing more was said concerning the end of the fourth book
of Moses, not even in answer to questions.*

The Fifth Book of Moses

On Deuteronomy 1–4

The angel remained serious and silent.

On Deuteronomy 18:18–19

The angel:
Isaiah was THE prophet.
The legend that a prophet shall arise applies to Isaiah!

On Deuteronomy 24:6–22

The angel:
Wise sayings.
Separate wisdom from commandments.
Commandments are laws from the source of life
for people of the spirit.

I read the fifth book of Moses to the end.

The angel:
The books on Moses are closed.
Learn from them: history — antiquity — the old laws —
laws of everlasting value — above all the greatness of God!

Read the book of Joshua:
God came down to him. He spoke to him — face to face.

On checking:
The angel:
No mistakes — go further.

Joshua

An angel:
Joshua — a strong, holy messenger!
Read the book of Joshua carefully.
It belongs to olden times. Love Joshua.
A great spiritual leap took place
between the time of Moses and the death of Joshua!

I read the whole book of Joshua.

An angel opened a book and read:
JOSHUA —— feared God!
He loved the laws of Moses.
He —— was —— the bridge
between the time of Moses and the time of "the Kings."

On Joshua 1–12

An angel:
The entry into the promised land
under the leadership of Joshua is true.

On Joshua 6:

"... Jericho ..."

The angel:
It was only a prolonged battle, a struggle before God.
Thus the power of prayer was necessary.
An exaggerated story was told later, which was not correct.

An angel:
It is true that God spoke with Joshua.
Through his obedience, God was with him in the battles.

On Joshua 3

I asked: What happened at the crossing of the river Jordan?

An angel:
God held back the waters. With God —— that is possible.

On Joshua 7

No answer.

On Joshua 8

An angel:
Unworthy!

On Joshua 9

An angel:
It belongs to ancient history.

On Joshua 10

An angel:
Told rightly.

On Joshua 11

An angel:
Told rightly.

On Joshua 12

An angel:
Told rightly.

On Joshua 13

An angel:
History.

On Joshua 15

An angel:
Rejoice and jubilate!

On Joshua 22:
"... The building of the altar near the river Jordan ..."

Mary with joy:
The first spreading of the faith, the preservation of the faith,
the worship of God!

This new beginning was completed by the great, holy man Joshua.
So it was right and good.

On Joshua 23:7

An angel:
If you present-day Christians *[said in 1976]*
would serve God alone —— there would be peace on earth.

But you love yourselves —— and take idols for yourselves!
Chaos upon earth is what follows.

Love Joshua! May he be an example for you.
Spiritually, let yourself be guided by Christ and his kingdom.

> *I spoke to Mary: We know where the people of Israel came*
> *from, and how they became a whole people, by this story*
> *of Moses and Joshua. But surely not all the Hebrews were*
> *at that time gathered in Egypt, only those who arrived*
> *because of the famine. Where were the others? What was*
> THEIR *history?*

Mary:
Thousands fled to Egypt, to the "breadbasket."
Need and distress drove them there.
Moses and Aaron were great men, leaders moved by God.
This story, of the people, was written down.

Whole tribes, thousands of people developed, grew, lived,
and served God. They were loved by God ——
and their descendants still live today.
Their story is written in the wind.
God knows it and loves it.
Your task is, first of all, to go through
the whole Bible, Old and New Testaments!
Later, words for the peoples of the earth may be added.

Do not go astray.

The Book of Judges

The angel:
A time of wisdom, not of faith.

An angel opened a book and read:
The time of the "Judges," a time of justice,
is similar to the present time.
No God —— a weak, a weakened church!

Over decades there were figures of light,
such as Othniel, Deborah, Gideon, and Jotham.

[Jotham spoke with wise words, Judges 9:7–15, "the fable of the trees."]

The angel continued:
This turning away from God degraded Israel at that time.
This turning away from Christ in the present time of today *[1976]*
degrades Europe, Africa, the West Indies,
the entire East, West, North, South, all of humankind.

Judges and seers will act as a bridge and
stand firm during this time.
Write about the song of Deborah for your times!

I then dared to ask: Who are the enemies of God today?
(Judges 5:31)

The angel:
I. The poppy —— traditions and practices from the East.
2. The flower that became a star, blood-drenched without God.

> *[The poppy implies opium and drugs. Traditions refer*
> *to those practices in Eastern religions, where redemp-*
> *tion of self is sought — without God. The flower is*
> *Russia; it became the red star, meaning Communism*
> *— without God.]*

The angel:
Read further.

On Judges 13–16

An angel:
SAMSON was a strong man. His lineage was from giants.
The Spirit of God was with him.

The angel, with severity:
A man of God is strong in spirit ——
as long as he is placed UNDER GOD ALONE!
Learn from this!

The woman gained power over Samson.
God's power was no longer the central power for him.

Never turn away from God.

You know about purity in God.

[Purity is to be oriented towards God, even in the smallest, most exacting matters.]

Every human who does not completely serve God is weakened.

On Judges 17 and 18

An angel:
The robbery of "Micah's carved image and sacred objects"
belongs to the misdeeds of these people.
RELIGIOUS PROPERTY MUST NOT BE STOLEN.

Religious property can be passed on to other people.
This is spiritual and farsighted thinking;
this is generosity, indeed love.
It is valid still today for icons and similar objects.
Whoever steals religious treasures *[also cultural ones, as in Africa]*
commits something like prostitution.

On Judges 19:
"The misdeeds of the Benjaminites and their punishment"

An angel:
It belongs to ancient history —
decline and fall, weakened development.

I asked: You are silent about so many tales?

The angel:
Those times were like that.
MANY TRIBES DID LIKEWISE.
IT WAS THAT TIME, indeed "history."

An angel:
Let us go further: to RUTH.

The Book of Ruth

An *angel:*
The book of Ruth is true.
The entire book of Ruth is true,
and it is important that it was written down.

Ruth was a maiden of God — obedient, pure.
TRUE — BEFORE GOD — IN HER SPIRITUAL LIFE.

The First Book of Samuel

Mary, *the mother of the Lord:*
To know God's laws — and not to act according to them —
brings death.
Whoever sees God — and does not remain in the light —
dies!

An angel:
THE SONS OF ELI were not God-fearing.
Likewise, THE SONS OF SAMUEL were not God-fearing.
In that way [*through the behavior of Samuel's sons*]
the kingship came upon Israel.

Samuel — loved God.
Samuel — was a man of light.
Samuel — IS loved by God.
Samuel's spirit was great!
Love the story of Samuel!

I asked: Why did Samuel blame the people for instituting kingship, and you blame his sons?

The angel:
Samuel was God-fearing; his sons were not.
It was through their fault that the people changed!

The angel:
The historical times from Samuel to Solomon were hard!

Saul

On 1 Samuel 9

An angel:
Write this down:
Saul —— was sent by God.
HOW he reigned was according to the times.

He —— was a great king!
As the full obedience to God dwindled,
and Saul thus lost his spiritual greatness ——
God gave the people a new king.

The spiritual bond between God and the people of Israel
was thus preserved.

David

On *1 Samuel 16*

A *saint:*
David came from the house of Jesse —
and belongs to those who should be called the sons of God.

DAVID IS SPIRITUALLY THE FATHER OF CHRIST.
If you could only appreciate
how the hereditary substances are spiritually handed down!

To help me understand this, they showed me a part of the brain.

The spiritual continuity from David to Joseph —
until Christ — is visible for us in heaven.

It happened not through flesh and blood,
BUT ACCORDING TO THE PLAN OF CREATION —
THROUGH SPIRITUAL HEREDITY — A SPIRITUAL TRANSMISSION.

A *saint:*
Said more simply:
From the time of David's manhood on,
this spiritual strength was passed down until Christ.
It was done with God's Spirit in the process of creation.

God's Spirit — moves the human spirit!
Whoever can grasp it — should grasp it!

THE STORY OF DAVID AND GOLIATH IS TRUE.

The way David's life is described and how his house was,
and about Saul and afterwards, corresponds to reality.

I asked: And Jonathan?

The saint:
It was a friendship between David and Jonathan:
a genuine and clean friendship, not a marriage!

On 1 Kings 1

A saint:
Solomon was a wise and spiritual man, a man of nobility.
Not more.
His time — was a time of recovery.
Unfortunately, there was later also a turning away from the laws.

An angel:
Write down THE NAMES OF THE PROPHETS:
Isaiah, Jeremiah, Daniel, Ezekiel,
Amos, Habakkuk, Zechariah, John the Baptist.

The Book of Esther

The angel:
Esther fulfilled the tasks given to her by God
with intelligence and love, and thus saved —
thousands of her people.

ESTHER AS A WOMAN IS AN EXAMPLE FOR ALL WOMEN.

To be an Esther is possible in every corner of the earth.

She was royal, wise, intelligent, just, courageous,
and in all things she acted with genuine, true love!

Learn from this!

The Book of Job

The angel:
A hymn of suffering.

The Psalms

My question: The Psalms?

The angel:
Love them, they are hymns of praise,
an expression of prayer, history.

The Book of Proverbs

The angel:
This, you may pass by.

*[This was no judgment. It was important for me to know that I was
not to receive visions on all the books of the Bible.]*

Ecclesiastes

The angel's answer:
Pass it by.

The Song of Songs

The angel:
A poetic work.

Elijah

The angel:
A just messenger of God. *(1 Kings 17)*

Elisha

The angel:
True in parts. *(1 Kings 19)*

On 2 Kings 7

The angel:
True.

On 2 Kings 13:14–25

The angel:
True. When reading about the kings,
you may pass by the books of Chronicles.

The Lamentations

The angel:
Be silent.

Joel

The angel:
Is loved.

Obadiah

The angel:
Good; do not ask further.

Jonah
"in the belly of the whale"

The angel:
Symbolism, wisdom. Jonah is loved.

Micah

The angel's answer:
History. Micah is loved.

Nahum

The angel's answer:
Be silent.

Zephaniah

The angel's answer:
Is loved.

Malachi

The angel's answer:
Just.

Mary added to this:
We have named the important, wise prophets who were close to God.

Isaiah

An angel:
Take the book of Isaiah in hand, so that you can understand
the birth of Jesus better.
The spirit was at that time very troubled.
A seeking —— a finding; there was also a losing of spiritual values.

Isaiah himself had difficulty finding
the spiritual path of light —— the new era.

Narrow was the path of light on which he wandered:
FORESEEING — ENVISAGING —
HE SAW THE DEVELOPMENT AND GROWTH UP TO OUR TIMES
[1987].

He saw the new epoch!

Thank him, Isaiah, for his seeking —— his not going astray!

> *So Isaiah had a vision that went further than the times in*
> *which we now live. Isaiah is not yet theologically under-*
> *stood, and he would be worth a study!*

An angel:
JEREMIAH —— the great prophet —— loved, suffered, stood before God ——
and became a figure of light. He became an example of living in God.
JEREMIAH —— lived his very own personal life.
ISAIAH was the great prophet for thousands of years.
He was formed so as to work and act for the people.

His seeing and hearing were not for him personally;
they were for everybody — for the peoples of the earth.

Other Prophets

The angel:
EZEKIEL: Love him!
His light — as one risen from the dead —
touches the peoples of the earth even today.

DANIEL lived for his time.
He was God's witness — in and for his time.

HOSEA: Weep that so much injustice was done to him.
Do penance, that this injustice shall be forgiven.

HABAKKUK: Read him accurately.
He asserts more than has been accepted until now by the scholars.

Mary, the mother of the Lord:
ZECHARIAH: I love him. Here also is history.

My question to Mary: Can one or should one ask, through prayer, saints of the Old Testament for something? Are ALL of them "available"?

Mary:
No. ABRAHAM was a figure of light.
His light radiates to the people on earth. *[See "Abram's Hymn," p. 251.]*

I asked: Moses? David?

Mary:
They are servants of Christ ——
and have other tasks now, to be and to work for God.

Mary:
SEPARATE
the shepherds —— the angels ——
Joseph and Mary —— the birth of Jesus,
which are THE EVENT,

from
the three kings *[wise men]* ——
the prophets, such as Isaiah ——
the apostles of Jesus,
which are THE HANDS THAT JOINED
THE OLD TESTAMENT TO THE NEW TESTAMENT,

from
THE FIRST CHRISTIANS, who are
Luke, Paul *[they did not know Jesus personally]*
and all those who spread the words of the New Testament.

Amen.

An angel:
Add to this work:
The greatness of God has become visible
in the story that is contained in the Old Testament.
The people of Israel found grace in God.
The development of the human being
is visible in the Old Testament.

Join the New Testament to the Old Testament.

Amen.

THE NEW TESTAMENT:
THE FOUR EVANGELISTS

Mary, *the mother of the Lord:*
Rejoice and jubilate!
The time of the Maccabees is over!

From now on concentrate fully on the birth of Christ!
Work further on the New Testament.

The books of the Maccabees are at the end of the Old Testament
(Catholic) or in the Apocrypha.

Mark the Evangelist

Mary:
MARK — was not present at the birth of Jesus,
nor in the stable at Bethlehem,
even though we already knew him long before the birth.
He, Mark, knew about the pregnancy — and about Joseph's dreams.
He did not know about the meeting with Elisabeth.

Mark often spent time with Jesus — and watched him.
He was the one who imparted to Jesus a great deal of knowledge.

He went for long walks with Jesus.
Their discussions on the workings of nature,
on experiences of God and the fear of God, were important.
The child Jesus spoke about his visions with the Evangelist Mark.

Mary continued:
He, Mark, was often our guest, at the "table of Joseph and Mary."

From his seventeenth to his twenty-seventh year,
Jesus dwelt with Mark and two God-fearing men
in different places —— spiritual centers.

The ancient tradition was to educate oneself spiritually,
to form oneself, receiving the light ——
so as to become a master and a man of knowledge.

Jesus, Mark, and the two men came back after some years.

After his twenty-ninth year,
JESUS LEARNED TO UNDERSTAND HIS PEOPLE.

He saw
the earth and its peoples,
the truth of heaven and the Father.

Thus —— strong within, and filled with the Holy Spirit,
he entered into **THE MIDST OF HUMANKIND.**
His work began!
Amen.

Mary:
Rejoice that you have received this knowledge.

I asked: Was Jesus — in Jewish centers?

Mary:
He was with the Essenes, old rabbis, philosophers, astronomers,
and people who were spiritually educated.
He was in different places, different spiritual centers.

Do not forget that he was highly sensitive —
a sensitivity enveloped in light.

HE SAW — HE KNEW —
HE RECOGNIZED WHAT WAS SPIRITUALLY
FROM THE FATHER OF FATHERS,
and what was therefore pure:
the highest, the best, the most important.
Jesus assimilated spiritually, and accepted,
what he recognized to be right.
That was his nature, to understand and decide alone! [29]

Amen

While Mary was speaking, I saw in visions:
The two men whom Mark took along were neither young nor old.
They made these journeys on foot, from center to center,
with great bags slung over their shoulders.
Israel's typical ranges of hills were to be seen — no woods.
Once they had a donkey with them, which carried the baggage.

Weeks later, Mary spoke:
PHILIP, of all the followers of Jesus, was the closest to Mark.
Philip lived in Greece, later in Jerusalem and Galilee.
Philip attended and cared for Mark in his old age, with love.

Mary:
Let us go on to Matthew.

But first you should know what joy is in me,
because you have heard about
Philip's Christian esteem and love for Mark.

Matthew the Evangelist

Mary:

MATTHEW —— a great man!
He received grace in the presence of God.
His words and actions were wise!

Don't you smell and inhale the fragrance of the flowers?
So —— was Matthew! *[He enjoyed the beauty of the earth.]*

Matthew lived —— enveloped in light.
He saw and experienced
everything very powerfully, in the spirit ——
and rendered it complete with HIS language.
In that way —— he completed HIS Gospel.

The making of the Gospel of Matthew
is as if a great painter, in all the details, was at work
from the birth of Jesus —— to the middle of his life —— until the end!

*[The end was the Resurrection and the commission to baptize and
teach all nations.]*

Rejoice about this!

Mary spoke further:
It is true that the Catholic Church
has accepted, interwoven, and integrated

much of Matthew's Gospel into church life.

My question: Mary — may I ask, what else was there between Jesus and Matthew?

Mary:
There was joy!
There was a strong presence and intensive work ——
for Jesus and with Jesus!
This was so until his, Matthew's, death.

I asked: Is anything incorrect in Matthew's Gospel?

Mary:
No.
Matthew experienced the life of Jesus in this way ——
according to his testimony.
He died early.

Luke the Evangelist

Mary:
You know Luke from earlier visions.
He examined and researched —— some of it with Paul ——
the whole life of Jesus and his disciples.

What he wrote —— is true.
He did not write down everything.

Let us work through the Gospel of Luke.
It is important!

On Luke 1:1–4

An angel:
True and right.

On Luke 1:5–25

The angel:
Everything took place just as the Evangelist Luke set it down.

**THE ANNOUNCEMENT OF THE BIRTH OF JOHN
HAPPENED IN THIS WAY, AND WAS THUS FULFILLED.**

Mary added:
It is important that Luke wrote it down.

*My question: Why did they take the name of John and not the name
of Zacharias?*

The angel:
A John or a Johanna[30]
is a person who is formed by God — a servant of God.
When a name like this is God-given,
one cannot choose one's own name.

The angel added:
BEFORE JESUS — came John the Baptist.
AFTER THE DEATH OF JESUS CHRIST came John the Evangelist
— he "whom he loved."

THE FIRST JOHN —
was the one who prepared the way for Christ. *(Luke 1:17)*

THE SECOND JOHN —
was the one who prepared the way for Christians.

John the Evangelist was
"the one who fulfilled the light and the Holy Spirit"
by completing the New Testament
with HIS GOSPEL and REVELATION,
as well as WRITINGS IN EPHESUS which have not yet been found.

My question: Was JOHN THE BAPTIST *"in the wilderness" (Luke
1:80) — in a monastery in order to learn?*

The angel:
Yes. Do not ask further.

*I still asked: Is it important that I go on asking about his life and
about his death?*

Mary:
No. He was a real servant of God.
Amen.

On Luke 1:26–38
The Annunciation

The angel:
It is GABRIEL'S task[31] to bring messages from God to human beings.
There are many angels who bring messages, also in dreams.

Angels brought messages in dreams
to JOSEPH, the betrothed of Mary.
They are all true. (*Matthew 1:20, 2:12, 2:13, 2:19*)
Joseph —— was pure, true, and authentic in his faith in God.

Mary added:
Gabriel was —— is —— an angel with intense radiance.
Learn from this.

The angel spoke further:
The light from the primal source ——
came to the earth —— to its people —— in human form.

THAT IS THE EVENT OF CHRISTMAS!

On Luke 1:26–38

An angel:
Luke —— was wise.
Luke recognized how important it is
to pass on word for word, recording in his Gospel,
the Annunciation of the birth of Jesus.
Every word that Gabriel spoke to Mary has its significance!

Do not alter the words of Luke *(1:32–33)!*
Allow them to be engraved upon your minds!
The words *(Luke 1:33)* are holy, true, and important historically.

Mary:
Place here the words of the hymn
"In the Middle of the Night."[32]
They too are important.

In the depth of night ——
as the shepherds delight ——
holy singing, sounding, and ringing,
light in the night.

Satz: Franz Eibner

In the depth of night —— the earth becomes bright!
Light from God.

Passing sun, moon, and stars to the earth —— light from God.

Sun, moon, and stars
created for revolving, turning in the light of God.
Light from God to earth, to humankind.

Mary:
The shepherds *(Luke 2:8–20)* were the first
to hear the birth of Jesus proclaimed.

They saw —— they heard —— they were chosen ——
BECAUSE THEY WERE FREE
from the usual conditions of human life!
Heaven —— earth —— animals were their life.
No limits prevented them
from accepting and spiritually assimilating all that happened.

The shepherds were the first to hear the message.
They were able to visit the child.
They praised and glorified God.
As the first ones, they "made known the Word."
They were the first preachers and missionaries.

Mary spoke further:
LUKE recorded the announcement to the shepherds.

MATTHEW passed on everything about the three wise men.
(Matthew 2:1–12)

The stargazers, the three wise men,
were not astrologers as we know them today.
They were God-fearing men who knew one another.
In order to see the star of Bethlehem,
the eyes of each one were opened.

They recognized the intense, strong radiance of the star ——
as an event of energy and light that was significant.

A LIGHT BETWEEN GOD AND THE EARTH!

Linked with God, they set out —— to search and to find ——

SO AS TO EXPERIENCE THE GREAT THINGS
THAT HAD COME TO PASS, AND TO GIVE GLORY TO GOD.

I had a question: Is there still further information about the actual birth of Jesus?

Mary smiled:
All that is important —— about this great event ——
is written down in the Gospel.

On Luke 2:21–40
The Circumcision of Jesus / The Presentation

An angel:
The spiritual aspect of the presentation
was greater than that of the circumcision.
Today —— after Christ's influence —— no circumcision is necessary.

Presentation and baptism,
whether in early youth or later, are not law.

A believing father or mother offers the child —— to God,
has it baptized.

The circumcision of Christ, however, is true.
Luke wrote it down intentionally.
(Luke 2:21)

On Luke 2:25–40

The angel:
Simeon and Anna are witnesses for you all.
To Simeon and Anna, this experience was
a personal sign of God's love.

On Luke 2:30–32

Mary:
CHRIST WAS BORN — FOR ALL HUMANKIND!
Churches, learn from this!

Christ —— was —— and is the one
through whom Israel lives spiritually!

On Luke 2:41–52
The Twelve-year-old Jesus in the Temple

Mary:
There is not much to add to that. The words of Jesus say it:
"Could you not tell that I need to be in the place
which belongs to my father?"   *(Luke 2:49)*
As a twelve-year-old,
he was already —— in spirit —— above "the teachers."

On Luke 3:21–22
The Baptism of Jesus in the River Jordan

Mary:
It was the first time Jesus was in public;
and he chose, with religious freedom, baptism.
It was the spiritual union
between God and the human being which Jesus sought.
That union is in baptism —— and Jesus said yes to it.

In this way Jesus also affirmed the workings of John the Baptist!

On Luke 4:1–13

The Temptations of Jesus:

"And Jesus being full of the Holy Spirit returned from the Jordan,
and was led by the Spirit into the wilderness, being forty days
tempted by the devil."

Mary:

The overcoming of the temptations
was a trial of strength against the power that reigns over the night.
The light — and the power of the Holy Spirit — were victorious!
(Stage I)

After such a victory — love finds its place in the heart.
This also happens with people
who have lived and fought through something similar.

**WITH THIS LOVE, AND FILLED WITH THE HOLY SPIRIT,
THE WORK OF JESUS BEGAN!**   *(Luke 4:14)*
(Stage II)

To truly become yourself —
it is of great importance to spiritually overcome evil.
Learn from this!

To overcome temptations, and all that is evil and negative,
makes you strong and free!

An angel:

It is an important process of spiritual growth and development.
IN FREEDOM LOVE LIVES, LOVE IS STRONG!

On Luke 4:33–37
The Healing of the Possessed Man

An angel:
You ask why did the demon speak?

Remember,
power against power —— light against darkness.
When you pray, you also speak.
The word is a spiritual force.

Jesus was not simply there!
Power went forth from him!

Here, during this healing, the powers of darkness spoke.

You cannot measure how great and manifold
the spiritual world of light is.

Hold fast to all that is pure and of God in yourselves ——
and the demons will flee when they meet you!
(Stage II)

An angel:
From the healings of the Gospel of Luke, learn this:
The greater part of the healings, that the people of light pray for,
take place through the power of the Holy Spirit.

JESUS, SON OF GOD, HAS POWER OVER EVIL *[demons]*.

These words, about healing and the casting out of demons,
are sufficient —— for the present time in which you live.

In a hundred years —— in a thousand years ——
humankind will be able to understand more.

324 • SO THAT YOU MAY BE ONE • The Visions of Joa Bolendas

On Luke 5:1–11
Peter's Draught of Fishes

An angel:
An example of the greatness of God
and a commission for EVERY Christian:
to convert the people, to show them the way,
TO BECOME FREE FROM THE SET WAYS OF THE WORLD.

If a human being is free —— he can free others!

On Luke 5:27–32
The Calling of Levi

An angel:
Levi —— heard the call, affirmed his true self,
and so came into that love which makes free,
and was fulfilled with the power and light —— of God.
He, Levi, was loved by God.

On Luke 6:12–16
The Calling of the Twelve Apostles

Mary spoke thoughtfully:
What happened then is holy.
Imagine this as a vocation —— and you sense something
of the holiness, the greatness, of the event.

Mary seriously:
You Christians pass too lightly over this event!

Mary spoke further:
This kind of calling is the third stage of spiritual awareness.

Reflect on it.
(Stage III)

He — Jesus — called twelve Apostles.
Who is ready — to be one of the twelve, regardless of where you live?

I asked: Are you speaking about theologians, pastors,
ordained priests?

Mary:
To take on the task of an apostle is to live, according to one's gifts,
fully and wholly in the power of love — filled with the Holy Spirit!

On Luke 6:20–49
The Sermon on the Mount

Mary:
The Beatitudes are not easy to understand.
Francis of Assisi recognized them partly.
The Sermon on the Mount is the center of Christ's teachings.

Mary continued:
You should know that those who come to him —
and hear his words — and act upon them —
to those he will show whom he is like.
(Luke 6:47–49)
Add to this the words which you have received earlier.

[May 1972]

Christ:
Blessed be the one who becomes pure through God.
Blessed be the one who is there for God.
Blessed be the one whose receiving

and giving is through God,
whose being is in the presence of God.[33]
This purity through God enables you to stand
whenever the earth breaks apart, the mountains fall,
the sun darkens, and dust rains on the earth.

Don't forget this —— at the present time!

[August 11, 1987]

> *Sister Clare, of the Franciscan Order, stood in front of me, to the right, in the choir of the church. She was gaunt, of medium height but on the tall side, and wrapped in a dark brown cloak. She looked at me for a long time and then said slowly:*

Only in the spiritual life of Brother Francis
did I find —— the very essence of life.

Before his encounter
with angels, and later with saints,
he lived as an intelligent and kind-hearted person, enjoying life.
Christ also visited him at that time.

HIS LIFE WAS TRANSFORMED INTO A GREAT LIFE —
SPIRITUAL AND FREE.
He was free from the set patterns of the world,
and free from an economic system and from money.
Only in poverty —— did he live freely.

This freedom is possible today ——
being independent from material concerns,
and living according to the Ten Commandments
and the commandment of love.

I asked if I had heard everything correctly.

Sister Clare answered:
Yes. To live as Brother Francis did
is to live freely and independently —
with God — in the power of love.

Silence.

Sister Clare:
Whoever loves his father or his mother more than Christ
is not free.
We, the order of the Poor Clares, try to serve God and Christ
in a simple way, with praise and love.

There have to be church regulations and servants of the church:
Yes!
Coercion in the church and power in the church:
No! No!

Listen! HE WAS FREE AND LIVED FREE
from spiritual and ecclesiastical constraints.

[August 14, 1987]

Mary added:
My love goes to the poor —
and those who are poor in spirit.
THE POOR IN SPIRIT SEEK JUSTICE, TRUTH,
AND LOVE, LOVE OF ONE'S NEIGHBOR.
They are not puffed up.

BLESSED ARE THEY WHO THIRST FOR ETERNAL LIFE.
BLESSED ARE THE POOR, FOR THEY SHALL BE RICH
AND INHERIT THE KINGDOM OF HEAVEN.
Francis of Assisi became rich in poverty!

Mary said to me:
May it be your wish to experience all the Beatitudes!

> *I saw in vision: Francis of Assisi — free — spiritually, alto-gether free There was nothing that could distract or hinder him. Thus — and only thus — could he meet birds, animals, and human beings with concentrated strength and unbroken spiri-tual power! He found spiritual strength because he was without earthly possessions and poor, and because he hungered and thirsted for the truth.*

On Luke 7:11–17
The Raising of the Widow's Son at Nain

An angel:
This was possible —— with the power and light of God ——
through Jesus Christ.

On Luke 7:36–50
Jesus Anointed by a Sinner

An angel:
It is a sign of love —— from all human beings —— for Jesus.

On Luke 8:1–3
The Women Disciples of Jesus

An angel:
Luke wrote it down; even if it is self-evident,
it is important that women were named, not only men.

On Luke 8:19–21
The True Relatives of Jesus

An angel:
Clear —— for one who is rooted in faith.

On Luke 8:40–48 and 8:49–56
*The Healing of the Woman with the Issue of Blood / The Raising of
the Daughter of Jairus*

Mary smiled and said:
The raising of the daughter of Jairus had
to be written down for future generations;
it is an experience that testifies against transmigration of the soul.
A human being's light —— with soul and spirit ——
does not return to another body!
Learn from this!

On Luke 9:1–10
The Sending out of the Twelve Apostles

Mary:
How I love this event.
"And they returned and told him all that they had done."
They were a community, a unity.
Learn from this, for the unity of the church.

On Luke 9:11–17
The Feeding of the Five Thousand

*To my question as to how the multiplying of bread and fishes hap-
pened, an angel answered:*
In a thousand years you shall understand it.

Fifty years ago you could not understand a voyage to the moon,
nor that spoken information
could be sent from the moon to the earth. It is progress.

On Luke 9:18–22
Jesus Foretelling His Own Death

The angel:
The announcement of Jesus' Passion,
and Resurrection on the third day,
was important for the disciples, to give them a perspective.

On Luke 9:23–27:
*"... there are some among you who will not taste of death until they
see the kingdom of God."*

Mary:
The saying was often misunderstood.
The correct understanding is that some
reach the light directly, without experiencing death.

On Luke 9:28–36
The Transfiguration of Jesus

Mary:
True! Jesus spoke with Moses and Elias!
Almost incomprehensible to you,
BUT THIS WAS A PREPARATION FOR DEATH —— the dying of Jesus.
(Luke 9:31)

On Luke 9:37–43
The Healing of the Epileptic Boy

Mary:
Yes. He, Jesus, had more spiritual strength and light to give
than the disciples!

On Luke 9:44–45
Jesus' Second Announcement of His Passion

Mary:
Whenever you remember this, then sing the hymn:
Glory to you, O Christ, Lamb of God.
Amen.

GLORY TO YOU, O CHRIST[34]
Glory
to you, O Christ ——
the Lamb of God.
Amen.

On Luke 9:6–48
The Disciples Argue over Their Rank

Mary:
It is to remind you that Christians are to love one another.

On Luke 9:57–62
Three Different Followers of Jesus

Mary:
To follow means to do God's will and his will alone ——
not the will of the church, nor to bend to its power.
Learn from Francis of Assisi
as well as from the baptism of Jesus.

On Luke 10:1–12
The Sending out of the Seventy Disciples

Mary:
Here Christians are called
to be ready to serve God and his creation.

On Luke 10:25–37
The Good Samaritan

Mary:
"A man went down to Jericho and fell among thieves ... But a Samaritan showed mercy on him. Jesus said, 'Go your way and do likewise.' "
This is love!

On Luke 10:38–42
Martha and Mary

Mary:
The story is very important.
Both of them were loved,
though to be with Christ means to receive light.
This comes first in the life of a human being.

On Luke 11:1–4
Jesus Teaching the Disciples How to Pray: "Father, hallowed be thy name ..."

Mary:
You have received the prayer in the form of a hymn:
The Our Father is at the heart of prayer
and one's being in the presence of God.

> *Here I, Joa Bolendas, would like to add my own words on the Our Father:*[35]
>
> FATHER — FATHER — OUR FATHER.
> *The Lord's Prayer is surely the greatest prayer. Love it, pray it, sing it! As the saints sang this prayer to me, there was, first of all, a searching that joins us with God the Father.*
>
> WHO ART IN HEAVEN —
> *Whether in prayer for others or for ourselves, we pray with all the angels, with the saints in heaven, and with all Christianity:*
> HALLOWED BE THY NAME —
> *and further the plea that is so important:*
> THY KINGDOM COME —
> *that Christ may come to us!*

THY WILL BE DONE ON EARTH,

AS IT IS IN HEAVEN.

GIVE US THIS DAY OUR DAILY BREAD.

We ask for the bread and chalice.

FORGIVE US OUR TRESPASSES,

AS WE FORGIVE THOSE WHO TRESPASS AGAINST US.

We ask that Christ may forgive us, that he may enable us to forgive.

LEAD US NOT INTO TEMPTATION;

BUT DELIVER US FROM EVIL —

that he may protect us from temptation and evil, with the Holy Spirit.

On Luke 11:24–26
On the Return of Impure Spirits

Mary:
Knowing this,
at every repentance and forgiveness, is important.
It is also important for every psychologist.

On Luke 11:27–28
A Woman Blessing the Mother of Jesus.

An angel:
Many have loved the mother of Jesus.

On Luke 11:37–54
Rebuking the Scribes and Pharisees

An angel:
Be silent;
nevertheless it is true what Luke wrote down.

On Luke 12:22–34
The Warning about Earthly Concerns

Mary:
Be sensible and wise in trusting God.

On Luke 12:49–53
Jesus Announcing a Time of Strife

An angel:
These words of preparation were important for the disciples.

On Luke 12:57–59
Warning to Be Reconciled with One's Adversary

An angel:
Do not forget! Never forget it!

On Luke 13:1–5
The Murdered Galilean

Mary:
Learn from it!

On Luke 13:6–9
The Parable of the Fig Tree

An angel:
Translate it for the people —— this is a parable of love!
Listen! Give the fig tree time, and work for it, too.

On Luke 14:7–14
Warning about the Seeking of High Places and Selfishness

Mary:
Learn from it!

On Luke 14:25–27
Jesus' Demand of His Followers

An angel:
Understand this —— and then work on yourself.

> *Concerning my question why no instruction came from Mary or from an angel about the records in Luke 14:28 up to 21:4, the angel answered:*

Let it remain so —— as you have received it.
Some of these chapters remain concealed;
it is good to understand part of them clearly.

> *The angel spoke further concerning Luke 21:5 up to 24:53, on the account of the last days (up to) the Ascension of Jesus:*

Write down the words of Mary which you have received.

Mary:
Weep for Israel.
The humiliation is great!
The woes of the world are:
Bloodshed —— death —— pain —— fear —— sickness ——
famine —— earthquake —— devastation.

GO THROUGH THIS TIME CONTEMPLATING
the Passion of Christ ——

the death of Christ ——
his Resurrection ——
his Ascension ——
the sending out of Christians
through the power of the Holy Spirit.

Mary:
Luke examined what he wrote
about the death and Resurrection of Jesus;
he wrote it down with reverence and love for Christ.
Praying —— embrace these words for the present time.

Silence

Mary:
Luke —— is buried —— in a rock grave not far from Jerusalem.

Silence

> *I implored: Mary — let me from time to time stand at his grave*
> *— in spirit. He, Luke — in his works and his acts gave much*
> *— gave a great deal to the people in his Gospel and the Acts of*
> *the Apostles.*

> *A year later, in prayer I heard a voice and, as in the shadow of*
> *the night, a man became visible; according to the form of his*
> *head, he could have been Luke ... and I asked: Who — are*
> *you, who is speaking?*

The answer:
Paul —— was ill —— in the hip, the hip-joint.[36]
He also often had a fever;
yet he received strength —— to live,
strength also in the face of death.

Know this — that he, Paul,
had a God-given task to live as an apostle.

**SEPARATE WHAT WAS TO BE FULFILLED AT THAT TIME
FROM WHAT HE PREACHED TO THE ENTIRE CHRISTIAN WORLD.**

I, LUKE, loved Peter and Paul.
I tried to research and gather together
what had come to pass through Jesus,
and then wrote the Gospel.

I met the mother of Jesus seven times.
I received from her the most important
and greater part of the Gospel, and wrote it down.

Mark — the Evangelist — gave his records to me
to complete this Gospel.

Then I made journeys to the places
where Jesus had preached, and inquired there —
and wrote down what I found.

Theophilus (*Luke 1:1-4*) was a spiritual follower of mine.
He preserved the documents.
I am, even today, astonished, joyful, and thankful,
feeling nothing but praise, that no word was lost.

I also wanted to tell you that there were no letters of mine.

Write everything down well — for God, Christ, and humankind.
Later I will see you — in the greater life!
Rejoice!
Luke went away — withdrew — disappeared ...

In the year 1985 Mary spoke:
Mark was the oldest of the Evangelists.

He was the first to write about Jesus.
Love him!
The other three Evangelists took over his records and added to them.
Mark was connected to the carpenter's family.
That is the reason why Mark wrote down so little.
Luke was the learned and wise one
concerning all that had come to pass.
Hold fast to him as an example.
Love Matthew — the great narrator.
He loved Jesus very much.
That is the reason for his rich, flowering language.
The Catholic Church was influenced by Matthew.

Take John separately. Amen.

Stretch out your arms to the whole world,
AND LET EVERYONE TAKE PART
IN THE GREAT WHEEL — THAT GOD TURNS!

Go out on the streets —
and call aloud — with the new book!

John the Evangelist

John the Evangelist is of such great significance that I did not dare to leave out any words which repeated themselves in the following records. I also omitted a summary, and thus I pass on the visions in the same order as I received them.

An angel:
Love John!

Try to understand the period of Greek philosophy ——
and the life of John.

He, John, washed
Jesus' feet —— on the cross —— with his tears.

John was the first human being
to recognize Jesus as a man of light ——
with primal light —— full of the Holy Spirit.

JOHN SAW — RECOGNIZED — LOVED JESUS.
HE KNEW WHO JESUS WAS AND IS.

John took Mary, the mother of Jesus,
as one of his own, after the death of Jesus.
He honored Mary —— and cared for her.
John —— was Lazarus —— whom Jesus awoke from the dead.[37]

A saint:
John — whom Christ loved —
had the gift of living in God's revelation.
He saw — heard — experienced — partly dwelt in —
the kingdom of God.

As John loved Christ —
so he loved the entire spiritual greatness of Christ.
He loved the image of God.

Whoever recognizes that, in John,
has found the chalice of light — the Eucharist.

*Mary spoke about Jesus. She appeared in vision, and beside her a
young boy growing up and becoming an adult.*

Mary:
MY SON — ON EARTH — WAS A BEING OF LIGHT —
AS A CHILD AND UNTIL THE END OF HIS LIFE — ON EARTH.

I understood: This was her child.

Mary:
HIS RESURRECTED BODY OF LIGHT —
IS CHRIST ALONE!
HE SEES ME — HEARS ME — LOVES ME.
I may serve.
HE IS NO LONGER MY SON:
HE IS CHRIST!
God and he, Jesus, are one!
Spiritually and in the life of light.
Do you see this? Do you understand it?
No eye on earth has seen this.

The knowledge of God, of Christ, and of myself,
who gave birth to Jesus, is important!

Theology should be adjusted, accordingly.

> *Expressed another way: In his lifetime, Jesus was the son of*
> *Mary. In heaven, Jesus is no longer the son of Mary, but solely*
> *at one with God — in spirit and light.*

Mary:
LOVE Mark, Matthew, and Luke.
They gave an account of the life of Jesus on earth.

LIVE with John!
He comprehended and was formed to live with
light —— Spirit —— the power of the Holy Spirit!

He, John, is the living church.
TO LIVE — TO EXPERIENCE ALL THINGS
TOGETHER WITH GOD AND CHRIST —
IS TO BE A CHRISTIAN.

> *I saw John, in an enormous vessel that lay partly above, partly*
> *beneath, the earth.*

Mary:
John experienced the "Spirit of the Earth" as a vessel;
he stood in the midst of it —— in the midst of creation on earth.
AND BECAUSE HE ABSORBED IN HIMSELF SPIRITUAL LIFE ON
EARTH, HE WAS CAPABLE OF EXPERIENCING
THE IMMENSE SPIRITUAL, HOLY POWER OF GOD.

Filled with the Holy Spirit, John's spirit —— waxed ——
AND HE COMPREHENDED THE GREATNESS OF HEAVEN,
THE EXISTENCE OF GOD, IN WHOSE LIGHT CHRIST STOOD.

This, until he became enveloped in a sphere of light.

Such —— was John, already on earth, and, for that reason,
he was the favorite disciple of Jesus Christ.
He whom he loved.

He, "John," is the church, the teachings of the church.

I wanted to ask further questions, but Mary pleaded:

Be silent —— it is more than the knowledge in "Eureka"! [38]

Mary, some days later:
Do not be afraid of the new theology.
Teach the people TO LIVE after the example of John!

Take in the light!
In prayer —— in being in the presence of God ——
and in the Word *[Old and New Testaments]*.

Take in primal light at the Lord's Supper.

Pray for the Holy Spirit to be active ——
and pray that you may recognize this activity in the creation earth.
Live the Ten Commandments.
Live the commandment of love.

Live and believe according to the life of Jesus.

Love Advent —— Christmas —— Lent ——
Maundy Thursday —— Good Friday —— the Resurrection ——
Easter —— Pentecost —— the sending out of the disciples,
the sending out of Christians.

In your ways —— be and live like John.

Hannes and I went into the church at midday in Einsiedeln, in order to pray. We hoped that only a few people would be there then. It was quite the reverse. The church was full of Slavic pilgrims. They were celebrating their Mass.

After the preceding words of Mary, there was silence. Then John appeared — a lean, tall figure — in the choir, in front of the door. He looked at me and said:

Do you hear them singing?

In the Slavic Mass they sing without an organ, without any instrument. The singing was fresh, strong, and joyful. I answered: Yes.

John:
Love them —— seek the true Church of the East,
which is without power! without the misuse of spiritual power!

You have heard about me from the mother of Jesus.
Yes —— I live —— you see it.
Read the second and third chapter of my Gospel.
Join them together.

John probably saw all my inner questions concerning theology, for he said:
Closest to my spiritual life are
—— the Protestant Church with
the Word, the Old and New Testaments,
and prayer for the Holy Spirit.
—— the Catholic Church with
the Eucharist of Christ
and prayer for the Holy Spirit.

Between twenty and fifty percent of my spiritual life is to be found
in the Protestant Church, and seventy percent in the Catholic Church.
I counted up the percentages quickly —— looking for the portion of the
Orthodox Church. John smiled kindly —— and said:
Eighty percent of the Orthodox Church is contained
in the Catholic Church ——
not its history nor the ways it has evolved, but its theology.
The people of the East need the icon,
the joy of the day of Resurrection.
They live more consciously with prayer for the Holy Spirit.

John spoke further:
I ask you to lay aside all power, all pretensions of power!
LIVE IN THE NAME OF THE FATHER — OF THE SON —
AND OF THE HOLY SPIRIT.

John:
My Gospel has been shortened;
nonetheless, as you read it
you will recognize and experience the truth,
and joy shall be in you.

Love! Be strong!
Greetings to Hannes.
I have now blessed him.
Joy will be in him.

John to me:
I will speak to you yet again.
A star is now shining.

Mary added:
When you build your house of Christians,
in accordance with the Protestant Church

and the Catholic Church,
and include the love of icons
and more prayer for the Holy Spirit ——
and this be done in freedom ——
then the Orthodox Church
will come toward it, step by step.

Mary spoke to me about "John":
SOUL — SPIRIT — BODY
MEET GOD'S SPIRIT AND LIGHT —
That means the human being meets God ——
and becomes one with God.

With the Jews —— the human being is soul and spirit.

WITH THE GREEKS , THE HUMAN BEING IS SOUL — SPIRIT — BODY.
TEMPLE — THEATER — STADIUM.
["Theater" here means culture, which includes language, art, architecture, science, theater, and other aspects of human behavior.]

C. G. JUNG, THE DEPTH PSYCHOLOGIST, SEPARATED SOUL AND
SPIRIT. WITH JOHN , THE HUMAN BEING IS SOUL — SPIRIT — BODY,
MEETING GOD'S SPIRIT AND LIGHT.

THE HUMAN BEING BECOMES RELIGIOUS, IS RELIGIOUS,
NEEDS RELIGION TO FULFILL HUMAN DEVELOPMENT.
John lived with the entire creation ——
bonded with the earth and his fellow human beings;
and in this life ——
he met and was united with God, with Christ.

Mary:
John took the unity of soul —— spirit —— body from Greek philosophy;
and thus affirmed life on earth in all its fullness.

If anybody has recognized Christ,
then it is John.
This happened when Christ lived on earth, and later ——
after his death and Resurrection —— in prayer and vision.

Mary added to this:
The commandment "Sundays you shall keep holy"
is one of the great commandments.
Through it, soul, spirit, and body recover.

But if you pass by a sick person,
whether he be sick in body or soul, on this seventh day ——
and you do not offer him any help ——
a shadow comes between you and God.

John recognized this when he lived with Jesus.

Peter, whom I knew on earth and who is risen from the dead:
Read parts of Greek philosophy.

If the soul is well developed,
then, according to John,
a rich spiritual life is important ——
this again following the example of Greek philosophy.

What John knew, experienced, and lived
is the full and entire development of the human being
through the stages of encounter with Christ,
God, and God's Spirit.
John —— saw —— into the heavens;
he knew about the resurrected Christ
and about the resurrection of the human being.
John knew through the faith taught by Christ,
that the human develops to become a person of light.
If this happens,

then the full and entire development of the human
is accomplished.

It is very, very important
that John recognized this truth and passed it on.
Thus — for people today
being a Christian is significant, bringing joy,
and giving spiritual meaning.

Understand also that C. G. Jung studied soul and spirit,
and rediscovered many things.
The development of the human being —
with God, the primal source,
with light through Christ,
and with the power of the Holy Spirit —
he did not recognize.
But he would have inevitably arrived at it later.

An angel read out of a book:
GREEK PHILOSOPHY is
to live — to exist —
with soul, spiritual life, culture,
and care of the body including the stadium *[contests]*.

To live consciously with soul — spirit — body,
to learn about them and cultivate them,
ANIMATES AND ACTIVATES THE CEREBRUM!
Discussion, as with the Greeks, also activates this part of the brain!

Saying yes to the body — ACTIVATES THE CEREBELLUM!
Learn from it.

It is OTHERWISE WITH THE JEWS in their faith:
There soul and spirit make up the whole human being.

C. G. Jung separated soul and spirit in the twentieth century —
so as to strengthen the soul
and to create an intellectual confidence in the reality of the soul.
Hence separate and then heal;
whenever possible, create again a unity of soul and spirit.

John loved the way the Greeks
spoke about and discussed the soul and the spirit —
also how they strengthened and cared for the body.
John affirmed all this in accordance with creation.
Science and medicine were areas which interested him, too.

For John — Greek thinking,
the Jewish faith,
and the life with Christ
were like a joining of three worlds!

John loved
the wisdom of the Greeks,
the faith of the fathers of the Jewish world,
and the spiritual life with Christ;
which he loved above all else.

He recognized that to be human, to exist here,
on this earth, in the earth, is important and right.
Therefore he truly lived with all that was of the earth —
with all that was worthy of experience.

The cultivation of soul and spirit
was the next development:
Live truly on the earth —
then soul and spirit develop themselves in the right way.

The highest development for him was

to recognize God through Jesus Christ.
John saw that God —— through the encounter with Christ
and life in union with him ——
belongs to the final development of the human being.

Through the workings of the Holy Spirit
and the light through Christ,
the final stage of development has been achieved.

Therefore the human being is religious;
therefore he needs religion!

Soul —— spirit —— body meet
God's Spirit and light:
That is the true process of human development.

Andrew, the holy brother of Peter:
Love John!
He affirmed and loved existence and life on earth, in its totality,
all contained in the magnificent creation of God.
He said, "He who does not love existence on earth ——
does not love God!" That was John.

The earth, living and dying ——
all in God —— all in the same light.

To turn away from God
is to resign oneself to the negative and to sin.
One who does penance returns to the light of creation.

Andrew, lovingly:
The union with God is in Christ.
WHOEVER RECOGNIZES THIS, LIVES.

Hence John's love and affirmation of existence on earth.

OF ALL THE EVANGELISTS
HE WAS THE ONE WHO MOST AFFIRMED LIFE,
because he lived in God through and with Jesus Christ.

The Greeks taught him to say yes to the body.
From the Greeks, he learned about a culture
that cultivated intellectual life.
Through science —— came understanding.

John observed also
the caring, cultivating, and educating
contained in the Greek religion.

He recognized and lived with Christ,
and created for the people the link to Christ and God.

KNOWINGLY —— through his own seeing *[visions]*,
through his own experiences that were linked with Christ ——
he sought to form, to understand all this for future generations,
and for the Christians after him.

Thus he prepared the way —— for the coming church.

He loved —— everyone —— who prayed to God.
He was at one with those people
who lived according to the life of Jesus Christ ——
who, in their path through life, followed him
on a path of light.

He affirmed whatever was done through love.
John was very strong, generous, great:
not narrow-minded toward the people.

He learned to incorporate life in all its manifestations
from living in Asia Minor, Greece ——

this in politics, in art, in science,
and in the life between people *[their discussions]*.

He said yes — not no — to life on earth.
HE LOVED THE SICK AND HEALED MANY.
HE SOUGHT JUSTICE *[human rights]*.

Again the risen Peter:
In the Gospel of John, of which a part is absent,
you see the powerful relationship linking John to God — to Christ.
Every word in his Gospel is a statement from a person
of spiritual discernment.
Hardly anyone has in this way recognized,
loved, and experienced God as John did.
That is why Jesus loved this disciple so much.

It was through providence that
after his life with Jesus and the disciples,
he was persecuted and fled to Ephesus.
He loved the Aegean; and from his life in Greece
he realized how science, intellectual life, culture
in the form of music, theater, lectures,
art, and sculpture based on a scientific study of the body
also belong to the life of a human being.

With their way of constantly discovering new things,
the Greeks started a creative era of science!
From then on all the bases of science were present and complete.

Then for the Greeks began
a spiritualization of religion,
a seeking — for a religion joined with morality.

A Questioning

At the same time, for them the greatest question arose,
the one concerning death — and a future life.
You see how this time laid the foundation for Christian teaching.

John with Paul and Luke brought the gospel to Asia Minor.
Over the years, John formulated the life of man in a new way.

Life — on earth — became important for John, very important.
He said yes to human development in its entirety.
He recognized that the last stage — religion —
joins the human to God's Spirit
and only then is the full development of the human attained.

Human beings are religious because
they want to attain the fulfillment of their humanity!
Humankind — needs — religion!

When John discerned all this,
he brought the Greeks the religion
that Christ had taught him,
filled with the Holy Spirit and with love.

He brought it to the Greeks — and to all of you.

Beside Mary stood an angel. The angel spoke:
Complete the Gospel of John
with the Gospel of Luke — for yourself personally.

With this addition you will have a lot
that has been taken out of the Gospel of John
or has not been written down.

John appeared in the vision, on the other side of a river. He called to me:
Come over!
Come to the table of the learned!

God created human beings with the potential to develop
as far as this table of the wise —
the table of the Greek spirit.[39]

My question: Is this an example of God's creation in process?

John:
Yes! Come! And see!
And from then on — continue to build a life with Christ.

And so I went [in vision] in a sailing boat over the river.

John:
After Israel
there came a further spiritual unfolding.

In the brain there was a new, quick development of centers.
There was a spiritual, scientific blossoming.
I — John — experienced in Asia Minor,
where I lived in different places, the blooming of an age.

I never turned aside from the Christian faith.
I never broke away spiritually from Christ —
not even for days, for hours.

Yet I wish to tell you that the discussions with the Greeks
were electrifying; they were spiritual fireworks!

I was really filled with enthusiasm.
I felt full of energy and joy
about how important living on earth is —
united with living in Christ:
From active, spiritual, joyful learning, in the midst of life,
WITH the Christian faith — and this is important —
I became a person of light!
I experienced this development and maturation
consciously, with my own eyes.
And so I was completely present on the earth —
and united with God in the hereafter —
through Christ — till death.

Soul — spirit — and body,
united with God and Christ
and the workings of the Holy Spirit,
are the wholeness in the order of God's creation.

Cultivate and love a strong soul —
and the development of spirit and body!

Development with religion is full development.

The risen Franz Eibner:[40]
John was filled with the Holy Spirit!

Write down:

Documents and writings of John
lie by the straight street —— in Ephesus.
They are records from his time with Jesus,
and from later times with the apostles.
They are important for you.

For John it was important to speak and to write about
WHY JESUS IS CHRIST — to affirm that Jesus is the Son of God!

JOHN WROTE THE GOSPEL WHEN HE WAS OLD.
He wrote it for his contemporaries, for the people of his time.
Over and over again he brought forward
statements and justifications about Jesus.

Write everything down and put it together.

*After all the words concerning John, I asked while I was praying: Can
I close the record concerning John? Is everything complete?*

Then John spoke once more:
No! Not quite yet.
Do you understand me?

I came into a land
where spirit, culture, science, and religion,
——including its philosophers, for example, Plato——
were great and powerful.

In my time, Greece was one of the most highly developed countries.
I came there as a persecuted Christian ——
following the calling of my master Jesus Christ ——
thus as a refugee and missionary!

In highly intellectual Greece
I talked about —— a carpenter's son!
I learned a lot from the Greeks,

and I told them what I had experienced through Jesus.
Over and over again,
I told them that Jesus Christ is truly the Son of God.

This was the principal content of my Gospel,
which I wrote in old age!
Jesus — Christ — is the Son of God.
Through him — and only through him —
can we attain complete human development.

From the Old Testament, I also spoke about many things.

The Greek soul absorbed the light of Christ.
The Greeks sought God.
They recognized the one, great God.
Many Christians let themselves be baptized in Ephesus.

So they lived
with the earth —
with the acquired knowledge of the times —
being genuinely human toward one another,[41]
joined with — receiving light from — God.

Achieved in freedom,
it was a pure era of spiritual development —
without pressure, without rigid laws,
and without confining limits [theology was implied]!

In freedom of thought,
I saw and experienced an important and great mission — for Christ.

I also suffered. That was part of my life, too.
You also: Love and be strong!

Sometime later, John said:
My room for service to God was a mystical room,
a room of prayer, a room for "the Lord's Supper."

I was a missionary ——
in conversations, in discussions,
in short lectures, and in telling the stories to the world outside.

> *In visions I saw John up high, lean, tall, a figure of light —*
> *light radiating over Greece, which radiated further — over*
> *Europe as well. A bright figure of light appeared. It was Saint*
> *Peter. He said:*
I am Peter.

It is good if, at the beginning of the work on John the Evangelist,
you refer to: "He came unto his own" *(John 1:11).*

He —— Jesus Christ —— came unto his own.[42]
John understood "his own" as the earth and all that develops upon it.
The whole of the earth —— was —— is —— his own!
It was important for John to name this entirety.

Concerning John 1:1–14, Peter continued:
"In the beginning was the Word. . . ."

The creative power —— through God's Word,
through the Holy Spirit —— this John recognized!
It is of foremost importance in the faith of John!

On John 6:22–65
The Bread of Life

Parts are missing from the Gospel of John;
complete it with the Gospel of Luke.

This chapter of John refers to
the Last Supper in Luke *(Luke 22:15–20)*.

THE BREAD OF LIFE —

HOLY COMMUNION —

PRIMAL LIGHT —

ARE THE LOVE AND LIFE

WITH AND IN CHRIST!

THE NEW TESTAMENT:
THE ACTS OF THE APOSTLES

A *saint:*
Paul, Peter, and Luke,
as well as the disciples of Jesus, men and women,
were the ones who proclaimed the Christian religion.

On their travels, they were
THE CARRIERS OF LIGHT INTO THE PAGAN WORLD.

Read the Acts of the Apostles up to chapter twelve,
and note exactly HOW they spoke about Christ.
Pay attention to the basic teaching and HOW they taught:

— THE BREAKING OF BREAD — in different homes and in
    community.
— REPENTANCE — CONVERSION — RENEWAL.
— UNDERSTANDING POVERTY and the SHARING OF GIFTS!
— ASKING for the HOLY SPIRIT.
— BELIEVING in RESURRECTION and in ETERNAL LIFE.
— GOING FORTH — and BAPTIZING.
— The MANDATE for MISSIONARY WORK.
— On TRUTH and on JUSTICE.

Then read further in the Acts of the Apostles.
WHAT DOES THE CHURCH DO —
AND WHAT DO YOU DO, PERSONALLY, TODAY?
Is your Christian teaching part of your life?
Is it a faith that has really been learned?

The saint spoke further:
THE ORIGINAL CHURCH WAS FILLED
WITH THE POWER OF THE HOLY SPIRIT —
A ROCK THAT WAS STRONG!
IT WAS ALIVE — IN CHRIST!

THE FIRST HUNDRED YEARS, AFTER CHRIST'S BIRTH,
WERE THE MOST LIVELY —
AND SPIRITUALLY THE MOST POWERFUL —
SINCE THE BIRTH OF HUMANKIND!
THEOLOGICAL QUARRELS, LEADING TO A LACK OF LOVE,
WERE HOW THE CHURCH DECLINED —
this during the time up to the fifth century!

In addition, from the fifth century onward
came a struggle for power.

RELIGION TOOK POSSESSION OF THE HUMAN SPIRIT!
[The human being was robbed of spiritual freedom.]

Theology and power lead to the great dispute
between the Church of the East and the Church of the West.

Had the Christian faith not become a religion of power,
then "East and West" would have accommodated themselves
to a genuine theology of the Father —— the Son —— the Holy Spirit!

If power, today, falls away in the East and West ——
the church will rediscover itself,
moving toward a genuine being in God
and a genuine encounter with Christ,
in a sincere asking for the Holy Spirit.

MAY A NEW ERA BEGIN FOR HUMANKIND
AFTER A PERIOD OF SUFFERING.

One risen from the dead read from a book:
Paul — loved God, sought God, and encountered Christ!
This encounter with Christ as a figure of light changed his spirit.
He became an itinerant preacher.
Not a pope! BUT A GREAT HERALD OF THE TRUTH!
Paul and Luke were learned.
Searching and inquiring, they discerned
the actual events which happened.
Thus involved, they passed on the gospel and the faith.

They were two important servants of Christ.
God brought these two people together!

A man in a bright garment:
I am Thomas, a disciple.
I was on earth — in Jerusalem —
at the time when Jesus lived, died, and rose from the dead.

I was a Christian, a disciple;
on hearing that Jesus had risen from the dead
I was critical. This is not unusual.

I speak to you now to give testimony:
I SAW HOW CHRIST DIED —
and I saw and heard Christ after his death.
I did not ask how Christ came through the walls.
I did not ask why he could eat.

I — saw — heard — felt him, touched him.
He lived, had risen from the dead, went through walls,
was once here, once there.
I saw — I did not question; I BELIEVED.

I needed months —— to integrate —— the Resurrection of Christ ——
into my life. I wanted to say this to you.

Saint Peter appeared, came nearer, and said:
I am Peter.

I —— was and remained —— very human.
Not just in the night when Christ was betrayed —— BY ME.
Nevertheless, Christ never turned away from me!

At Pentecost strength came into me —— to work.

LOVE GOD —— the Father —— the Creator
of heaven and earth, and of the universe.

LOVE MY LORD, Jesus Christ, Son of God.

REPENT so that you may be one with Christ and with God.

ASK FOR THE HOLY SPIRIT so that you may be strong ——
and in the light!

Give God —— and Jesus Christ ——
the glory! All glory!

> *In the Acts of the Apostles, Peter, Paul, Luke, and all the*
> *disciples, men and women, took none of the glory for*
> *themselves! And Saint Paul, who was also present, added:*
Beloved in the Lord!

Jesus Christ sent me TO THE PAGANS —
TO PREACH, TO BAPTIZE in the name of Jesus Christ.
It was hard, so hard, to preach among the pagans.
The power of the Holy Spirit gave me strength.
I RECEIVED KNOWLEDGE AND REVELATION
from Christ —— from THE RISEN CHRIST.

What he said to me was the same truth
which Peter and the disciples preached about Christ.

How shall I explain it to you?

There was the old Judaism, with its fathers and prophets.
Jesus Christ brought to the Jews a new religious life.
And it was out of love that God passed on, by revelations,
the teaching of Christ — through Peter and me —
to the pagans, to all the people of the world.

Through Jesus the God of Israel gave
to the whole world, and to the cosmos,
UNION WITH THE PRIMAL SOURCE — WITH GOD.

To preach **TO THE PAGANS** was a great step
ACROSS THE BORDERS OF ISRAEL — TO THE GREATER WORLD.
A DEVELOPMENT. Give thanks for it!

A *saint:*
"Peace be with you and with the whole house of the Lord."
THUS SPOKE PAUL, and thus he addressed
the people and the Christian community,
whether in their houses or in their congregations.

Truth is to be found in "the period of Paul."
The letters are one-sided exhortations.
Yet he had a strong love within himself.
His personality was kind, humble, and just.
His task is over, but not the teachings of Christ —
not the Christian faith.

Paul was the one chosen to put into practice a life in Christ
as opposed to a life according to the Law
[*circumcision and other Jewish rules*].

With the Christian teaching,
he liberated the Jews from their laws.

Through Christian teaching, he brought freedom
to the pagans, the Greeks, and the Romans as well.

Great was Paul —
filled with the Holy Spirit and the revelations through Christ.

Amen.

> *Saint Peter, Saint Paul, and Saint Luke stood there. Peter*
> *looked at me a long time, as if he were reflecting on his life*
> *and actions on earth. He said, first pensively, then suddenly*
> *joyfully:*

THAT WAS MY TASK.
Paul had an equally great task:
to preach to the Jews and pagans — to proclaim Christ to them!

Peter added:
John, "the one whom he loved," lived in the Spirit and with love.
HE — BROKE — EVERY RULE.
HE LIVED THE SPIRITUAL FREEDOM OF HUMANKIND!

He, John, loved God, his Son Jesus Christ, and the Holy Spirit.
These three — God, Christ, and the Holy Spirit —
were for him absolute love,
and provided for the development of the human being.
Luke, whom I love,
brought forth the true gospel on papyrus scrolls.
He wrote the Acts of the Apostles —
and was a physician in the light of Christ.
He had a task which was great and fulfilling.

As a painter, he liked
blue, light blue, bright green, yellow, and some red.
He liked dark yellow to orange, the colors of ripe corn and wine, several earthy
colors and the colors of rock.

Peter added:
Love the Evangelists Mark and Matthew.
Likewise love all servants, apostles, bishops, deacons.
THEY ARE ALL SERVANTS OF THE COMMUNITY.

Peter spoke again to me:
You have grasped —— much of the Bible.
It is the foundation for all the ages of humankind.
And this foundation was laid
in the time of the Old and New Testaments.

You —— and others —— have been given understanding
about the human need for religion ——
how human beings can live and develop in a religious way.
Pass on to the people of the world the message
that you have received, with wisdom and love!

Trust in God, Jesus Christ, and the Holy Spirit.

I no longer saw the saints Peter, Paul, and Luke. But John was there!
He put a ball of light in my hand and said:
From Christ —— take the light.
You have need of it.
I look forward to the new Johannine Church!

While I was still praying, there appeared a tall figure in a robe.
This figure came nearer and said:
JOSEPH. I am Joseph,

and I ask you to leave in the books Maria Immaculata.
Mary's spirit was sensitive, pure, uncorrupted, and full of light.

Joseph:
Mary received her first child through the Holy Spirit —
without me — without a man.
Jesus had four natural brothers who were begotten by Mary and me.
All four brothers, even as laborers and craftsmen,
were followers of Jesus.

Thus God was good to us.
Life would have been more difficult
for Mary and me — and Jesus —
had he been an only child conceived by God.
As it was, we were a normal family.

All five sons were educated in the same way.
Mary was almost a perfect human being.
She was full of love, and had within herself the joy of life.

I died early in life.
When Jesus was twenty-eight years old,
I was living in the "great life hereafter."

You look at me questioningly.
Include my words in the books.
They are true.

At the end of my earthly life,
I praised and thanked God for the richness I had received;
you call it an experience of God.

Write down: Luke wrote the truth.
Mary loved the inquiring mind and personality of Luke.

Silence.

> I said: First of all, Joseph, I want to thank you, because you
> are here and have spoken. I am still astonished that you
> have appeared. Yet I wish to ask you so many things about
> your family.

Saint Joseph, very slowly:
What — do you still want to know?

Fish, grain, fruits, figs were our staple food;
some wine, much water, oil of the olives,
often fig compress as a remedy.
We had a wood fire indoors and outdoors,
sheepskins on the floor, handwoven woolen clothes,
a little cotton and very little silk;
wooden chairs, a table, shelves.
What do you still want to know?

Joseph smiled:
If the children fought?
O yes! Jesus was the stronger one,
but in the games he joined in well.
Don't you say bright, lively, active?

> I asked: Please wait. Let me ask: Can the Holy Spirit cause a preg-
> nancy as with Mary?

Joseph:
The Holy Spirit "cannot" do that!
IT WAS GOD WHO BROUGHT ABOUT THIS CREATION
through the Holy Spirit.
The Holy Spirit can only pass on information and impulses from God.

This happened later also through Christ.
At Holy Communion, which Christians
have celebrated since the death of Jesus Christ,
the Holy Spirit does not change the offerings ——
but in the Communion Jesus Christ is present!
He gives you of his own life!

When Christ is present in the Communion,
then any request for the work of the Holy Spirit is full of strength!
Do you really understand what a great thing happens?

*My question: May I still ask: Was Mark at your home? And was he
on the way with Jesus later, as I have seen in visions?*

Joseph's whole face radiated kindness:
Yes! All that you have written down is true.

I asked: And the visions on the Acts of the Apostles and the letters?

Joseph:
Yes! You have heard and seen correctly.
For the passing on of the hymns,
I — THANK — YOU!
You are to make haste —— in working through this.

I pleaded: Joseph — wait —

> *But Joseph's figure of light went away — further and further,
> without turning around once. For thirty years I have had
> visions — and only now Joseph said:*
"She, Mary, had her first child from God."

A saint:
Joseph radiates a strong light —— like Abraham and Moses.

*A month later, Joseph appeared once more. He looked at me
and said:*
I died early.
Not by accident, but with a fever —— because of a fever illness.
It was God's will that I did not survive the illness.

When Jesus died, I was in the great life hereafter.
While on earth I was his father,
and as such gave him his name.

I WAS BEFORE HIM —

BEFORE HIS BIRTH ON EARTH —

AND BEFORE HIM ALSO IN HEAVEN.

God let my spirit experience his last years on earth.
His death was horrible.
It hurt his brothers, his disciples, and his mother terribly.

Joseph in a lively way:
But after his death, he was —— in the light.
He was a man of light —— in magnitude above all the risen ones.
Greater than the angels!

I asked: What happened between his death — and Easter?

Joseph:
You call it the stillness of the grave —— holy, pure stillness.
Yes, it was so;
but —— he conquered death indeed!

Through Jesus the most wonderful
and the most unbelievable event happened:
From then on, a human being after dying
spiritually lives, ON THE SAME DAY,
lives as a figure of light, lives in full consciousness.

"Today you shall be with me in Paradise"
(*Luke 23:43*).
Thus spoke Jesus on the cross
to the one who was crucified with him.
This happened;
Christ —— fulfilled it in the time between Good Friday and Easter!
At Easter he revealed himself to the women and to the disciples.

Joseph added further:
And, as you know, at Pentecost the power of the Holy Spirit
was given to all human beings!

He, Christ, is the link from God to the people.
Many call him mediator.

Joseph:
Did I have contact with him in the life hereafter?

Yes.
Once I saw him —— and he saw me —— from a distance, far away.
His countenance radiated with pure, deep, golden light.
Kindness was in his face —— a "tear" in the corner of his eye ——
[why this was so, I did not know]
and he, Jesus, said with love, quietly:
"I thank you —— you are in the light —— love the people and worship."

Slowly:
We love the people, their life, and their being!
Praise be to God —— Our Father.
Amen.

Joseph:
This was a lot for you to experience and to take in.
I wished to say all this to you ——
and asked Christ and his mother if I could do so.

I love the unity in spirit of Christ and Mary,
and therefore I included Mary in my request.

I asked: Do you see Mary, now, as a different spiritual being?

Joseph:
Mary was an exceptional woman, rich in love, on earth.
An inner greatness formed her life.
We all loved her deeply.

As a figure of light in heaven,
she is even more noble, tender, true —
indeed, a queen of heaven, a queen of love.

Not sweet, as painters often paint her.

She was spiritually a great woman on earth,
and is loved — now — in heaven.

Do not be afraid; I will speak to you yet again.

After Easter, Mary Magdalene read in a book:
**BLESSED BE CHRIST, THE RISEN ONE — THE LIVING ONE,
THE ONE WHO TRIUMPHED OVER SIN AND DEATH.**
Gloria!
To the one who is and who lives!
To the one who links God and humankind!
To Christ, who was prepared to understand
the source of life and all creation!
Because of this awareness,
he became the one who joins God to man!

In the greatness and fullness of God —
in the greatness of the cosmos, earth, and moon —
in this power and in this light,

he overcame death and sin.
Whoever discerns this can forgive.

A saint added:
Christ saw, understood, and experienced!
Without the understanding given by God and God's Spirit,
he would not have been capable of CONQUERING DEATH.

In the ongoing of creation,
THIS ACHIEVEMENT — OF JESUS CHRIST —
IS AS GREAT AS THE GIVING OF LIFE
AT THE BEGINNING OF EARTH'S CREATION.

The saint continued:
Therefore live your magnificence!
Death is conquered.
Sin becomes annulled[43] and is forgiven.
The human being lives — in eternity.

Christ added:
I give you light —
for earthly as well as for eternal life.
Take, eat, my body, my blood;
in this communion is life: eternal, imperishable life.

Days later, a saint said seriously:
I AM THE BROTHER OF JESUS.

You have received much from God — through Christ;
pensively:
very much!

Think over what you have received before God!
Be strong!

I, the brother of Jesus, experienced with him the days of youth.
I experienced the way he informed and educated himself
in spiritual centers with Mark and his two companions.
I experienced his work as the Son of God.

Near him, I experienced
how he was spiritually in the presence of God.
Often his lips moved, and his expression changed.
He was — in a state of timelessness — in the presence of God.
My greatest experience on earth was:
I was often permitted to see him living in the presence of God.

It is important, what you write about the Gospels.
Do not cross out anything!

John the Evangelist,
with his family, his parents and siblings,
belonged to the intimate circle of people around Jesus.
Because John UNDERSTOOD Jesus, Jesus loved him.

Lazarus/John wrote the Gospel.
It is true that parts are missing.
They were taken out, because John had not been understood.
Complete it — with Luke.

I asked: Have you seen Jesus also after his death?

The brother of Jesus:
No. The other brothers saw him, as did our mother.
I heard and saw Jesus, in a vision, while awake.
He said to me: "Love — believe!
Collect my writings, works written about Jesus,
and give them to Luke."

He continued seriously:
And now —
I ASK YOU to collect and pass on what you have received —
to the Christians, the Jews, and the pagans.

I thank you.

The brother of Jesus was no longer visible.

Another saint:
John says that you have now grasped the true church.
Write everything down —
also what you have learned from the wisdom and words of Joseph!

Joseph of Arimathea appeared. He said:
I am Joseph of Arimathea.

To live — with the risen one
requires knowledge which means:
   — a process of learning;
   — seeking the truth;
   — being true to oneself and God.

THE RISEN ONE — IS PRESENT. LOVE HIM!

Joseph of Arimathea looked at me searchingly:
In the New Testament and in the Acts of the Apostles —
the Evangelists, the apostles, disciples, and Christians
tell about the risen Christ.

What do you do with their accounts?

You — many of you — expect a "road to Damascus experience"! [44]
This is wrong.
It can happen, but it is not a necessary part
of becoming a Christian in order to meet the risen one.

I took the chalice with me throughout my entire life.
In Communion, I was at all times near to Christ
— facing the risen one.

Living with Christ means that in your life as a Christian
you become sensitive, finely attuned to the presence of Christ.
Whenever Christ is near — you become joyful, for joy is within.
This gives impetus, light, fire to the spirit and soul;
and from this newly received energy,
the love for God and your neighbor becomes so strong —
that you become capable
of passing things on in a life-furthering way.

This new love is like a ray of light:
vertically — from the head to God and Christ;
horizontally — from the soul and spirit to your neighbor.

When we are present before Christ,
in prayer, song, and Holy Communion,
we receive: life — and pass it on — to our neighbor.

Try it.
This is the strong and joyful existence of a human being.

To understand the Bible correctly — is important;
work on it! Please do!

It was Christ who spoke:
Mark preached and baptized in the Nile area.

Peter undertook great journeys.
He preached with the strength of the Spirit, and
LAID THE FOUNDATION STONE FOR THE CHURCH IN THE WEST.
Peter dwelt also with Mark among the Copts.

Paul was among the pagans.

John, whom I love, recognized me spiritually!
He became a brother to me and a son to my mother
under the cross.
John loved the Aegean area — the Aegean Sea.
He made great journeys with Peter, Paul,
Luke, and Mark in Asia Minor, in the Aegean,
in the south of France and the south of Italy.
HE — JOHN — "LENT WINGS"
TO THE SPIRIT OF THE GREEKS AND CRETANS,
and in later years to the New World and to southern Ireland.
He lived in God's light.
His spirit and understanding came from God's Spirit.

Suffering

Luke, the great speaker and narrator,
was the one who inquired, searched, and recorded what happened!
He wrote it down, and what he wrote is genuine and true.

Christ spoke slowly:
Matthew is loved.
He experienced these great events with his soul
as well as with his eyes.
He experienced them in the same way as the people,
the disciples and the baptized, did.
Love him!

Silence.

Christ:
Just as these followers were different,
so also are the churches.

THE CHURCH OF LUKE —— the largest one —— is the narrative church
[the church of the biblical stories and parables, and the like].
MARK brought the faith to the Copts and the Armenians.
MATTHEW had a strong influence on the Catholic Church.
JOHN is to be found even today in the Eastern Church
and in the Catholic Church.
JOHN honored and loved my father and my natural brothers.
JOHN WAS THE SPIRITUAL GUARDIAN OF THE CHURCH.
He "surveyed" the disciples and baptized ——
and with me he could talk, in prayer, to the Father.
PETER WAS THE EARTHLY GUARDIAN OF THE CHURCH.
Learn from this.

> *My question: What about Philip, James, and the others? Did*
> *Bartholomew and Thaddaeus also work among the Armenians*
> *and die there the death of martyrs?*

A Martyr

Christ:
They belong to the early Christian world.
The Copts and Armenians worked together with Mark.
He had great influence on the first Christians.

My question: Does the Russian Orthodox Church stem from the Armenian Church?

Christ:
The Russian Orthodox Church was
influenced by different spiritual leaders.
They accepted what was in accordance with their ways,
much from the Armenian Church and from the Irish Church.

Missionaries traveled through Greece,
through Slavic lands — toward the North,
and brought the Word to Russia.

My question: Who influenced Russia?

Christ:
Russian men traveled also to the South ——
and to Rome —— as observers.
They changed everything, according to their ways,
in praying, in singing, and in celebrating the paschal meal.

Georgia was essential.
There was a missionary and evangelist ——
she was Nino who "built" the church,
the Russian Orthodox Church.

Silence.

Then Christ spoke:
Nino was active and influential in the way my mother was.
She was formed in the spirit of Mary —— my mother.

I asked: A second Mary?

Christ:
No! and not a reincarnation!

Nevertheless, she, Nino, was formed like Mary ——
and later light was around her.
She was accompanied in spirit by Mary.

She did not give birth to a son, as Mary bore me ——
but men, women, and children
became figures of light through her!

A mediator, linking heaven and earth, was not born.
It was light that was given,
and a Christian community came into being!

"Christ" was preached; baptism followed.
The faith grew — concentrated in the East — like a field of light!
A stronger field of light was then shown — Asia Minor.

My question: Who influenced Africa?

Christ:
Mark.

The Catholic Church influenced Mexico —
and later China.

Christ became thoughtful; he looked into the distance. Then he
spoke earnestly:
WOMEN HAVE HAD A STRONG INFLUENCE IN FORMING EUROPE.
And women — who became Christians through Paul —
have influenced Greece.

In Rome were three great female personalities:
Patricia, Theosophia, Eusebia.
They were people of light, powerfully linked with God.
Pray to them!
These three women know that it is I who ask you.

Amen.

A saint of the Eastern Church:
In the time from the eighth to the eleventh century,
THE CATHOLIC CHURCH SEPARATED
FROM THE EASTERN CHURCH.
[The official schism was in 1054.]

In the sixteenth century,
THE PROTESTANTS SEPARATED
FROM THE CATHOLIC CHURCH.

In the twentieth century,
**CHRISTIANS ARE IN THE PROCESS OF SEPARATING
FROM POWER — IN THE CHURCHES.**

**THE TEACHINGS OF CHRIST WILL BE BUILT UP ANEW
IN CHURCHES — WHICH HAVE BECOME ONE.**

Give them the records of John!

Also in the churches
the human being is to remain human,
with spirit, word, music, song, and movement ——
in the encounter with God ——
in the encounter with fellow human beings.

Therefore with prayer and love,
with knowledge and healing,
with joy and suffering:

All of you, hold out your hands to one another!
Be brothers, sisters,
sons, daughters,
God's children!

THE NEW TESTAMENT:
THE REVELATION OF JOHN

These visions are better understood after a preliminary reading of the whole text of John's Revelation in the New Testament. They were received in November 1987.

A saint, radiating great light, looked at me for a long time and said:
John's Revelation begins!
Listen well!
We in heaven shall watch over you.

I made the sign of the cross and waited. Appearing in a bright white light, Luke spoke:
John sent me.

And he read from a scroll:
I, John,
heard and saw the words and images of light.
The seven churches that were named understood the message.
They no longer exist.
The same words shall again be addressed to
SEVEN CHURCHES OF TODAY.

On Revelation 2:17:
"Write to the angel of the church in Ephesus."

Luke continued to read:
Ephesus —— how I have loved and still love this area.
My words were addressed to that community,
**AND TODAY THE SAME WORDS ARE ADDRESSED
TO THE EASTERN ORTHODOX CHURCH.**

It will live
after a long period of distress!
It will arise anew, be purified, and become great once again,
in Asia Minor as well as in Russia.

"Your first love" (*Revelation 2:4*) will grow again.
Let us praise the Lord!

On Revelation 2:8–11:
"Write to the angel of the church in Smyrna."

Luke continued:
Smyrna —— no longer exists.
TODAY THOSE IMPRISONED IN THE GHETTOS SHOULD BE FREED.
This in Russia where communism threatens the Jew.
Weep! Today (1987) Jewish people
participate in this betrayal in order to save themselves.

On Revelation 2:12–17:
"Write to the angel of the church in Pergamum."

Luke:
Today Pergamum means the age of theological training
with its intellectual approach to religion.

PERGAMUM IS THE CHURCH THAT BRINGS IN FOREIGN FAITHS.

The "white stone" is John and the whole New Testament!
Mixing different faiths
weakens the individual's spiritual strength.

On Revelation 2:18–29:

"Write to the angel of the church in Thyatira."

Luke continued:
Hear!
TODAY THERE ARE CHRISTIANS THROUGHOUT THE WORLD,
WHO, GUIDED BY THE BIBLE, LIVE IN GOD'S TRUTH AND LOVE.
They feed the poor and give drink to the thirsty.

Jezebel —— the power of the rich!
Jezebel —— the power of war!
Listen and learn!
Jezebel —— those Christians today who are rich and support war!

On Revelation 3:1–6:

"Write to the angel of the church in Sardis."

Luke looked at me questioningly, waited, and then read:
Weep! It is the heads of the churches;
the heads of the Orthodox Church ——
of the Catholic Church ——
and of the Anglican Church ——
who should do penance.

There are a few —— very few —— in white garments.

On Revelation 3:7-13:
"Write to the angel of the church in Philadelphia."

Luke:
These are disciples —— men and women —— startsi and all Christians
who bear love within themselves and live it in their daily life.
Whoever weaves the link between Christ and human beings
receives the crown of life!

Luke looked toward me with love and kindness, as if I had understood everything.

On Revelation 3:14-22:
"Write to the angel of the church in Laodicea."

Luke continued:
John brought "gold" and "white robes" to Asia Minor.
He was the messenger.

In France, in its south,
there were people who lived in white robes —— the Huguenots.
They were persecuted by the Sun King!

In Russia as well, there were many people
who wore and still wear the white robe!

Israel and its people too wore white robes,
and wear them still today, throughout many countries.

Africa's people will receive "gold" from Jesus,
and they will be clothed.

I saw Africans who were poor and starving — including those who suffer under apartheid.

Love! Repent and you will be clothed!
Amen.

On Revelation 4:1–11:

*"I saw a throne standing in heaven and the one who was sitting on
the throne ... Round the throne in a circle were twenty-four thrones
and on them twenty-four elders."*

Luke:
Listen to the Word of the Lord!
These are symbols —— symbols to reveal the greatness of the Lord!
The twenty-four elders with crowns on their heads
SHOW THE WORSHIP of the twelve tribes of the Old Testament
and the twelve apostles of the New Testament.

Listen!
The symbols were important
for the period between A.D. 100 and 1000.
From then on the symbols faded, but not the greatness of God.

God does not sit on a throne!
It is a sign of status —— a sign of the Almighty.

On Revelation 5:1 up to 8:1:

"The seven seals."

Luke read:
The book with the seven seals
contains the levels of spiritual knowledge.

Luke slowly:
Wise are they who live in the faith
and recognize that it is the Son of God who opens the book

because he is God's Son and because he is at one with God.

WHAT JOHN DISCERNED AND SPIRITUALLY UNDERSTOOD LONG AGO,
and what we are now in the twentieth century
learning to understand, is again interwoven with many symbols.

HE, JESUS, HAS THE SPIRIT, LIGHT, STRENGTH, AND KNOWLEDGE TO OPEN OR TO SEAL WHAT HUMAN BEINGS ARE TO DISCERN SPIRITUALLY.

You, Joa Bolendas, know the six seals:

"I saw the Lamb break one of the seven seals ... I saw a white horse appear, and its rider was holding a bow; he was given a victor's crown ..."

Luke:
The first seal has happened: It is Christ.

"He broke the second seal ... out came another horse, bright red, and its rider ... was to take away peace from the earth ..."

Luke:
The second seal is happening and will happen again —— war.

"He broke the third seal ... a black horse appeared, and its rider was holding a pair of scales ... I seemed to hear a voice ... 'a day's wages for a quart of corn'..."

Luke:
The third seal will come and is already present in the South —— famine.

"He broke the fourth seal ... I saw another horse appear, deathly pale, and its rider was called Death ..."

Luke:
The fourth seal will come.

"*He broke the fifth seal; I saw underneath the altar the souls of all the people who had been killed on account of the Word of God.*"

Luke:
The fifth seal has happened.
They, the souls of those who have died for the Word, have moved on.

"*He broke the sixth seal ... there was a violent earthquake ... the stars of the sky fell onto the earth ... the sky disappeared like a scroll rolling up ... the Great Day of his retribution has come ...*"

Luke:
The sixth seal: Call the churches to do penance
so that they may live.
Build the southern part of the city, Jerusalem,
in this period — your period of history.

> *I did not know what this meant. Could it refer to the Protestant and Catholic work for the unity of the churches?*

Luke continued:
Mountains will fall and valleys will be filled.
Storms, floods, fires, and earthquakes will come.
There will be hunger and distress, and the sun will burn
[damage to the ozone layer].
Feed my lambs, says the Lord.

Hear, Israel!
Build the new city —
after the storm, and the stillness that follows, have passed.

On Revelation 8:2–13:

"Next I saw seven trumpets being given to the seven angels."

Luke read:
Hear!
And you will discern and be able
to heal the spirit of man's madness,
which wants to destroy the entire earth!

IT IS YOUR TIME:
war —— Chernobyl —— pollution of the environment.
Make the sign of the cross.

After I had done this, Luke continued:
Chapter eight is about your time.

Chapter nine is about the end of your time.
It is about separating
those people of goodwill from those with evil intentions.

On Revelation 10:1–11:

*"Take that open scroll from the hand of the angel ... take it and eat
it; it will turn your stomach sour, but it will taste as sweet as honey."*

Luke:
THIS WAS THE PAST.

JOHN WILL SPEAK AGAIN THROUGH THE JOHANNINE CHURCH!

John ate the scroll ——
and so, he dissolved a period of the church!
He did not throw away the scroll;
he swallowed it!
He took it inside himself and digested it!

The theology of the early church was as sweet as honey.
From the eleventh century onward
it became as bitter as wormwood.
Afterward the Johannine period begins!

Luke severely:
Hear!
The temple — the Johannine Church —
will not be built according to the old traditions!
It will be built so that there will be no spiritual domination.
It will not serve any military power,
nor will it open its doors to Mammon!

Woe unto you all!
The prophets watch over you!
The Evangelists watch over you!

Do not be afraid;
practice the truth and remain in God's love.

John also described your time in the eleventh chapter.
The symbolic language from the period of John's Revelation
describes the sinister aspects of all the different dangers
of the present day.

On Revelation 12:

"*A great sign appeared in heaven: a woman robed with the sun. . . .*
She was pregnant, crying aloud in the pangs of birth. . . .
A second sign appeared: there was a huge dragon."

Luke:
Write down:
The church became pregnant and bore sons and daughters.

The spiritual and political
persecutions of the church followed.
It was also persecuted
by foreign religions such as Islam and Buddhism.
Sin, too, persecuted the church.

The paths that lead through the stillness and
wilderness are still with us today and will remain.
The mountain of two thousand meters has fallen.
For "half a time" the woman and her child
will still remain silent.

On Revelation 13:
"Then I saw a beast emerge from the sea."

Luke:
Write down:
The saints will be afraid, but they will receive
strength to stand upright in the time of evil power.
They will stand like pillars of strength ⸺
prudent, wise, and without pretense.

Luke did not say anything about chapter 14.

On Revelation 15 and 16:
*"I heard a loud voice from the sanctuary calling to the seven angels,
'Go and empty the seven bowls of God's anger over the earth.'"*

Luke and an angel:
Days ⸺ long days ⸺ will come
where the comfort of shadow is far away.
This is the torment of the first and second cup of anger.[45]
The third cup is war.

The fourth cup is hunger, thirst, and death.
The fifth cup is cruelty and crime.
The sixth cup is when the bearing of children will be forbidden,
when to pass on life means to spread disease
[*I wondered if this referred to AIDS*].
The seventh cup is when voices will fall silent;
after cries of anguish, silence comes over the earth.

Luke:
Pass on the message —— the message of all creation ——
both of heaven and earth.
When the people have understood it, life will return to earth.

On Revelation 17 and 18:
"Babylon the Great ... The seven heads are the seven hills ...
Babylon has fallen."

Luke:
And the city of the seven hills will fall: Rome.
And the truth that Luke, Peter, Paul, John, Mark, and Matthew
brought us will win!

Stay close to the Four Evangelists, the Acts of the Apostles and
the Revelation —— which you have written down.
Hear! Whoever has ears, let him hear!

On Revelation 19–22:
"Praise our God ... Come here, gather together at God's great feast ...
I saw a new heaven and a new earth ... God lives among human
beings."

Luke:
Such will be the rejoicing in heaven and on earth!
Bring your records to a close —— a testimony for a thousand years.

After years another will pass on records.
Those records will be for the needs of the people of that time,
so that they may live life, in all its fullness, on earth.

Amen.

TWELVE VISIONLIEDER

Translated by Miriam Mason

Music Calligraphy by Therese Schroeder-Sheker

HOVER, YE ANGELS

HONOR TO YOU, O CHRIST

THREE MYSTICAL SONGS

> *Em e re re re*
>
> *Ro ho – ro ho*
>
> *Romio*

EL—EL—EL—EL

JESUS CHRIST, WE PRAY TO YOU

JESUS, I LOVE YOU

FATHER—FATHER—OUR FATHER

PRAISE, PRAISE BE TO YOU, MARY!

TWO SONGS TO PRAISE AND THANK MARIA

> *Maria, Maria, You Maiden of the Lord*
>
> *Honor to You, Maria*

Hover, Ye Angels
(Schwebet ihr Engel)

Young *people were lost in the mountains and the rescue crew had given up the search.*

I was asked to pray. In the vision this song was given—to sing and pray together. Saints sang this song until, in the vision, the rescue of the young people was shown—and they were saved!

SONG
Hover, ye Angels!
Hover over the mountains!
Hover thither!
Seek the lost (ones)!
Guide them to the shepherd!
Hover along!

Schwebet ihr Engel

Schwe-bet ihr En-gel! Schwebt uber die Ber-ge! Schwe-bet da-hin! Sucht die Ver- -irr-ten! Fuhrt sie zum Hir-ten! – - - - - - Schwe-bet da-hin!

D.c. a. v. ad lib.

(This calls for great refinement – to be sung effortlessly, as if one were carried along, born aloft on the lyricism.)

Honor to You, O Christ
(Ehre sei Dir Christe)

Several priests were in disagreement. During an intercession about this, Mary spoke earnestly: "Go before the Lord!"

From the angels I learned how to be in timeless prayer before the Lord. They sang: "Honor to You, O Christ, the Lamb of God. Amen."

This song works not only as an intercession, it also makes those in prayer quite strong.

SONG
Honor to You, O Christ,
the Lamb of God.
Amen.
D.c.a.v.ad lib.

Ehre sei Dir Christe, dem Lamm Gottes

Eh - - - - - re, sei Dir Chris -

te, dem Lamm Got - tes, A - - - - - - men.

D. c. a. v. ad lib.

THREE MYSTICAL SONGS

Which language do angels speak? I was often asked this question. To us they speak, so that we can understand them!

Some songs however, can be understood only in the visionary context. The language of the heavens is such that we can neither fully grasp nor understand it.

The following three songs are prayers:

"EM E RE RE RE" is a prayer for those with heart sicknesses, for weakened people.

Mary stood before a large ray of light and sang purely and softly this prayer: "RO HO–RO HO . . ." Through repetition of this song the golden yellow light moved—gently up and down—and from this, a ray of light came down on a suffering, searching person.

"ROMIO" is a song of penance, to be sung for individuals, for all kinds of addicted people. It is also to be sung as a song of penance for all humanity.

Em e re re re

Em e re re re——em e re re re——

em e re re re , em e re re re——

em e re re re——em e re re.

Ro ho–ro ho

Ro ho——ro ho——

ro ho ho ho ho ho——

o o o o o——o o

o o o o o.

Romio

Romio, Romio, Romio

Romio, Romio

Romio o o o o

Romio o o o o

Romio——oo, Romiooo oo

Romio, Romio

Romio o o o o, Romiooo oo

Romio, Romio, o Romio.

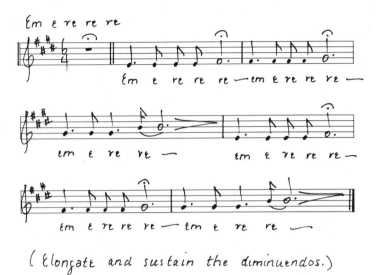

(Elongate and sustain the diminuendos.)

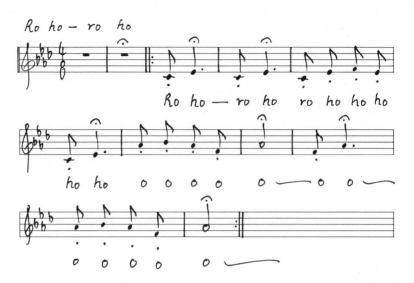

Ro ho — ro ho

Ro ho — ro ho   ro ho ho ho

ho ho   o   o   o   o   o ⌣ o   o ⌣

o   o   o   o   o ⌣

(Notice the intunal echo. To be sung as if one is
calling and then listening for the response.)

Romio

El—El—El—El

"**E**l—El" *is Hebrew. "El" means: God—and* elei: *my God.*

We didn't know what "echma" meant. So I asked an elderly Jewish scholar, Mr. Mannheimer.

He listened to the tape recording of the song "El" and translated: "God, my God, see, what I bring, what I offer You."

The word "echma" is pronounced "eschma" rather than phonetically.

This meaning correlates with the vision that I had.

During the prayer I saw an angel, kneeling down, the head almost touching the ground. The angel's hands were stretched out forward, as if holding out a light: The soul of a human being!

The angel sang the "El" song—until the offered soul shone brightly.

It is therefore a song of intercession.

SONG
El-El-El-El
El-El-El, ä,

em e-lem

e-chma, e-chma, e-chma,

e-lei, e-lei, e-lei.

Jesus Christ, We Pray to You
(Jesus Christus, wir bitten Dich)

At Pentecost, when the breathing of the Holy Spirit is more strongly felt, I love to think of people in prayer.

And so it happened, that I heard this short song during my prayers:

"Jesus Christ,
we pray to You,
through the strength of the Holy Spirit,
for: Light!"

As always, I joined in the singing in order to learn it, and was astounded how, throughout the singing, rays of Light went to sick people and often to unexpected weak or ill areas of their bodies.

We sang this song again and again for sick people.

Jesus Christus, wir bitten Dich

Je-sus Chris-tus, wir bitten Dich durch die

kraft des Hei-li-gen Geistes um: Licht!

D.c. a. v. ad lib.

Jesus, I Love You
(Jesu, ich liebe Dich)

The song: "Jesus, I love you, Jesus! Jesus, Jesus, Jesus!" is a prayer!

I was feeling burdened, worried by the problems of people around me, and then angels sang this song to me. They asked me to sing it until I became spiritually balanced and nothing could distract me from Christ anymore.

It is not a soft lullaby, but rather a prayer that enables us to think of and pray for people, through Christ, whether one feels love for them or not.

SONG
Jesus, I love you!

Jesus!

Jesus, Jesus, Jesus!

D.c.a.b.ad lib.

Jesu, ich liebe Dich

Je - su, ich lie-be Dich,

Je - - - - · su! Je-su, Je-su, Je - - -

- - su!   D. c. a. v. ad lib.

(To be sung with the greatest intensity, as if one
is searching and listening at the same time.)

The Lord

Father—Father—Our Father
(Vater—Vater—Vater Unser)

Probably the greatest prayer is the Lord's Prayer.
Love it—pray it, sing it!
As saints sang this song to me, it began as a searching for the
connection—with God—with the Father: Father—Father—Our Father—.
Whether sung as a prayer for another or as a personal prayer, we
pray with all the angels and saints in heaven, and with all
Christianity: Hallowed be Thy Name, and further the important prayer:
Thy Kingdom come—may Christ come to us!
Thy will be done—in heaven, and also here on earth.
We ask for the bread and the cup.
We ask that Christ forgive us and enable us to forgive.
May He protect us with His Holy Spirit from temptation and evil.

SONG

Father, Father, Our Father,

Thou who art in the heavens!

Hallowed be Thy Name,

Thy Kingdom come,

Thy will be done in heaven,

so also on earth.

Give us this day our daily bread.

Forgive us our trespasses,

as we forgive those who trespass against us.

Lead us not into temptation,

deliver us from evil.

Amen.

unsern Schuldern   Führe uns nicht in Ver-su-chung

er-lö- se uns von dem Bösen. A - - - -

men!

Praise, Praise Be to You, Mary!
(Lob, Lob, Lob sei Dir Marie!)

And we?—We must thank Mary with this song of praise, for her life—:
Praise! Praise!
Praise be to you, Mary!
Praise be to you!
Praise! Praise!

Praise! Praise!
Praise be to you, Mary!
Praise be to you!
Praise! Praise!

TWO SONGS TO PRAISE AND THANK MARIA*

Maria, Maria, You Maiden of the Lord (Maria, Maria, du Magd des Herrn)

Maria, Maria, Maria.
You maiden of the Lord,
we love You,
You maiden of the Lord,
we greet You,
You Queen of Heaven,
You mother of the church!
Praise to You!
Honor to You!
Light be with You and thanks!

Honor to You, Maria (Ehre sei dir, Maria)

Honor, honor,
to You, Maria,
We love You,
You Queen of Heaven.
We greet You,
Maria, our mother!
Sancta Maria!

*The original German "Maria" has not been translated here as "Mary" since the melody is easier to sing with three syllables.

Maria, Maria, du Magd des Herrn

(with joy)

Ma-ri- a, Ma-ri- a, Ma-

Ma- ri- a, Ma-ri- a, Ma-ri ....

Ma-ri- a, Ma-ri- a, Ma-ri- ....

Ma-ri- a, Ma-ri - a, Ma-ri - .

ri - a. Du Magd des Herrn, wir lieben Dich

.... -a. Du Magd des Herrn, wir lie ben Dich

.... a. Du Magd des Herrn, wir lie ben Dich

..... a. Du Magd des Herrn, wir lie ben Dich

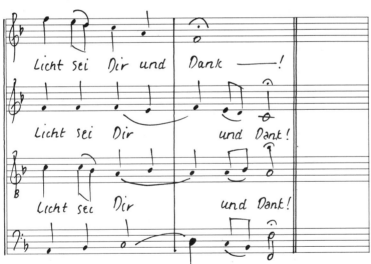

NOTES

1. I, John Hill, have translated the German, *Geist/geistig* into the English, "spirit/spiritual." The German does not always connote an immaterial or transcendent reality but when applied to human nature may include intellectual and cultural activity.

2. The Catholic small sign of the cross is made on the forehead, the mouth, and the chest.

3. The German original, *allgemeines Priestertum*, means "the priesthood of all baptized Christians."

4. Nicholas von Flue (1417–1487), hermit of Ranft and patron saint of Switzerland.

5. The service in the Catholic Church was the exposition and adoration of the Blessed Sacrament in the monstrance. Christ spoke these words with regard to this kind of adoration. I, Joa Bolendas, took this to mean that the Holy Bread alone is not to be worshipped — only Christ. In Communion, the Bread of Life is given to nourish the poor, the hungry, the thirsty — all who seek to renew soul and spirit, to all who seek God's presence in their lives. I know that the Bread is to be preserved worthily and Christ is truly present in the Eucharistic celebration.

6. An outline of this rosary with musical notation is to be found in the appendix of this volume.

7. Joa Bolendas: As this book was being prepared for publication (July 1996), a student asked what is meant by: "But it is better to live in purity, so that the love for his fellow human beings is great." St. Paul, who was known to practice his faith severely, answered: "Sexuality is a creation of God. It can bring beauty, joy, and relationship between two people. Sexuality must not cast a shadow over spiritual life—over the link to Christ and

God. It must not weaken the link with God or divert a person's attention away from God. In this way you will learn to love your neighbor more. To live in purity does not mean to live without sexuality, but to put your relationship to God, Christ, and your love for your fellow human beings first and foremost. If sexuality casts a shadow over your love of God then it is better to live without it—and live a life of purity in God." I, Joa Bolendas, would like to add that these words on the rights of a priest are also valid for women priests, pastors, and rabbis.

8. The original German word *Mensch* is the collective term for man and woman. In most cases I have translated it with "human being" or "human." However, sometimes I have used the word "man" for stylistic reasons only, and not to signify gender.

9. Add to this the Tenth Message of Wisdom in this volume. The German prefix *Ur-* has been translated throughout as "primal."

10. This refers to Glastonbury's earliest church, built from timber and wattles, some of which came from the legendary thornbush that grew from a twig of the crown of thorns.

11. Joa Bolendas composed music for this rosary, similar to the "Twelve Visionlider" on pages 395–421.

12. The original German word *Jungfrau* means "virgin". Following the words of Joa Bolendas, "maid of light" is also an appropriate translation of the meaning of this word. The arrangement of words describing the mysteries follow the German text and is an attempt to adapt the English translation to the musical rhythm of the rosary.

13. The *starets* (plural, *startsi*) is a characteristic figure in Orthodox monasticism. As an "elder" or "old man," he is a kind of spiritual father—a monk of spiritual discernment and wisdom, whom others adopt as a guide and spiritual director. He is sometimes a priest, but often a lay monk. He receives no special ordination to the work of eldership, but is guided by the direct inspiration of the Spirit. (See T. Ware, *The Orthodox Church*, Penguin Books, 1975, p. 47.)

14. Saint Mary was a harlot of Alexandria who suddenly converted while in Jerusalem, crossed the River Jordan, and lived a solitary life in the wilderness for the rest of her days.

15. Saint Zossima was a priest who witnessed miracles of Saint Mary.

16. This refers to the earlier visions on the Old Testament.

17. Saint Patrick (388–461 A.D.) is the patron saint of Ireland.

18. Joa Bolendas, "The Universe," in part three of this volume.

19. Jean Charon, *The Unknown Spirit* (London: Coventure Ltd., 1983).

20. Ibid., p. 139.

21. Teilhard de Chardin, *The Phenomenon of Man* (New York: Harper and Row, 1965), p. 35.

22. Ibid, p. 285.

23. The German original: *geistige Energie-Materie.*

24. The German original: *geschaffener Christus.* In February 1996, I asked Joa, Does this mean that Christ was created? Joa received the following answer. It was an angel who spoke: "At the moment of Christ's conception, God gave of his light, life, and energy. He gave his own son to the earth. This conception took place without a man. God gave his life, light, and the Holy Spirit in human form to the earth. This life of light existed before the creation of the earth, exists now, and exists in eternity. Christ gave of his light and love to humankind. With the power of the Holy Spirit, Christ linked heaven and earth. Christ suffered and overcame spiritual death, when he died on the cross. He made possible eternal life for humankind — the path towards the final great unfolding of human life in the hereafter. After Easter, there was to be no break in the spiritual life of man and woman at death. That is why Jesus spoke the words on the cross: *'Today you will be with me in paradise.'* You may use the phrase 'brought forth' (*hervorgebrachter Christus*)."

25. In the following passages, whenever a speaker is not named, it is a saint who speaks.

26. I, John Hill, asked Joa Bolendas for further clarification about this passage. She conveyed to me the following message of a saint: "The sons of Noah and their descendents were a people of fair complexion. They were not the only people who dwelt on earth at that time. This is about the migrations of the peoples of the earth."

27. On the name Abram, see Genesis 17:5: "*And you are no longer to be called Abram; your name is to be Abraham, for I am making you father of many nations.*"

    Here I, Joa Bolendas, would like to add that all the hymns in this book were received in vision. They were sung by the angels or by saints risen from the dead. I put them on tape and later Professor Franz Eibner from the Musikhochschule of Vienna notated the music for piano or organ accompaniment. "Abram's Hymn" was published in *Mit den Händen loben wir* (Jom-Verlag, 1986), p. 64.

28. See *Mit den Händen loben wir* (Jom-Verlag, 1986), p. 35.

29. Joa Bolendas: With these last words, the independent life, which only Jesus Christ lived, is implied. All the spiritual centers and the companions were important; however, he alone knew what is from God and for God!

30. The original German text: *Johannes, Johanna.*

31. The angel Gabriel.

32. Hymn published in *Mit den Händen loben wir*, pp. 66–69.

33. German original: *im Sein vor Gott.*

34. See *Mit den Händen loben wir*, p. 20.

35. Ibid., pp. 40–44. For the Our Father in song form, see the appendix of this volume.

36. The original German: *Hüftkugel*, which literally translated is "head of femur."

37. See Johannes Hemleben, *Johannes der Evangelist* (Rororo, 1987).

38. See Eureka!, in part two of this volume.

39. Joa Bolendas: The words of John, "Come over — to the table of the learned" (a large, square table with a thick wooden top and wooden benches), I understood to mean not only to read Greek philosophy but also generally about Greek antiquity, history, art, culture, religion, warfare, social and scientific matters, etc. A real help for me was the book: *Geschichte der alten Welt — Der Orient und Griechenland*, by Michael Rostovtzeff.

40. Franz Eibner died in 1986. Before the end of his life on earth, he wrote down the music given to me in vision. I remain deeply grateful for this work.

41. The original German text:
    im Sein der Erde —
    im Sein der Wissenschaft —
    im Sein — des Menschlichen

42. Joa Bolendas: I placed the words of Peter at the end consciously. Readers will understand them here.

43. The original German text: *Die Schulden werden getilgt.*

44. The original German text: *eine Saulus-Begegnung!*

45. In July 1996, a student asked Joa Bolendas what is meant by "the cup of anger." It was St. Luke who answered: "The cup of anger is an old symbol. When a cup is full with anger, then human beings have not followed God's laws. Then they are responsible for the cups of anger being full. Today this is mainly due to the misuse of the sciences. Now one would say, God is sad that human beings do so much evil, and this evil will return to them again and again."

46. Published in *Mit den Händen loben wir*, pp. 70–86.

JOA BOLENDAS was born in Zurich in 1917.
When twenty-one years old, she married a parson of the Swiss
Reformed Church.
From this marriage she had three sons.
In 1957 Joa Bolendas experienced the first visions.
She continued to receive visions throughout her life.
In 1980, she and her husband retired from active parish life.
The visions of this book have been published under a pseudonym.
The author believes that it is not her personal identity
but God's work that is important.